D1497903

DESTROYER SKIPPER

Commander Sheppard inspects the troops.

DESTROYER SKIPPER

A Memoir of Command at Sea

Don Sheppard

PRESIDIO

Copyright © 1996 by Don Sheppard

Published by Presidio Press
505 B San Marin Drive, Suite 300
Novato, CA 94945-1340

Library of Congress-in-Publication Data

Don Sheppard
Destroyer skipper : a memoir of command at sea / Don Sheppard.
    p. cm.
  ISBN 0-89141-555-6 (hardcover)
  1. Sheppard, Don. 2. United States. Navy—Officers—Biography.
I. Title.
  V63.S53A3   1996b
  359'.0092—dc20
  [B]   96-26259
                              CIP

Printed in the United States of America

DESTROYER SKIPPER

A Memoir of Command at Sea

Don Sheppard

PRESIDIO

Published by Presidio Press
505 B San Marin Drive, Suite 300
Novato, CA 94945-1340

Library of Congress-in-Publication Data

Don Sheppard
Destroyer skipper : a memoir of command at sea / Don Sheppard.
    p. cm.
  ISBN 0-89141-555-6 (hardcover)
   1. Sheppard, Don. 2. United States. Navy—Officers—Biography.
I. Title.
V63.S53A3   1996b
359'.0092—dc20
[B]   96-26259
                                    CIP

Printed in the United States of America

To my grandchildren. May their life be just as adventurous.

To Carolyn Martin, for being there and reading the words over and over, and talking to me about them.

To E. J. McCarthy, my editor at Presidio Press, who made the words stronger.

And to Bob Kane, publisher, Presidio Press, who found merit in my work, and encouraged me.

Destroyer

I've looked into the maelstrom,
    and seen the devil's eye.
I've fought its dreadful fury,
    where only brave survive.

I've taken waves upon my bow,
    t'would frighten lesser men.
The seas in all their fury,
    can never hope to win.

My turbines spin a happy song,
    bow waves curling free.
My hull, a work of beauty,
    cutting throught the sea.

I'm here to take your young ones,
    to pass them through the breach.
Awaken them to manhood,
    teach them how to reach.

Tender me your children,
    those within your kin.
Parade them on my weather decks,
    and you will get back men.

—*Don Sheppard*

Foreword

Destroyer Skipper is the last of a three-book odyssey dealing with my life in the U.S. Navy from when I joined as a seaman recruit in 1948 to my retirement as a full commander in 1977.

Chronologically, the first of the series is *Blue Water Sailor*, the story of my life as a junior officer, mostly aboard destroyers, and my ascension from seaman to lieutenant commander.

Blue Water Sailor chronicles my fight for shipboard acceptance, my struggle to overcome feelings of inadequacy caused within me by my lack of a college degree and the intellectual numbness of growing up in a small midwest mill town. It tells what worked for me as all the while constant seasickness gnawed away at me, ever lurking to destroy my naval career.

The second book, *Riverine* is about the river war in Vietnam, my year as a combat commander of PBR gunboats in the Mekong Delta. It outlines how I was driven to war by the memory of the relentless pounding of the United States' propaganda machine during World War II, its fiery words beating into my young ears, extolling me to fight for the greatness of America.

Riverine reflects on my search to prove my worthiness while pushing my men to greater deeds of valor. It weaves in my leadership techniques and the management of combat. They proved to be the same as on a ship. The same methods applied, just in another arena, a bloodier arena.

Destroyer Skipper is an accounting of my senior officer days and the culmination of my naval career as a destroyer captain and duty on a major European staff. Everything comes together in the third volume you hold in your hand.

I wrote these books out of a compulsion to share my experiences, to show what worked and what didn't. I wrote them to share my successes and my failures, all with a hope that the lessons learned can be applied, not only to the navy, or the armed forces, but to every management and leadership situation.

The people in this book, for the most part, are composites of those I have met and served with along the way. Names have been changed, but some of you will recognize yourselves. I trust I have rendered you satisfactorily.

Some will not recognize themselves, for they have never seen themselves through the eyes of others.

The ships are real, their names have been changed. The events are real, but not always the sequence.

Dialogue has been reconstructed to the best of my memory.

For the techno buffs, you may find fault with too little description. This is a story of men; the equipment they used are backdrops.

This is what I remember, twenty to forty-five years later.

Prologue

The U.S. Navy destroyer *Henshaw* rolled gently in the quartering sea while my stomach spewed out its retched green bile and foul dry heaves. I was sick, gut-wrenching, toilet-clutching sick, and had been since reporting aboard as a fresh-caught ensign three weeks earlier. My shins, torn and bleeding from smashing into watertight door coaming, stood in awesome testimony to my inability to become a naval officer.

I was ex-enlisted. I'd come up through the ranks, a mustang. I'd flown as an aircrewman in S2Fs and P2Vs and watched a hydrogen bomb explode in the South China Sea.

In a violent North Sea storm, I sat helplessly strapped into a seat while the pilot tried to claw his way aboard the pitching, rolling, flight deck of our ice-encrusted carrier. On the thirteenth time, the hook caught.

We chased a Russian submarine across the Atlantic while it disdainfully sailed away from us at forty knots.

OCS followed, and I was allowed to wear the trappings of a naval officer. But my stomach wasn't.

I reported aboard the USS *Henshaw*, my first destroyer. My captain took me under his wing, taught me, nurtured me, and my stomach's curse faded away . . . well, mostly so.

Handling the ship and shipboard life came easy. I learned what being an officer meant while battling the wretched specter of inadequacy that hung over me, eating into me like a rampant cancer,

1

since childhood. I fought it down, performed, did well, learned the trade, became as one with the ship.

As *Henshaw's* chief engineer, learning the plant was easy, but not the battle with the leading machinist for dominance over it.

While aboard a U.S. submarine in the South China Sea, her clandestine ways came to me, as well as how to use them against her in her subsurface domain.

In the Formosa Straits we fought off pirates and tracked a Chinese submarine, forcing it to surface with our depth charges and suicidal maneuvering.

Learning, always learning.

There was a fear-crazed night in a Filipino jungle hunting wild boar. Having to kill a giant python taught me never to go into a jungle again. But the lesson was forgotten.

A killer typhoon in Hong Kong piled ships up on the rocks, and a merchantman begged us for assistance as it pulled its anchor chains across the bottom, the ship heading for destruction, taking Hong Kong's underwater cables with it. We could do nothing for it—we, too, were anchored and fought the storm for our own survival.

I served on a fleet staff, hated it, and found action was my forte, not paperwork. At the naval postgraduate school I received a bachelor's degree and volunteered for Vietnam . . . and was chosen.

Vietnam. 1967. Our battle ensigns flapped boldly as the Mekong Delta's hot wind blew across the muddy waters of the Bassac River. My gunboat, and three others behind me, turned in to the attack, hurled ourselves toward the tree line, our .50-caliber machine guns slicing out a fearful pounding of half-inch slugs against the Vietcong, who gave us bullet for bullet, rocket for rocket.

The low swoop of Huey helicopter gunships firing their miniguns, spewing 9.62mm rounds over our heads and into the enemy in an attempt to thwart their crossing of the river.

It was a firefight, a classic firefight, the likes of which repeated itself day after day along the jungle-lined river. A day's work, count the dead, count the wounded, and thank God you're still alive.

In February 1968, a tall lieutenant commander stepped off an army transport aircraft at the Can Tho, Vietnam, airport. Thousands of little gnats buzzed around my black beret, and around his freshly pressed khaki hat. He smiled at me, hand extended. He didn't look used up, his eyes weren't dark pools devoid of expression, like mine. My shoulders drooped, his didn't.

Two days later he relieved me. It was all his now: the heat, the blood, the anguish, the futility of it all.

It was his first command, and he didn't have an idea in hell on what to do or how to do it. Neither had I.

Chapter 1

Japan, Late Winter 1968

I gathered my bridge coat closer around me. I pulled its high collar up to stave off the harsh March wind whipping in from the Sea of Japan. The snowflakes, all of them, aimed directly for my exposed, reddened face. My heat-thinned blood from the Mekong Delta offered no resistance. I was thirty-eight years old, and nervous over my new assignment, an assignment whose duties I could not conceive.

My just-shined black shoes crunched against the gathering white carpet as I made my way through the storm's haze to a low building in front of me. My cloud-forming breath distorted its view. My toes had already given up the fight for survival, they offered no feeling. My fingers lasted a minute longer, then joined my feet in sympathy. I couldn't feel my briefcase's weight in my left hand.

I stood huddled outside a small guard shack attached to a squat green building surrounded by an eight-foot chain-link fence with barbed wire on top and an Air Force Policeman circling a squad car around it, and around it.

The wind whirled the snow into twisting devils dancing about me in their Arctic two-step as I banged on a four-by-five-inch wooden window cover. In ten seconds a hand pulled it up. Heat rushed out. I could feel it. My face hadn't been destroyed after all. A stern face looked out at me.

"Is this the Pacom Elint Center?" I asked. He stared at me through the little hole, saying angrily that he couldn't give that information out.

"I'm Lieutenant Commander Sheppard, reporting aboard. They described the building at the main gate . . . this looks like it."

"Reporting a board?" the voice growled.

"Reporting for duty . . ."

The wind freshened in the ten-second pause.

My teeth chattered like a clicking Chinese monster as my lower jaw assaulted my upper. "You ain't on the list, sir."

"Can you call someone, Sergeant . . . are you a sergeant? *Call someone, goddamnit. I'm freezing my ass off out here.*"

"Nobody gets in unless he's on the list. This place is secret, sir, you gotta be on the list," he proclaimed, slamming down the little wooden window with a bang of finality. *Damn, it's cold.*

I thought of my poor little fan back in Vietnam. It lasted the year for me, kept me alive in the heat. Now I'm going to freeze to death on an air force base thirty miles west of Tokyo.

The squad car pulled up to me. The driver leaned over and pushed open the passenger door. He motioned me in, saying I looked cold as he twisted the heater knob to full. He put the car in gear and continued his circumnavigation of the prisonlike compound.

I thanked him, my chattering teeth chopping up my words. I took off my gloves, opened my coat, and leaned over the heater vent. He asked me what I wanted in there, adding that it was a secret place.

"I'm trying to report in . . . there seems to be some list I'm not on."

"The access list . . . you ain't on it . . . you ain't in it," he chuckled.

That bit of wisdom passed around me as thoughts of how I ended up here trickled through me. We were on the third turn of the building as my body melted back to normal.

Assignment to anyplace in the world where the navy had sailors was one of the perks received for volunteering for Vietnam. I chose Japan. Its history and how it handled itself after World War II fascinated me, this fascination overwhelming my wartime, propaganda-based fear of how bloodthirsty it was. The fear I still felt when I had first arrived in Japan on the destroyer *Henshaw*, my first ship, ten years ago.

Orders to the naval station at Yokosuka, or some other naval installation were expected. We had a lot of them. I barely knew what a

PACOMELINT center was. I pointed to the radio microphone on the dashboard, asking if he could call someone. He asked why.

So they'll let me into the building. I'm reporting aboard."

"Reporting a board? You ain't on the list!"

"Corporal . . . maybe there's someone who is."

He picked up the microphone, relief on his face. He was probably wondering what he was going to do with a stray naval officer not on the *list*. "Doghouse, this is Rover One, have a navy officer here who wants to get into the place."

Someone called Doghouse answered. "So?"

"He says he's reporting a board . . . there ain't no boards around here . . . he ain't on the list!"

I reached over and took the microphone from his hand. "Doghouse, this is Lieutenant Commander Sheppard. I have orders to report to the PACOMELINT center and I can't get in. I *ain't* on the list.

"This is Doghouse, wait one . . ."

"Cute, uh, sir . . . they're Doghouse and I'm Rover One . . . get it?"

"Yes, very clever, Corporal, thank you for explaining it to me."

"Oh, that's okay, sir."

Doghouse came back over the radio and told my savior to take me to the entrance, where someone would meet me. Two armed Air Policemen met me outside the little shack; sandwiching me between them and as we entered the holy temple of secrecy, they escorted me to a small office. I was glad they hadn't cuffed me, for it seemed more like a prison cell than my next duty station.

The plain office had nothing personal to prove someone worked in it. It had only the foul odor of steam-heated, baked paint and a lone, crooked picture of a B-52 in flight hanging on the rear wall.

In a few minutes a full navy commander came in, saying his name was Jacob G. Robbins, the deputy commander. He offered his hand stiffly, like a ventriloquist's dummy. We shook. His palms were wet.

"Welcome aboard. Sit down, please. Coffee?" We sat in silence while he pretended to read my service jacket. The friction of my hands rubbing against each other warmed them enough that I could hold them steady. My body wasn't there yet, it shimmied on the hard oak chair it was trying to sit in. The stifling heat of the room made it hard to breathe, but I sucked it up like a man lost in the desert who craves water.

Periodically Commander Robbins's eyes darted to the ribbons on my chest. A woman finally appeared with two cups of coffee. I held the hot mug dearly.

"Silver Star?" he asked as the woman left the room.

"Yes, sir," I answered, feeling ashamed, since I didn't feel I really deserved it.

"Not too shabby, don't see many of those around here," he replied in admiration.

"Thank you, sir . . . it's really nothing," I replied, not looking at him. "They pass these out like candy in the Delta," I lied.

"And two Purple Hearts?" he said, pointing at my chest, at the purple ribbon with a star indicating a second award, a second wounding.

"Just a little more expensive candy, sir," I answered, feeling the stab of the dozens of small pieces of shrapnel still embedded in my body and left to "work their way out," as the doctors said. I was never free of their painful journey, and a change in the weather seemed to triple their size and speed.

He paused, obviously uncomfortable as he said apoligetically that they didn't have a job for me and I didn't even have a background investigation or any decent clearances. His face was all frown as he asked the room how could *they* have possibly assigned me here.

I answered I didn't know, and told him the obvious that the Bureau of Naval Personnel, BUPERS, sent me there. I was ashamed of myself for not having whatever he was talking about. "I do have a secret clearance," I boasted in defense.

His eyes tried to be kind, like a coach telling a handicapped kid he shouldn't even be trying to make the team. Even the third string. "Secret clearance?" He paused, pointing his pencil at me as if it were a ray gun. "Mr. Sheppard, even the janitors here have secret clearances. We do ELINT, do you know what that means?"

Of course I know what that meant.

"Electronic intelligence, sir, maybe I could be sent to the naval station at Yokosuka, or someplace else."

"Colonel Spinner's already tried that. Naval intelligence said they wanted to put some 'kick-'em-in-the-ass' new blood in here . . . you're assigned, and we're stuck with you," he answered, looking ashamed for the terseness of his statement. "C'mon, the colonel wants to see you."

We waited in silence outside the colonel's office in hard straight-back chairs. The longer we waited, the more my fantasy drifted away, like leaves in an autumn wind. I had envisioned being a spy. It was an intelligence center, wasn't it? I'd be a secret agent . . . not really, but maybe something like that.

I had seen myself sitting in a fancy club in Hong Kong or maybe Macao playing baccarat while wearing my impeccably tailored tuxedo. I would be going for the limit when a Chinese girl, sleek and sensuous, like a jaguar, would come up behind me with a drink in her hand. She'd offer it to me. "Vodka martini . . . stirred not shaken," she'd coo while her free hand caressed my arm.

I'd look at her. She'd smile. "Sheppard . . . Don Sheppard," I'd offer, and we'd walk away to her penthouse suite to the envy of every male in the place. But I'd never tell her any secrets . . . well, not important ones anyway. That is, if I knew any secrets.

We waited outside for about fifteen minutes before a gruff "come" fought its way through the door.

"We don't have a job for you," said Colonel Stephen B. Spinner, USAF, the commander of the tri-service, army, navy, air force, ELINT center. He clicked out the words as if he'd memorized them.

He sneered, looking at my ribbons as I stood in front of his desk at parade rest. The smell of his cheap cigar fouled the room. His tall frame didn't even get up to shake my hand. I reached over his desk to shake his. His hand barely touched mine before he yanked it back as if I were a leper, his face hostile, like a lee shore in a storm.

He wore an Air Force Academy ring and had only a single row of three ribbons, one was a theater medal showing he was in the service, somewhere, anywhere, while the U.S. was in Vietnam. Another was the American Service ribbon which everyone got for just being in the service and breathing. His highest was an Air Force Commendation ribbon. I wondered why he didn't have the deep-blue expert pistol shot ribbon; everybody from the military academies had one of those.

"We run a tight ship here, Sheppard, as you swabbies like to say. Do your job well, and we'll get along okay, we don't need any *new blood*," he said curtly, his head going back to a paper he was reading, which he had quickly covered when we entered his office.

"Aye, aye, sir," I said, turning to walk out of the windowless room, wondering what job I could do well at.

Back in Commander Robbins's fake office, an army lieutenant colonel waited. "You'll be working for Colonel Penske here," Robbins said, introducing me. The green-uniformed officer extended his hand as if in fear he would catch some nameless tropical disease if he touched me. We shook. He smiled as if relieved that he hadn't been struck dead—or at least paralyzed—by being this close, touching someone with only a secret clearance.

"He's all yours, Colonel . . . keep him busy . . . idle hands, you know," the puffy face of Commander Robbins said, laughing as he waved us out of his fake office with the back of his hand.

Lieutenant Colonel Penske set up a desk for me in an innocuous corner of an office where I couldn't detect any "top secrets" being talked about around me. Three air force captains came up to me, huddled together, as if in mutual support. They introduced themselves, then scurried away, their duty done. An army major was next. He braved it on his own. Then two navy lieutenant commanders appeared, talking down to me as if I had embarrassed them by even being here. An air force sergeant came up with a paper sack and dropped it on my bare desk. "Colonel Penske . . . said you might need these, ah . . . ah . . ."

"Try sir, Sergeant."

"Ah . . . yes, of course, *sir!*" He ambled away.

After ten minutes of making myself busy putting away the office supplies the sergeant had delivered, a navy lieutenant sauntered over, offering his hand. I rose and shook it. He said his name was Baldwin, then pointed to a chair next to my desk. "May I?"

"Yes, sit down, if your career can take it."

"It can, only got a year left . . . know what you're going through, I came here with no clearance." He pronounced *clearance* as if it were a dirty word. "They put me in the base admin office for six months while the magic of the FBI checking me out was working; I guess they can't do that to a genuine war hero."

"War hero?"

"Got your dossier . . . genuine war hero, sure enough. It was distributed. You make 'em nervous, Mr. Sheppard. They don't like operators; it makes them uneasy. You might ask some embarrassing questions about the clandestine brotherhood." He raised an eyebrow and chuckled.

"I'm in the computer department . . . if I can help you with anything, let me know."

I spent the rest of the three hours of the morning with the five-minute job of readjusting my desk supplies and checking that I had enough staples in my standard government-issue stapler. I wanted to be sure they weren't communist staples. I wanted only *cleared* staples in my stapler.

The clock shaved off thin slices of the day as my ego banged itself against reality. I wallowed in the self-pity of disappointment. But a few months before, I had lead men in combat. I was invincible. Important. Before coming here, I briefed admirals, they listened and thanked me, all the while looking enviously at my medals and sun-bronzed face. I lectured CIA and State Department officers, who listened in appreciation. People paid attention when I spoke. I was important.

No longer. I was a staffie in a staffie's foreign world. How swift glory passes.

In the afternoon I read four issues of the *Navy Times,* one copy of the *Air Force Times,* and, masochistically, three *Army Times*es. Remarkably, they were all the same except for the pictures and the lead articles. It was something to do instead of watching the clock not move. Three back issues of *The Stars and Stripes* served as a break.

The vegetating days passed. Boredom was one thing, I'd been bored a lot at sea. It was the inactivity that ate away at me. It was an unfamiliar feeling, I had no defenses against it, no sword to fight it off. But I tried to, by reading all the books and magazines in the center's library.

It was a standard library of technical magazines from all over the world plus U.S. and friendly country intelligence documents up to secret classification. I had that much of a clearance at least.

Having a little knowledge of computers, I got together with Lieutenant Baldwin and designed a computerized cross-indexing system to make the library more useful by cutting down the time it took for someone to research a given subject. Colonel Spinner reluctantly acknowledged it wasn't too bad a job. And he took credit for it.

After six months of meaningless activity, working at simple, demeaning jobs, my clearance came through: Special Intelligence—code word, SI. I was glad to hear I was a loyal American citizen.

Now the real stuff. It wasn't much. We collected bearings and electronic characteristics of enemy radars from satellites orbiting high above Vietnam and from our aircraft flying close to and over as well. We cross-checked them with other "intercepts" and reported the "suspected" locations of enemy surface-to-air missile (SAM) sites and search radars. These reports went to the carriers off North Vietnam and to the air force bases that launched strikes into the north.

A commendable job and one needed a top secret clearance to know the *compartmentalization* of the sources. The special intelligence was for the satellites, which were the most sensitive sources we had. One had to have their "code word" clearance to know about them. The SI clearance got you to the door and the code word got you into the room and to your desk. I already knew about the satellites and all the other stuff from reading magazine articles in the library.

Cross-checking all these intercepts on a drafting table took time and introduced errors. I got with Lieutenant Baldwin again and together we figured out how to computerize the intercepts so they would plot themselves automatically. This also allowed us to bring in old intercepts to compare with current data.

We increased accuracy and drastically cut down the time needed to process the signals. The colonel begrudgingly allowed it wasn't too bad a job, and in his reporting of it suggested that it was his idea.

But I wasn't a "spook," as these ELINT center guys liked to call themselves. They considered themselves professional spies, and they didn't like outsiders like me, a mere naval line officer, sullying their holy domain. They were the priesthood of clandestinity. They were the back door, unsung heroes surreptitiously protecting the free world from the godless Communists by processing their recorded electronic signals from thousands of miles away. I found it sad that they suffered such delusions of adventurous grandeur. They marched to a drummer I could not hear.

Sometimes, after a few drinks, I couldn't contain myself from making reference to it. It didn't make me popular, except with the junior officers, who pretty well felt the same way I did, even though they were intelligence staffies. They wanted to be in the *field,* wherever that was.

The *field* and I thought about another intelligence staffie who showed up in my office in Vietnam early one morning in the later stages of my tour. He flashed his air force ID card and another card identifying him as a member of COMACV, General Westmoreland's J-2 intelligence staff in Saigon. He pouted as I took them from his hand and examined them without awe.

"White Knight," he had said pompously. "When you hear that code word, you'll get a set of coordinates on a point somewhere along the riverbank." He got up and peered out the window. He stepped to the door, glanced out, then shut it. "When you get the coordinates, take it under fire and report."

"No."

"*No!* Whaddaya mean, no?" I asked him which part of no he didn't you understand.

"Now, see here, Commander. I'm from MACV," he answered, his face flushing, his lower lip quivering as he ran his hands over his balding head.

I remembered asking him if he was really serious that I take an area under fire from a radio call. And I recalled asking where was the voice getting its coordinates from.

He tried to recover his composure, saying he couldn't tell me. "Why not?" I asked.

He paused, his lips pursed as if he were trying to frame an answer I could understand. He said I wasn't cleared. I told him either I know what the source is or I ignore it. He said I didn't understand, and asked if I had forgotten he was from MACV.

"Major, tell you what . . . you have MACV send a message to my boss and explain it to him, and he'll tell me what to do . . . okay?"

"We can't." His reddened face snapped.

"Why?"

"He's not cleared," came the smug answer.

I stood and opened the door. "Good day, Major."

Now, with my magic clearances, I knew that White Knight was no more than an airplane flying around listening to the Vietcong radios, the few they had. Big deal, what was so secret about that?

I had another problem. Every month the colonel had an officer's call meeting, which included all hands attached to the center. At these get-togethers, things such as promotions, births, marriages, transfers, and general items of interest were announced. One of the more senior officers would always give a leadership pep talk. Also, awards and medals appeared at these forced-attendance affairs.

Citations explaining the reasons for the medals had to be read with the presentation, and their flowery wording read like an adventure story—like David slaying Goliath.

The time between the action and the award of a medal took several months; consequently, many of mine arrived after I'd been in Japan for a while. Colonel Spinner read the first one, a Bronze Star. It spoke of courage and tenacity. With disdain, pretending to be proud of me, he asked me to speak about how courageous I was.

I straightened my shoulders, trying to ignore the pain the citation had mustered to the forefront of my mind. I grasped the microphone with both hands. The heat of the Delta boiled in the cool room. I sweated as my mind cringed at the imaginary bullets zinging around me.

I took a deep breath. What can I say? Courage? Courage is a state of mind. My hands steadied as I pried their death grip loose of the microphone.

My mind cleared in the coolness of the room. I coughed. "Gentlemen," I started to say, catching each set of eyes on every face. "I have no admiration for courage within itself . . . it is a mental trick, an ability to blind oneself to the consequences of one's actions by focusing all thought to the task at hand. I dislike being told I am courageous, it labels me to something I am not. And I am not modest. I see a job to be done, and I do it. . . ."

I stepped away from the lectern. Fifty-two faces looked at me as if they expected more. I had no more. One man clapped, stood . . . then another, and the entire room broke out in applause as I returned to my seat.

"Thank you." I bowed and sat down.

After that Colonel Spinner refused to read anymore citations, and when I started getting them once a month he didn't even show up at the meetings. In all, it embarrassed me to appear like a Sergeant York or an Audie Murphy. They were heroes, I was not.

They finally ended with my award of the Legion of Merit, a strikingly beautiful medal in the finest French tradition. It was a most coveted medal, usually awarded only to very senior officers for outstanding performance. Almost never with a combat "V" for valor attached to it like mine had. I had heard it was the medal the colonel hoped for more than anything else.

The next officer's call was chaired by an army lieutenant colonel, an O-5 pay grade. It was too high a medal for a mere O-5 to award, and Colonel Spinner feigned unavailability. To my pleasure, a couple of naval officer friends on the staff dug up an admiral somewhere in Yokosuka, fifty miles to the southeast, and he came up to award the medal to me. He had one. I cannot recall the colonel ever saying another civil word to me.

Time hung laboriously heavy, and I passed it by reading everything that came into the center. I devoured the intell reports from sources such as the HUMINT, human intelligence; the spy; COMINT, voice communications recordings; and ELINT, electronic intelligence readings. Minute indications hinted Russian Mikoyan-Gurevich 17s, the MiG-17s, might be appearing in Red China. No publication on it had surfaced because of the paucity of information.

I strove to verify it. I had a mission, a goal, something to do. I threw myself into it as day after day I dug deeper into everything I could get my hands on. And as luck always falls on those who bust their ass, the voluminous information started falling into place. Finally, I felt I could show, unequivocally, MiG-17 presence. I took it to my boss, Lieutenant Colonel Penske, and he said it had credibility. I took it to Commander Robbins, he said it looked good and congratulated me on a fine piece of intell research.

A briefing for the colonel was next. He arrived a half hour late. Rigorously I outlined my reasons and data. He opened a document he'd brought with him to the briefing. Rudely, he read it while I talked, glancing up at me, grunting disapproval, about once every three or four minutes.

I finished, and waited, waited for him to say well done and that he had been wrong about me. Five minutes passed as the waves of silence cut into my feelings of accomplishment. He put down the document he was reading and looked around, frowning at the men attending the briefing. He yawned as he stood, putting me off guard.

"*Nonsense,*" he barked like a drill instructor, and his aquiline face snapped around to each of his *real* intelligence officers. "A piece of junk? Is this what new blood is suppose to give us . . . haven't you taught him anything yet? Work on what you're supposed to work on, SAM sites and radars." He waved his arm to the briefing easel. "Not this kind of bullshit," he sputtered, scowling around at the rest of his cowed officers, who were all busying themselves with important matters like keeping out of the line of fire. He cleared his throat, grunted, and left.

Three weeks later MiG-17s roared up from Phuc Yin, the Lyndon B. Johnson sanctuary for the North Vietnamese Air Force, just north of Hanoi, to harass our unalerted pilots putting strikes in against North Vietnam.

The gods smiled. Word came that the PACOMELINT center was to be moved to Hawaii. All personnel that didn't wish to extend their tour of duty and go would be transferred at their request. I requested.

And twenty months from my bitterly cold arrival, I received orders to become the executive officer of a destroyer, an XO.

Chapter 2

XO

The man sat slumped, skin pale, his gaunt face drained, his eyes not focusing. His wayward attempt at a smile made him even more pathetic as I introduced myself, reaching for his outstretched hand. "John Givens," he said softly, exhaling a breath as if a yoke had been lifted from his shoulders. "Glad . . . glad to see you."

The USS *Kramer* had just arrived back in Long Beach, California, a week before from its western Pacific tour, called WESTPAC, and its crew was enjoying a two-week stand-down period. His hands shook when he told me the captain wanted to see me as soon as I reported aboard.

John Givens knocked on the door to the captain's in-port cabin. No answer. He waited for ten seconds and knocked again. A loud, snarling "Wait" bounced back at us through the fake-wood door. We stood there silently for three minutes, Givens's eyes not meeting mine. He fumbled with his academy ring, pulling it up and down over his left ring finger. In two more minutes a growling "Come in" sounded.

The five-foot-eight, rotund little man with silver oak leaves on his collar turned slowly and stared at us as if we were animals in the zoo. "You," he said, pointing a stubby finger at the XO. "We don't need you here, get out there and see if you can at least get this shit bucket cleaned up for once . . . show Sheppard here what a real XO should be," the captain snarled, dismissing John Givens with a pompous sweep of his hand.

Givens's face puckered in an imitation of anger, but there wasn't enough emotion left in him to hold it as it loosened into wet clay faster than it formed. He glanced at me, his eyes begging for understanding as he slinked out of the room, his head almost lying on his chest.

The captain turned back to his desk, ignoring me for another minute. "So you're a mustang, Sheppard, I guess you think that makes you some kind of hotshot officer with the men . . . eh?"

"No, sir," I replied, still standing while he sat. He hadn't even offered to shake my hand.

"What makes you think you can be an XO on my ship . . . I've known a lot of mustangs and I'm not impressed."

"I can do the job, Captain," I answered a little too softly.

"I can do the job, Captain," he mimicked in a falsetto voice, his cheeks pulled back in a phony smile, half closing his eyes. I didn't reply. "Well, I've heard that before, and if you can't hack it, I'm kicking your ass out of here, you understand me?"

"Yes, sir."

He turned, busying himself with a sheet of paper on his desk. I waited, standing at parade rest as if I were a seaman recruit waiting for my boot camp chief to note my insignificant presence. After five minutes, with my fresh white shirt dripping sweat through my dress blue jacket, he turned again for the attack. "You think all those hero ribbons you're wearing mean shit to me?"

"No, sir."

"So you were in Vietnam . . . you're not the only fake hero here, we were there bravely shelling the coast for nothing . . . how many babies you kill, Sheppard?"

The light grew dimmer as my eyes narrowed and the muscles in my jaw clenched. "None, sir," I answered after three seconds of keeping my breathing easy and slow. I was thankful for the navy's survival training and prison camp interrogation techniques I'd received before going to Vietnam. I never suspected I'd have to use the knowledge meeting my CO as his prospective executive officer. His attempts to rattle me were at best amateurish. I persevered, a triumph of training over nerves.

Five more minutes of silence passed as I stood there. He got up and went to his private head. The toilet flushed. He came out drying his hands. He didn't even look at me as he sat down again with his back toward me. Three minutes later, still pretending to read the lone paper on his clean desk, he muttered, "Dismissed, Sheppard."

I left without a word, his conduct lessening and spoiling my moment of happiness over becoming an XO.

Lieutenant Commander Givens sat in the wardroom holding a cup of coffee. His hands shook as he carefully lifted the cup and just as carefully drank it down. I smiled. He inhaled and tried a smile in return. It wasn't much, more like a wild animal first encountering a human being. I looked at him and chuckled. "You poor sonofabitch." He focused on me for a second, winced, then exploded into laughter.

"The captain wants me off the ship in forty-eight hours," he said as we sat in his stateroom just forward of the wardroom with the OPS officer in the stateroom just across the narrow passageway.

"I'm sorry, Don, but it'll have to be quick . . . we're not in good shape. Our remaining OPTAR funds are very low, but all in order. Material conditions are bad. I'm sorry I can't give you anything better. Morale is low and I don't wish to comment further.

"The competence of the officers, you'll have to judge for yourself, I don't wanna say anything about it. We have no commitments for three weeks, and by that time all the crew will be back aboard off postdeployment leave." He stopped and lit another cigarette from the one he'd just finished. He'd gone through two packs in the two and a half hours we'd been talking. Between packs he chugged Maalox down his throat as if it were water. His shallow eyes looked at me. "I'm sure glad you're here . . . please don't think ill of me."

I couldn't answer.

At lunch, which the XO was too busy to attend, the captain started on me again. "I read your service jacket . . . you think you're an intelligence officer, eh?"

Only four junior officers were there for lunch. Two of them had the duty. The other two, being brown-baggers, married officers, were probably too strapped for money to eat ashore with the other junior officers. Economics overcame unpleasantness.

A pimple-faced young sailor came in to give the twelve o'clock reports, those reports that showed the ship's position when at sea and the fuel and water quantities. But before his nervous voice got the first two words out, the captain snatched the reports out of his hand, berating him for a filthy uniform and squeaky voice.

I felt ashamed of being a naval officer.

"Well, Sheppard, did you think you were an intelligence officer or not?" he snarled. The junior officers winced.

"No, sir, we just analyzed data," I answered, which constituted the entire mealtime conversation. Twenty minutes passed without the usual banter and good cheer until the captain folded his napkin, and, without a word, left.

Commander Baker, my first CO on *Henshaw,* had often said one must feed his mind as well as his stomach at the wardroom table. I guess *Kramer* never heard that one before, or maybe the press of their responsibilities kept their minds occupied.

At just after 1900 the next evening, Lt. Comdr. John H. Givens, USN, USNA, departed the ship.

As he shuffled aft to the quarterdeck, his bloodshot eyes knifed into each dark spot. His breathing came hard, mostly gasps. He leaned toward me, the smell of sweat on him as he whispered, his eyes still shifting, "Don't worry, Don, I have friends, he won't be around long, now that I'm detached."

As his foot stepped off the gangway, his shoulders came back, his head came up. He turned to me, saluted, smiled, then marched down the pier, ramrod straight, a stride any marine corps drill instructor would envy.

Four weeks later. "Under way." The captain had the conn. I, with my additional duty as navigator, bent over the nav table, laying in the sightings the quartermasters fed to me as I tried to keep from being seasick. The curse had stayed with me. The lines of bearing cut beautifully, and as I called out course recommendations, my confidence returned. The captain ignored every recommendation I gave him, but that was okay, I was at sea again.

This part was easy. I had worried that I might have forgotten. It was just past seven years since I had been to sea in a position of authority on the bridge.

Long Beach Harbor was a sailor's dream. You could back out of the berth, turn south for a few minutes, then sail to open water in less than fifteen minutes. Not like San Diego, with its sailboat-filled, twisting, narrow harbor, or San Francisco, with its murderous tides, fogs, and currents. Long Beach was a straight shot and superheaters could be lit off ten minutes from under way.

Separately fired superheater furnaces were a major concern on this class of destroyers, which had two fireboxes in the boilers. One brought the water to a pressurized six hundred pounds of steam pressure. This was routed through the second firebox, where the temperature was raised by the superheater furnace to eight hundred fifty degrees. This gave us greater efficiency through the turbines, and thus greater speed.

When the superheater furnaces were lit off, however, there had to be sufficient steam flowing through their tubes, or the boiler would melt down. This meant we had to maintain at least ten knots when they were firing. And that, sometimes, could be a royal pain. Consequently, we never lit off the superheaters until well at sea.

The captain kept the conn well out of the harbor, then gave it to the OPS officer. Only the three line department heads: weapons, operations, and engineering, stood OOD watches. It had been that way for the entire time the captain was aboard.

Luckily, our operation area was close to land, and I could use the surface search radar for fixes. I had no confidence in my celestial navigational ability. At very best, previously on *Henshaw* my star lines crossed uselessly in a large ten-mile triangle for our position, it should have been just a point. I hated it.

At breakfast that morning, the other officers had eaten early, glancing at the door with apprehension each time it opened. Only two ensigns were left when he came in. The temperature dropped ten degrees. I was just finishing as he sat down. Hell, the least I could do was have a cup of coffee with him.

"Sheppard!" He should be calling me XO. "Blue Monday . . . eh?" he said expansively, unrolling his white linen napkin from its sterling silver napkin ring with CAPTAIN engraved upon it. I had been admiring it.

I told him it looked like a great day to me. The steward swiftly appeared from the pantry, shakily carrying the captain's breakfast plate. He put it down gingerly and slunk out of sight.

"No, Sheppard, blue Monday. In the good ol' days, on the sailing ships . . . on Mondays they lined up all the defaulters and flogged them till they were black and blue. You know . . . blue Monday. Get it?" He laughed, a phlegmatic laugh that sounded like a chicken clucking.

"Don't they teach you mustangs anything at the ranch? He must have thought that was awfully funny too, as he laughed so hard, the coffee cup he was bringing to his lips splashed over the white linen tablecloth.

"Wish they'd bring back flogging for this ship . . . could use it," he said more seriously, calling for the steward to bring him more coffee.

"This ship needs something much stronger than flogging," I said before my better sense shut down my mouth. I meant leadership, but he didn't get it.

He looked at me, his eyes squinting. "What, oh, yeah . . . know what you mean." He looked toward the serving window between the wardroom and pantry and bellowed, *"Steward, bring me more coffee."*

He started talking again, I wasn't interested. I had too many things to do. He babbled about how bad the crew was, how incompetent his officers were. He droned on, unmindful of the thousand things I had to attend to on the first day at sea after thirty days in port. I tried to pay attention, but thinking about the tasks awaiting me took precedence. The sound of his deep voice had no more import than the constant whirling hum of the vent blowers.

Then something different. The hum of the vent fans was all there was. I glanced at him, he had stopped talking. He looked at me, he expected an answer. Shit! What do I say? In a second I said, "Yes, sir, I'll have to work on that." A good answer, it'd cover most everything.

"Right, Sheppard . . . take care of it . . . you've got the right attitude." He stood and left. I'll be damned, it worked.

Later, at about 1000, we were contacted by another destroyer, call sign Tango Alpha. Ships at sea changed their two-letter call signs every twenty-four hours according to a communications pamphlet that listed the daily call signs for each ship for a month. This was for security, so spies wouldn't know which ships were under way. Supposedly.

Tango Alpha was steaming in an adjacent op area, and she wanted to join us for tactical maneuvers. The captain agreed, but took the conn every time the other ship got within five thousand yards of us and, worse, ran the tactical OOD drills himself. He was good at it, but he should have been letting his officers do them. That's what they were for. The lackluster performance of CIC and the bridge, including the officers, did not surprise me. It bothered me, but I held my tongue.

I pondered over the authority I had yet to exercise. Mostly, I told myself I was waiting until I got the feel of the ship. In truth, I held back because of the harangue the captain gave me twice a day on how incompetent the old XO had been and how poor a job I was doing, and how his disloyal officers fought him on everything he tried to do.

He bemoaned that because of this, he had trouble running a decent ship. "But I'll get even," he insisted.

Hadn't I read a book like that somewhere?

I left the bridge, the CO's domain, and headed to mine, the ship's office. I fought down the rising bile in my throat each time the ship rolled. Thank God the seas were calm. The chief yeoman and his petty officers reported directly to me. I hadn't paid much attention to them on *Henshaw*. Actually, at that time I thought our XO had a nice, cushy billet. I was wrong. The door was closed. Odd.

I knocked once and walked in. The chief yeoman and his two men danced a little jig, laughing and patting each other on the back as they circled in the tiny, cramped space.

"What the hell is going on in here?" I demanded with what I considered my tough XO voice.

The chief handed me a letter from BUPERS. "Orders for the captain to be detached . . . in two weeks. Just came in. Detached . . . hot damn! Detached. Here, XO, see for yourself," he said, not containing his excitement.

"Hallelujah, there is a God," Smitty, the yeoman striker, yelled out.

"That's enough of this shit. Knock it off, Chief!"

"Yes, sir . . . two weeks . . . knock it off, Chief . . . yes, sir, yes, sir."

I returned to the bridge, looked around, and handed the letter to the captain as the signalman tried to tell him we were to go alongside the other destroyer's port side in ten minutes for a practice high line. "What?" he snarled at the signalman, then to me he grunted out, "Whaddaya got, more crap for me?" He had been maneuvering in, heading for a point a thousand yards behind the lead ship, and he hadn't taken his speed off yet.

I told him he would be interested but it could wait. He snatched the letter out of my hand and looked at it, his eyes widening in pained surprise, his mouth contorting into a hateful sneer. Our bow headed toward the other ship's stern.

"Umph," he snorted, his face muscles wrestling between a sneer and a smile. "Too soon, too early," he chanted. "Rotten orders . . . too early, too early."

"Can I take it alongside, Captain?" I asked, knowing his feelings on only himself conning the ship in tight situations. His eyes, like a rodent searching out danger, darted about the bridge as if he were trying to orient himself. He clung to his chair with his left hand while the other petted its simulated leather back. His head swiveled to me. Demonic eyes consumed me.

"What? How dare you, Sheppard!" he blurted out as if I'd slapped him across the face.

"Can I take it alongside, Captain? *Captain!* We're getting too god-damn close," I yelled.

In reading his orders and his astonishment and anger at my committing the sin of asking to conn the ship, his attention diverted. The lead ship was a bare six hundred yards ahead of us, and we were closing her fast.

"Tell Main Control to stand by for a backing bell," I turned, shouting to the lee helm, then added, "Superheaters?"

"Secured," a voice replied.

"Captain, may I have the conn?" I asked softly. He glowered at me. His lips moved, but no words came out. A slight tremor danced his hands in front of him as if he were playing a toy piano. He'd lost it.

I asked again, even more softly.

"What? Yeah, what?" he stammered, looking at the approaching stern of the destroyer ahead, then at me, then at his orders. His eyes glazed over as if he were in shock. I took the yeah to mean permission granted.

"Sheppard here, I've got the conn, all engines emergency back full." The sweating lee helmsman yanked the engine order telegraph handles to back full, rammed them up to ahead full, and brought them back to rest on back full. I could feel the stern dig into the water as I rushed to the bridge wing to check my stern free. "Right full rudder," I ordered to swing my bow away from the lead ship.

The helmsman frantically spun his wheel clockwise. "Right full aye, sir. No new course given. My rudder is at right full, sir," the helmsman reported in the fine tradition of the navy. But his voice came out too loudly, rushed on the edge of panic.

"All engines back emergency full, sir," the lee helm, the man on the engine order telegraph, reported, as was the custom.

"Two hundred yards and closing, head's coming over to starboard," the OOD yelled out. The stern of the ship ahead of us kicked up a froth as she threw her engines ahead full, realizing we were closing her too fast and from the wrong position. *Thank God!*

"One hundred yards and holding," the OPS officer said. Thirty seconds passed.

"Lee helm tell Main Control to stand by for an ahead two-thirds bell. Boatswain's Mate, set the high line detail . . . on the double . . . rig starboard side to . . . move it."

"Aye, sir, Main Control acknowledges."

"Two hundred and opening." Thirty seconds ticked by. "Five hundred yards. Opening."

"All engines ahead two-thirds, rudder amidships," I ordered.

"My rudder is amidships, no new course given. Passing 040, sir."

"Eight hundred yards and . . ."

"Knock off ranges . . . signalman make to Tango Alpha, 'We are prepared to come alongside your port side, two minutes.' Lee helm tell Main Control well done on that backing bell."

In precisely one hundred twenty seconds the signal flag indicating 'come alongside my port side' was hauled up to half mast on Tango Alpha, a preparatory command. Our signalmen raised the same flags to half mast: We understood. Tango Alpha instantly hauled her flags to the yardarm and flashed them down meaning execute.

"Pass the word, Boatswain's Mate, 'We are commencing our approach starboard side to.' Lee helm, all engines ahead full, make turns for twenty knots. Helmsman, steer course 049."

I stood on the starboard wing, absorbing the ship's power as a tonic to my long absence, its vibration welcoming me aboard. No sound could be heard save the soothing squish of our rapierlike bow parting the water, curling away, announcing the passage of the ship. The sea air cleansed me, washed away the dourness of the land. I was home again, as if I'd never left. The captain sat silently in his chair, staring at me, his blank face registering no emotion.

We closed fast with our five-knot speed advantage. I wanted to look good after that near collision. The calm sea and mild wind offered heady encouragement. We passed her screw's "suck in" point at one hundred twenty feet out. I looked in to caution the helmsman, and noticed Willie, my first class quartermaster and leading hand, had taken over the helm. And from his nod I knew he knew.

With a flash of luck I took my speed off at precisely the right point and eased in to eighty feet to allow an easier haul on the line. "Stand by for shot line aft," Tango Alpha's 1MC blared out.

The high line aft started coming over as well as the distance line forward. In two minutes the distance line pulled taut. Not too shabby. I eased out to the green flag on the distance line, which indicated one hundred feet, and held us there.

We passed dummy loads back and forth aft as the captain lifted himself from his chair and came up and stood behind me. He was silent, but his nearness offended me. He looked fore and aft and at the other destroyer. He looked down into the turbulent water between us and said softly, "Aren't you a little close, XO?" It wasn't really a question but more an observation. *XO! That's a welcome change.*

"No, sir, one hundred feet, Captain. She's holding beautifully," I answered, expecting—fearing—another tirade. To my relief, he didn't respond as he picked up the phone connected to the sound-powered phone line that came across with the distance line. He apologized for the closing incident and thanked them for helping out by going ahead full. "Trouble with communications," I heard him say. *Too right, trouble with communications.*

"All lines clear aft," came the report.

"Lee helm, tell Main Control to stand by for twenty knots . . . tell them to watch the smoke."

"All lines clear forward, all lines clear," Lieutenant Sanders shouted.

I verified with a glance and ordered all ahead full, turns for twenty knots. Nothing happened for six seconds, then the stern dropped and the fantail skewed slightly toward Tango Alpha as our fast-turning screws created their low pressure area. Willie caught it. He was good.

I eased out to one hundred and fifty feet and increased speed to twenty-three knots. We raced forward, and clearing her bow, I ordered left full rudder. The ship, in obedience, swung smartly to port, and with all the not-forgotten skill honed under Captain Baker, we eased into station only ten yards short of our assigned one thousand yards astern.

No one on the bridge spoke. We wavered from our course by two degrees. "Mind your rudder," I whispered to Willie as I passed him. His face crimsoned as he overcorrected to bring us back on station.

"Secure the high line detail, Mr. Sanders," I said to the OOD, the OPS officer, ". . . and take the conn." I walked over to the captain, who was sitting in his elevated chair again just as two flags drew up on Tango Alpha's halyards.

"Bravo Zulu," shouted the lead signalman. "Well done."

"Understood," Mr. Sanders shouted back, his face lighting in a smile.

"Thank you, Captain, for letting me take her alongside. I enjoyed it and appreciate your confidence, sir. Request permission to lay below."

The morose face grunted an answer I couldn't decipher. I turned to walk away when, like a striking cobra, his hand shot out, grabbing my arm. But he remained silent as if a great churning in his brain did not know what to say but wanted to say something. "I—" He tried to speak, but from the depth of his madness he couldn't.

"Understand, Captain," I said as his hand released my arm. He didn't have to say anything, I'd won.

"*Kramer* Departing"

I sat in my stateroom, trying unsuccessfully to hold my pipe steady enough to light it. In the emptiness of the room, I was unable to avoid myself. The enormity of what I had done struck me like a hammer's blow. I had taken the conn away from the captain, a heinous act in the navy's book. I kept pushing the events through my mind, trying to find out if I had generated the incident or was I just there at the wrong time. The orders certainly precipitated events, and I could have held off, giving them to him until I saw he was completely free. *Why hadn't I?*

Seeing his reaction, did I really have to ask to take us alongside? His attitude on this was plain. I'd pushed too hard, too fast. He never did say I could take the conn. I effectively did it when I gave an order to the lee helm to tell Main Control to stand by for a backing bell. It was a reflex action. I saw the ship in danger and reacted when no one else did. I wondered what the crew must think of me for usurping the captain's authority.

But it was done, and better now to ride with the shape of the events than the substance.

Lieutenant Sanders knocked once on my open door and poked his head in. "XO . . . ah, may I, ah, say something?" he asked, his voice shaky.

"Sure, what?" Here it starts. The OPS officer, being the senior junior officer, would naturally be the one to say something. It would take balls to approach an XO with something this delicate. The department heads had been told emphatically during our first meeting that I wanted complete communications between us, and for them to tell me when they thought I was screwing up.

"We've . . . ah . . . never seen ship handling like that on this ship. The captain never lets us take the conn for maneuvering . . . a beautiful job, XO, beautiful, and we thank you."

"Thank me for what?"

He cleared his throat before he spoke again, his hands holding on to the doorjamb as his body consumed the easy roll of the ship. "XO, you know, thank you. Ah . . . is it true about his orders? It's all over the ship."

"Yes, Larry, it's true . . . two weeks."

The captain didn't come down for lunch. The officers' festive mood was much like the norm had been on *Henshaw.* Joking and congratulations on my ship handling filled the conversation. My ego sucked it up, but I cautioned the officers enough was enough, there'd be no more talk of the incident. But I loved the power and their adulation.

The captain didn't come down for supper either. He was still sitting in his chair as I came up near twilight to shoot the evening stars. His body sat rigid, as if made of concrete. I greeted him cordially, asking if he wanted anything special in the night orders. The XO wrote them, the CO signed them, adding a personal note if desired. He grunted no, continuing to look out to sea.

I walked down one level to the chart house. The evening offered no clouds, a slight breeze rippled the seas. The stars were just blinking on. None of it impressed me as I girded up for my first official bout with the evening star fix. I could have plotted our twenty hundred hour, 2000, position with the radar, we were close enough in, but custom demanded we take a star fix. I'd boned up on celestial navigation after I got my orders and on the entire trip back from Japan—and for the last two hours in my stateroom. Still, I lacked confidence.

Notwithstanding a ten-minute psyching-up session and repeating the story of the little engine that could, thirteen times, I still knew I couldn't do it. I didn't have the eye. The journey to the chart house was long. I was about to be exposed as a naval officer who just couldn't hack the mysteries of celestial navigation, though tens of thousands before me had.

Actually it was simple. All you had to do was measure the angle from certain stars or planets to the horizon, and knowing what time it was from the chronometer, a very accurate clock set to Greenwich mean time, you compared your angles with a book that told you what the angles would be at different times of the day for different locations. From this you drew lines of position from at least three stars and plotted them. With skill they each crossed over one another. And that was where you were.

Of course, you had to know your approximate location to start with. Locating the stars and measuring their angle was the difficult part for me.

First Class Quartermaster Dan Wilhelmson waited for me as I stepped into the chart house. "Got things lined up, XO . . . how'd you want to do it? You shoot, I record?"

"Whaddaya got?" I asked professionally, knowing the quartermasters usually picked the most likely candidate stars and plotted out an estimated location. The mighty navigator then came on the scene with his "special" sextant, tuned for his own eye, and swiftly identified the stars in seconds, then, with magical, deft use of the angled moving mirrors on the sextant, adjusted the angle indicator until the star appeared to be on the horizon, the angle.

The lowly assistant noted the time and recorded the angles and went through the drudge work of computing the star lines. One did this at twilight and daybreak so the stars and horizon were both visible.

"Ah, Willie, I'm not very good at this."

"Yes, sir, like you're not very good at ship handling either."

"I ain't shit'n', Willie, I've never plotted a box smaller than five miles in my life." I referred to the size of the area the star's lines of position cut into. A perfect fix was a point; as you increased from there, the fix became progressively poorer. "I'll give it a try again," I said, adjusting the sextant as Willie pointed out the stars.

With my usual skill, the box cut with a seven-and-a-half-mile polygon. Willie conceded that I was telling the truth, and handed me his, which he'd just plotted before I came up. He handed me a position report indicating our latitude and longitude advanced to 2000. I glanced at his cut; five lines crossed over each other. I shamefully signed the report in the navigator block and asked him what he was doing on the helm when we came alongside that morning.

He looked at me, his jet-black hair framing a smiling face. He didn't answer for a moment, then his tall, lean frame stood erect from the chart table. He slowly turned, snapping his hand up in salute.

"Sir, with all due respect, the minute I heard your first command to the lee helm, I knew we had a hot stick aboard and we'd be coming in fast and close. I didn't want that fucked up—excuse me, sir—by an inexperienced hand on the wheel." His arm came down, slapping his side.

"XO, you're number one on old Krammy Pooh, and I'll gladly take all the fixes we need."

Too embarrassed to answer, I turned to leave.

"Willie," I said at the door as I held his 2000 position report. "One thing . . . if you would."

"Yes, sir?"

"Remember, the helmsman doesn't automatically adjust back to station once he's off. We pay the officer of the deck, the OODs, to do that."

"You saw that?" he answered, his face burning red, his mouth curling into a little grin.

"No, didn't see a thing, just making a casual comment. Thanks for the assist."

"Now on deck all eight o'clock reports . . . eight o'clock reports will be taken outside the chart house," the 1MC, the ship's main announcing system, blasted out at 1930. This intrusive call summoned all department heads to lay to the chart house to report the condition of their departments. It also rudely awakened those of the crew trying to get some sleep before their mid watch.

The department heads stood at attention in the narrow passageway outside the chart house. Awfully formal of them, I thought. But then, I had never taken eight o'clock reports from them before, and they were feeling me out. Nothing new should be reported here; if it was important enough to mention at eight o'clock reports, the captain and I should have already known about it. I cleared my throat with a nervous cough and told them a little less formality would do quite well.

Lieutenant Larry J. Sanders, USN, USNA, spoke first, as was his due, being the senior lieutenant onboard. His short-framed body weaved majestically in synch with the rolling deck as he said he had nothing new to report, but added that the SPS-10 surface search radar was still acting up, and the captain was worried about the night steam area.

He should not have been, their area for the night was a thirty-mile-per-side box well out of the shipping channels. But tyrants always carried the burden of fear upon their shoulders.

Lieutenant Jeff J. Hobson, USN, ROTC, the weapons officer, spoke next. His body stood straight but his muscles sagged. Obviously there was a time when he ran and lifted weights. He spoke softly with a self-effacing tone that indicated great confidence and self-assurance. "Nothing new, XO, except I hear we got us one hot ship handler onboard that backed the captain down this morning."

"That'll be enough, Mr. Hobson. I will hear no more of that kind of talk . . . do you all understand . . . all of you, do you all understand?" I barked a little harder than I meant to. They nodded yes, knowing I couldn't allow criticism of the captain. But I silently forgave them; they, too, had suffered just as badly as the old XO.

Lieutenant Joe Raven, USN, ROTC, the chief engineer, reported the fuel and water status and that the number one main feed pump was out of commission along with a bilge pump and the small set of evaps. I knew about them, and asked for the estimated time of repair on the number one main feed pump. His phlegmatic body slumped.

He said haltingly that he wasn't sure, maybe tomorrow afternoon, and he'd have to check with the chief.

I just looked at him, not saying anything for five seconds, letting him ponder his answer. "Shouldn't a chief engineer know that sort of thing, Mr. Raven?" I asked. He didn't answer. I didn't push. He understood.

The supply officer spoke last, as was his place, being only a lieutenant junior grade, the junior department head. "Nothing new, XO, we're topped off on provisions, and we're due to change mess cooks in a few days, and these other department heads are still sending me their deadbeats," he chuckled, his eyes sweeping the faces of his uncomfortable mates.

Goddammit, that same old problem: How do you take your best seamen and firemen and rotate them to mess cooking . . . a tough, thankless job. When I was a chief engineer, I'd sent my deadbeats to mess cooking, the army's KP. But how do I fix it? Your good men had to be nurtured, not relegated to the necessary but menial task of mess cooking duties. Same with the damage control party assignments. I'm going to fix it.

"We'll talk about that later, Mr. Jellico," I answered as he still stood at attention. Lieutenant (jg) Alfred B. Jellico, USN, Supply Corp (SC), USNA, stood six feet three inches tall, an imposing man with the athletic body of a linebacker. The thick glasses he wore—because of a football injury—had forced him into the supply corps. He'd wanted to be a fighter pilot.

"Oh, the steam press in the laundry is OOC, out of commission, but Joe there"—he pointed to the chief engineer—"said they'll try to fix it."

I looked back at Lieutenant Raven. He shrugged, saying he'd try. I asked him if he knew we'd be having a change-of-command ceremony in a couple of weeks, and the steam press may well be an essential item to have around. He answered that he'd check with the DCA.

"Do that, Mr. Raven, and let me know . . . it should be on your report, Mr. Raven, I like to know about such things," I answered, trying to keep sarcasm out of my voice. "Also, gentlemen, it is no longer required you make eight o'clock reports yourself. If you have the mid watch, sleep in. Have your next senior officer give them."

They looked at each other in disbelief. Eight o'clock reports were a major pain in the ass for watch-keeping officers, especially those with the mids. You couldn't get to bed as early as you wanted to. I hated it on *Henshaw* when the XO insisted department heads make the reports in person. They glanced at each other and smiled.

Larry Sanders asked when the change of command would take place. "No word yet, he just got his orders this morning. I'll let you know . . . and one last thing, gentlemen. There is nothing too small or too insignificant for me not to know about, and I'd rather know it from you. Please try to understand that. And another last thing, let me emphasize it again. I want you guys to talk to me. I want your trust; I will earn it. If you think I'm fucking up, grab your balls in both hands and tell me. And another last thing, I'd be mighty embarrassed if the captain knows anything from you guys . . . and I don't. Long speech, sorry, carry on."

"Sir, do you know who the new CO is?" Mr. Jellico asked as the department heads broke up.

"No, but you'll be kept informed."

"Can't be any worse," came *sotto voce*, which I chose to ignore.

The captain still sat in his bridge chair. "Eight o'clock reports, Captain," I said as I had seen *Henshaw*'s XO do so many times.

"About goddamned time," he snarled, all his earlier humbleness gone.

It was 1945, fifteen minutes before eight o'clock, and every XO on every ship under way in this time zone was presently reporting to his captain. "My regrets, sir, what time would the captain desire eight o'clock reports?" I answered, keeping my composure and using the third person, which to me marked disrespect.

"Umph! . . . I guess you can't do any better considering the quality of department heads I have on this rust bucket," he said, sighing as if the gods had cursed him with an incompetent crew. Then, yanking his head toward me, his hand shot to grab the reports from me. Instinctively I pulled back, causing his arm to swing wildly, foolishly, in an awkward gesture, into empty air. The bridge crew stood silent, afraid to talk, too often having seen this drama unfold in the past.

I saluted, coming to attention. "With all due respect, Captain, I can have eight o'clock reports to the captain anytime it pleases the captain . . . and the department heads seem to be a competent lot. Would the captain like the reports earlier or later, *sir!*"

I spoke with all the officialism of a marine sergeant reporting to his colonel, snapping down my salute just as I ended the sentence, thrusting the reports into his hand.

"Reports, *sir!*"

It took him five minutes to read them as I stood rigidly at attention. It should have taken thirty seconds. "What's this position, Sheppard?"

"Call me XO, sir, if you would," I snapped back, not letting him slight me by addressing me by my last name as I called off the latitude and longitude to the second. His eyes went wide as he stared at me in silence. Willie, bless his heart, had warned me about the captain asking for the position verbally, checking the numbers as he listened. I had memorized them. "Any special night orders, sir?" I should be addressing him "Captain," but he didn't deserve the title.

I still stood at attention, waiting another three minutes for his answer. My stomach churned and my nerves fought one another for relief. He was putting on this little spectacle just to show me his power. I winced, knowing the negative effect it had on the crew. I stood straighter. I wondered if Givens had left any of his Maalox behind.

The watch changed silently around our little charade, and I knew it would be but seconds before the entire ship learned of the drama, if they didn't know already from the sound-powered phone talkers whispering out a blow-by-blow. Normally, a captain would have done all this in the privacy of his sea cabin.

"No, nothing special."

I thrust the night order book into his hand. He signed without reading what I had written, stepped down from his chair, coughed twice, and stomped into his sea cabin. "Captain left the bridge," the boatswain's mate of the watch called out, unable to hide the pleasure in his voice.

Willie touched my arm as I passed through the after-bridge door. "Good work, XO," he whispered.

"Knock it off, Wilhelmson," I barked, instantly ashamed of taking my frustration out on him.

I sat in my stateroom, pondering my actions. One more time I had openly defied the captain in front of the bridge team. What could he do to me? I had ten years of outstanding fitness reports and a chest full of medals. Navy tradition says you're not supposed to write a fitness report on an officer if you haven't observed him for at least ninety days. It would be barely fifty days for the captain and me. Even my nemesis, Lieutenant Colonel Spinner, USAF, from the PA-COMELINT center, had given me an outstanding fitness report even though he hated my guts. I sat with my rolling stomach and worried about it.

Normally fitness reports were written once a year or when the CO is transferred. Department heads wrote the fitness reports on their officers. The XO wrote them on the department heads and the CO wrote the XO's. The CO signed them all after reviewing them with each man. An officer lived and died with his fitness reports. It was all the navy had to base promotion and duty assignments on. One bad fitness report could seriously hamper a man's career. Especially if one aspired to command, and every good naval officer did.

Of course the old boy network as well as "The U.S. Naval Academy Protective Society" operated but they couldn't do much if your fitreps were bad.

In our case now, the captain wrote the fitreps for the department heads, surprisingly asking my advice based upon my short knowledge. I thought Joe Raven as chief engineer was weaker than the captain indicated, but I didn't comment, afraid my own engineering experience might add a negative bias. All the fitreps were good.

For me he wrote a glowing report, extolling my "organizational ability," my "take-charge attitude," and my "superb skill at ship handling." I felt like an asshole. I knew he had written John Givens a good fitrep even though verbally he proclaimed him woefully incompetent. I guess the captain couldn't help it if the pressure and responsibility of command had been too much for him. I'd seen it before. Maybe Givens had actually let him down, but I doubted it.

It takes a special kind of man to be a ship's captain. And even though I had proved myself as a commander in Vietnam, maybe being the captain of a ship was different. I hoped not.

The captain stood at the lectern to make the requisite speech to the crew. He simply said, "Thank you," and read his orders. Commander Frank J. Macaby, USN, NROTC, a qualified submariner, then read his orders and added, "I relieve you, sir." Then, turning to the assembled crew, he said, "I look forward to being your captain."

Ignobly, the old captain walked down the gangway as the sun appeared through an opening in the dark clouds.

Chapter 3

Morale

The new captain and I sat in his in-port cabin, chatting, after the change of command ceremony. He had been on staff duty and surprised when he received his orders. He was taken aback when I told him I had been aboard for only six weeks. He confessed he'd spent just a year on a destroyer as an ensign before going to sub school and had never handled a surface ship before. He was a sub driver and the ex-skipper of an attack boat. With complete candor he expressed doubts on his destroyer-handling ability.

I assured him I could handle the ship and the department heads seemed competent enough, although they had very little ship-handling experience under the previous CO. He asked why. I said I didn't know. He asked what I knew of the man he relieved. "Very little," I replied after a few moments. He stared at me, not accepting the answer. We both waited in silence, I hoped I didn't have to say anything more.

"How was your relationship, XO?" his voice almost demanded.

"I think he wore his underwear a little too tight, Captain," I replied after a moment, hoping it was a good enough answer. He said nothing for thirty seconds, then smiled and offered his hand. I was sure he knew all about the previous captain. That's how things worked. My answer was good enough; I'd served the system of not criticizing a senior officer, and he knew he'd get no more from me. He'd let me win. Captain Macaby was okay.

We decided on our relationship. He would be the good guy, I would be the bad, the usual arrangement. "Run the ship, XO, and keep me informed, I don't know much about destroyers . . . all I know is how to sink 'em."

"Yes, sir, submarines and targets," I chuckled. "We can sure learn a lot about ASW from an ex-sub driver, Captain."

He gave the standard answer that there was no way a destroyer could catch and sink a nuc boat on its own. His words came out egotistically with the same smugness I had heard on *Catfish* when I was on *Henshaw* and had been an exchange officer in WESTPAC for several days, several years ago.

He asked what *our* greatest problem was, though I knew he knew. It hadn't taken him long to discover the low state of morale during his relieving time, especially among the officers. A tinge of pride went through me as he used the word *our*. I wasn't alone anymore, stuck out on the weak branch of insubordination.

I told him our most obvious was morale, then added that our officers felt cheated because they never got a chance to handle the ship. They wanted to experience the power and majesty of the sixty-thousand shaft horsepower we had. I knew the feeling.

"Let's fix it, XO, but not by swatting the mosquitoes, but by draining the swamp."

The next day, at the captain's suggestion, we started the Thursday Planning Board for Training. I told the department heads that the captain knows about the past problems and wants us to put them aside. "During these Thursday meetings," I went on, we'll plan what training and work is needed for the next week and set priorities. And most important, we'll carry them out. Too many times I've seen all kinds of plans worked out and never executed." The four department heads exchanged quizzical glances.

"I hope, gentlemen, to establish a good enough relationship between us that we can get to the heart of problems and solve them together." The four naval officers glanced at one another and nodded their heads.

The head steward, First Class Petty Officer Ramon M. Santos, USN, with eighteen years in the navy, brought in fresh coffee in a sterling silver server. He placed fresh cups in front of us and filled each one. He placed a silver sugar bowl and creamer in the center of the table and laid out four silver teaspoons. I winked at him; he smiled and left.

Santos was a good man with a degree in accounting from the University of Manila. Not being able to find work in the Philippines in the mid-fifties, he, like many Filipino men, joined the U.S. Navy under a program that allowed them to be stewards—stewards only—and gain U.S. citizenship.

Though there was some breakout, for the most part they were stuck as being stewards for their entire career. They did a fine job, and I felt the navy suffered by underutilizing their talent in this blatant display of racism. Those that had broken out of the mold were assigned to duties in the supply and disbursing departments. Their foreign background prevented them from branching out to other rates because they couldn't get a security clearance. They didn't seem to favor the engineering ratings. Santos played a wicked game of chess and had beaten me all three times we had played. And I was no slouch on the board.

I continued my little speech by telling them that morale sucked on *Kramer*. As if they didn't know it, and their surprised faces smiled as I asked for suggestions.

None of the four answered, all looking down at the table as if I'd asked them about their wives' sexual habits. Naval officers didn't lightly criticize their senior officers, especially in front of another senior officer.

Silence danced around the bulkheads as it permeated the room, covering each one of them. I committed myself to sitting here until I could get them to talk about it. I filled and lit my pipe, letting its strong, aromatic pungency overwhelm the anemic cigarette smoke of the others. Five minutes passed with fidgeting and throat clearing.

"Liberty, XO, why are we still on three sections when all the other ships are on one-in-four?" Jeff Hobson, the WEPS officer, finally blurted out. "Why do we have to stay aboard every third night and every third weekend when there's no special alert and the rest of the fleet has to do it only every fourth night and weekend?"

I asked Larry Summers, the OPS officer, to comment. He answered that OPS can handle four-section liberty easily.

Joe Raven, the chief engineer, didn't volunteer a statement when I looked at him. He stared down at the green felt tablecloth that covered the wardroom table, as they did on every other wardroom table in the fleet. "Joe?"

He hesitated, as if struggling with himself. I knew his answer. He had to keep as many engineers aboard as necessary so the duty section could get under way and fight the ship. Unless the engineers were trained sufficiently, they wouldn't be able to do it, unless, maybe, if the chief machinist were aboard, but other than that it would be difficult.

He told me this and finished with "I'm sorry, XO."

"Thank you, Joe, a lesser man might have tried to fake it, not wanting to look bad because he hadn't trained his men well enough." His face dropped as if I'd slapped him. "No, no, Joe, I didn't mean that as a criticism but just a statement of fact. I know you haven't been able to train your men very much. I understand the old captain never allowed drills."

Al Jellico buoyantly spoke up next without a prompt. "No problem with the Supply Department."

"What does the senior watch officer have to add?" I asked socratically to Larry Summers. It startled him, as it focused his mind, causing his coffee to splash on the tablecloth.

"Hell! We have only three CDOs," Larry Summers said, sweeping his hand to the other department heads, seemingly embarrassed for not considering this before.

"Who do you have ready?"

He looked at his peers for support. The three line department heads were the only qualified CDOs on the ship. The old captain would allow no others. When a department head went on leave, the other two had to stand port and starboard, that is, one on, one off, watch and watch.

Al Jellico, not concerned with these line officer things since he was not in a duty section, broke in, saying he had only three cooks. "They can't go one in four. Sorry, I didn't think about that."

"Anybody you know wants to strike for cook?" I asked.

His baby face lit up. "Why, yes, yes, I do, XO."

One down, three to go.

Then Larry Summers spoke, telling me that only the three line department heads were qualified OODs and thereby the only ones by navy regulations allowed to stand command duty officer, or CDO, watches in port because of the requirement to get the ship under way. In the absences of the captain and the XO, the CDO is in complete control of the ship.

I answered that it was a simple fix; we qualify another OOD and then train him to be a CDO. I asked him who he had in mind, concealing my exhilaration on how well the meeting was going.

He looked at Jeff Hobson. "I think Lt. (jg) Vince Baldachino, the ASW officer, is maybe the best junior officer of the deck, JOOD, we've got, but frankly, I don't know; he's never been allowed to do anything . . . but he stands a good watch when the captain's not on his ass. The old captain, I mean. Whaddaya guys think?"

Joe Raven grunted, seemingly still in thought about his failure with the engineers. Not much of an answer there, but Jeff Hobson agreed Baldachino was the best they had for the job.

"Joe," I said, trying to bring the chief engineer back into the decision-making chain.

"What?"

"Forget about your snipes for a minute. What do you think of Vince Baldachino for OOD?"

"Oh, I'm sorry, he's a good man, learned the engineering plant on his own time . . . knows what he's doing on the bridge and CIC. Good man. Academy."

I asked who was senior to him that we might consider, remembering the trouble I had when I qualified for OOD before an officer senior to me on *Henshaw*.

Jeff Hobson looked at Larry and, shrugging his shoulders, blurted out, "The first lieutenant, but he's a basket case right now . . . almost as bad as the old XO . . . he had to take too much shit from the old captain. Hell, sir, every evolution we had in WESTPAC ended up with the 1MC demanding he and I report to the captain on the bridge on the double. Then he'd chew out our ass in front of everybody no matter how well we'd done. It was never good enough," he ended, breathlessly trying to light a cigarette.

I shrugged, telling them again to forget what used to be and concentrate on salvage. "How did Mr. Maxwell appear before he went
over the edge, if that isn't too strong a word?" I asked, sweeping my
eyes over each of them.

They all agreed he was okay, and Jeff added he was the JOOD when
I took us alongside. "He thinks you walk with God."

"Well, I can't fault the man's perception," I chuckled, asking, "You
guys agree?"

"That you walk with God, sir?" Al Jellico chided.

"No, gentlemen. Do you think he's okay to qualify as an OOD?"

"He'd be okay," Jeff Hobson answered, the others nodding agreement.

I reminded Larry that the quartermasters come under me oper-
ationally, and they'd need at least one more striker to be able to go
into four-section liberty.

"Okay, thank you, gentlemen. It's 0945. Get a plan together so we
can go to four-section liberty and we'll get together at, say, 1400 . . .
can you do that?" They nodded yes.

Larry Sanders stood, ready to leave, then stopped and said, "I've
handled a ship only once getting under way, and once mooring.
Joe has never done it and, Jeff, what did you tell me, twice, several
years ago?"

I flipped my hand into the air and said we'd fix that, then walked
out of the wardroom to the main deck. I strolled around the ship,
inspecting everything. We were in bad shape and little things around
the ship showed it.

There Are No Bad Ships, Only Bad Captains

I tried desperately to remember everyone's name as I walked through
the compartments and work spaces, glad they all had their names
stenciled on their blue dungaree shirts. I stopped often, chatting to
the sailors as they worked. They were courteous but distant. There
was no camaraderie here, and the men did their jobs just enough to
get by, no more. It broke my heart to see such a waste of America's
finest.

In the wardroom, everybody knew lunch was supposed to be carefree and light and tried to act that way, but failed. The captain and
I tried to bring them into conversation, but failed. Psychologically,

they were no better than whipped dogs. Even the department heads had lost the enthusiasm they had begun to show at the planning board for training. The wardroom's faith in the navy and its leadership had been savaged.

The captain, obviously uncomfortable, rolled his white linen napkin tightly into his napkin ring. This, to everyone's delight, signaled lunch was over.

I joined him in his in-port cabin, a pall hanging over the room like a hundred graves. He opened his mouth to speak, but couldn't. He tried looking me in the eye, but couldn't. Finally he stammered, "I tried to walk the ship this morning and I was aghast. The men cowered away from me as if I had a cat-o'-nine-tails to swing across their backs. It was awful, XO, awful. You'd thought I was Captain Bligh on the *Bounty*."

"Yes, sir, I know. You're the symbol of all their hate and frustration, but we'll turn it around, Captain," I said with more conviction than I had. I outlined again the plans we had earlier discussed, especially about four-section liberty.

1400. The department heads rose as I walked into the wardroom. "Knock off standing when I come into a room. We don't have time for that. You guys have a plan?" I looked at Larry Sanders, the senior department head. This was the tough part. I had my own agenda and had given them enough to think about, hoping they'd come up with the same plan the captain and I wanted. The solution was obvious, but one had to have the participants feel it was their plan, buy into it, so to speak.

They pointed out that morale was our greatest problem, and if we could get that up, our readiness state would follow. To do this, four-section liberty would have to come as the first step, and we needed to train for that. As they spoke, I nodded agreement. In an hour we had a plan and a method of execution, rough around the edges, perhaps, but we could adjust. It was pretty close to what the captain and I had decided, and it was their plan.

"Okay, gentlemen, anything else?" They looked at one another, each shaking his head. "Okay, the plan goes into effect immediately, thank you. Carry it out."

I stood gathering my notes, when Jeff Hobson broke in with a nervous cough and a voice two octaves higher than normal. "But, but, XO, we didn't think right away . . . what about the captain? We need more time to think about this. We—"

"We need our asses off top dead center and to make this hulk a destroyer again, Mr. Hobson," I said, stuffing my papers into an envelope, taking overly long to do it just for effect. I knew this part was coming. It's always scary when your plan is accepted when you didn't think it would be and you were only playing the game. I'd surprised them with direct approval.

"But, XO, we . . ." Joe Raven whined.

I sat again, pulling my papers out of the envelope and spreading them out with a flair in front of me. "Let's go over it again and make up a new plan if this one worries you so much. We can—"

Larry Sanders broke in heroically, saying it wasn't necessary, that they were just a little surprised, that's all. Then he turned to his fellow department heads. "It's a good plan, you guys know it . . . we'll go with it." He was exercising his authority as the senior department head, which in itself didn't carry any weight, but it made him the senior watch officer, and that was a powerful position.

The SWO controlled every watch on the ship except engineering watches in the main spaces. He did, however, control the bridge watches for the engineering officers.

I put my papers back into the envelope but didn't get up. "Thinking about it, gentlemen, we've left out one important item." They looked at me. I could almost see them rummaging through the databanks of their minds.

"Ship handling, XO?" Larry spoke up, he hadn't forgotten, but that was the captain's bag, and Larry was still under the intimidation of the old regime.

"Yeah, what can we do about it?" I asked, searching their faces for an answer.

Each looked down at his notes. It was now 1600 as I waited out the silence. The 1MC sounded liberty call. "Stop a minute, gentlemen . . . liberty call just sounded. What's going on on the quarterdeck right now?"

Only silence answered such a seemingly stupid question: The liberty sections were going ashore for liberty or to go home. "Whaddaya mean, XO, what's going on on the quarterdeck right now?" Al Jellico finally asked, his face skewed in thought.

"Tell me, what is the procedure to go on liberty on *Kramer?* Tell me, Mr. Jellico, what's happening right now, this very minute, back there?"

He told me what I already knew. The men would be in a clean uniform of the day, and they'd walk up and show their ID card and liberty card to the OOD or JOOD and request permission to go ashore. The OOD or JOOD will glance at the cards and the man. If he is presentable, he'll get permission to leave the ship.

"What do the officers and chiefs do?"

Jeff Hobson answered immediately, getting into the game of educating an addle-minded executive officer. "They walk up and request permission to go ashore and the OOD or JOOD gives permission."

"What about a liberty card or ID card?" I asked.

"Why, XO, they don't need one," Larry answered, raising his eyebrows.

"Why not?"

"XO, ah, well, I guess because we trust them!" Larry's exasperated answer shot out.

I shifted myself in my chair as I paused, taking a sip of coffee. "When I took the conn the other day, under circumstances we need not talk about, do you think I trusted the helmsman? I didn't even know his name. Willie didn't trust him, but I did. Do you think I trusted your throttle men would do okay, Mr. Raven, or your check men. Each one could have ended my naval career in a second. How about the lee helm, did I trust that he'd pass my exact order to Main Control? I trusted them; I took them on the blind faith that they'd do what had to be done. Blind faith, gentlemen, pure blind faith with no bullshit."

Silence. I continued, trying to control and hold my emotions in check. "When I was a white hat, the thing that pissed me off the most was some wise-ass chief or first class playing God with my liberty card . . . some power-mad Neanderthal acting like the big dog while he made me beg for my card, for my right to go ashore. It was degrading, humiliating, dehumanizing." Sweat poured down my forehead, my coffee cup rattled in its saucer that I held.

The department heads stared at me in silence. "After quarters tomorrow, I want every liberty card on this ship collected, taken to the ship's office, and I'll have them laminated and given back to you. You in turn will give them to your men on a *permanent* basis, and they'll be no Mickey Mouse on this, gentlemen, this is a pure no-shitter."

I reached for my pipe to calm myself and continued. "So the young sailors get hassled leaving the ship, then they have to hitch a ride or take a bus to go to a locker club, where they pay a fortune for a skimpy place to change into civilian clothes so they won't be harassed by every con man and whore in the area. And the locker clubs sell cheap junk and phony schemes to prey on and intimidate the very sailors the navy depends upon to keep it going. It's demeaning . . . destroys pride, and pride is the watchdog of efficiency.

"And to crown it, there's the permanent shore patrol, storm-trooping, Nazi bastards, that take delight in degrading our men with constant checks and demands to see their identification and liberty card as if they were searching for someone on the ten-most-wanted list. Life is not always pleasant out there for our boys in blue."

I paused, I'd said enough. I'd blown a point by not letting them come up with the conclusion of permanent liberty cards. "Sorry, gentlemen, we were talking about . . . ?"

"You have any strong feelings on the issue, XO?" Al Jellico asked jokingly with a tentative smile.

I answered, "Fuck you, Al," and laughed. "No, it just popped into my mind."

And we got back to the issues of ship-handling training. Each time a ship sailed, only one under way and only one landing was available. Al Jellico, the least concerned with these matters, came up first with an idea. "How about when we get under way, we just go in to the pier and out again, over and over?"

"We'd have to stay at sea detail all the time, and that's hard on the men," Jeff Hobson offered in defense of his deck division.

Ignoring the comment, Joe Raven said, "There's the fuel pier down from us a way, we could use that, it's nice and sturdy and rarely used." He paused, looking around for concurrence as he lit a cigarette. "And besides, we could use the duty sections and give them training . . . damn good idea."

Larry came up with the political side of it. "Don't know if the captain would buy it, what with the admiral's staff sitting on the tender watching us to see if we screw up." The captain had already suggested using the fuel pier for training. I mentioned the admiral's flagship, and he'd scoffed at it as meaningless.

"I think it's great, gentlemen, we'll let the captain worry about that. I don't think Frank Macaby worries much about what admirals think. Larry, get us permission to go to sea for three days on Monday and for us to use the fueling pier on Monday morning for training. When we return on Wednesday night, with any luck we might be in four-section liberty. Pass the word, gentlemen. Work hard."

I knocked and entered the CO's in-port cabin. He looked at me, his eyes begging an answer. I extended my right arm out in front of me with my thumb up. He smiled, picking up the phone. "Quarter-deck, Captain here, I'll be leaving in three minutes . . . thank you." A good captain always alerted the OOD when he was leaving. This gave the OOD time to call the CDO so he could meet the captain on the quarterdeck and receive any last-minute instructions. It also let the OOD and his watch team have a few minutes to square away their watch and look good. It was the professional and courteous thing to do.

The next day, bright and sunny outside, our wardroom officers sat listening to my ship-handling brief. "So keep that one point in mind, gentlemen, keep your eye on your stern and the stern in the right place, and you'll always be okay. Any more questions?" I finished my lecture to the fourteen officers in the wardroom. The captain sat in back, taking it all in, I suspected he knew more about ship handling than he let on to me. The principles applied to submarines as well as surface ships, and I understood subs were harder to handle than destroyers.

"Captain, comment?"

"Not about ship handling, XO, you've covered that adequately, but I would like to talk about us. It's rare we can all get together like this. I'm a submariner and think like a submariner and that means I like to know everything whether it's good or bad, nothing should be a surprise to any one of us. If it deals directly with the operation of the ship, talk to me personally—on all other matters, to the XO. He'll keep me informed. And at any time, if any officer wants to speak to me on a personal level, I am always, and I mean always, available.

"The object of next week is to qualify people and to do it fast. If you think we're pushing you or your men too fast, for Christ's sake, let us know . . . it takes more courage to stand up and say slow down than it does to fake it out. And a helluva lot safer. Let's go the safe way."

Some of the junior officers squirmed nervously in their chairs, uncomfortable even being in the same room with a captain. Others slouched in indifference. And from the looks on their faces, they not only didn't believe him, they didn't care.

"It is my policy that the officer who has the watch does the duty. If you're the CDO, you get the ship ready and get under way. If you've got the watch and we're going alongside, you do it . . . or your JOOD, and so forth. An exception, of course, is if the XO or I want to give it a fling or for some other reason, but that won't happen often.

"It is my intention to qualify Lieutenants (jg) Baldachino and Maxwell for OOD and CDO while we're at sea next week, if they're up to it that fast." The two JGs, startled at the sound of their names, bolted upright in their chairs, flashing broad grins. "It is my intention to put the OODs and CDOs on five-section watches at sea and in port by the time we get back on Wednesday night, and it is my intention to make this ship a fighting machine. It is my intention to make you and your men proud to be on *Kramer* and proud to look me directly in the eye and say 'Good morning, Captain' and mean it.

"Thank you for your time, gentlemen . . . XO."

Not a word passed as he left the wardroom; the officers, bewildered, sat silently in their chairs.

Alongside

"You're twisting the wrong way, Mr. Baldachino, reverse your rudder and engines. That's it, not bad, not bad, let the wind help you," I coached. We'd been shooting landings for three hours now. Men on the ship and dock ran back and forth, inserting bamboo fenders between us and the dock to stave off damage caused by inexperience. Mr. Maxwell and the other OODs had two under ways and two landings each. And the men's asses were dragging.

Vince Baldachino, the last of the five, let his nervousness cause a few errors. "Settle down, Vince, I've made that same error several times. Think of the engines as a bicycle's handlebars," I said, demonstrating with my arms outstretched pulling them back and forth as if steering a bicycle. "And just turn your rudder the way you want the bow to go . . . yeah, that's it . . . good, good."

"Moored."

"One more time, Vince, then take us out to sea."

"Under way."

I leaned against the chart desk as we passed the tender with the admiral aboard. The captain had observed the first landing with intense interest and for the rest of the time sat seemingly unconcerned in his chair. He must have balls of iron.

I'd been on my feet for six hours, starting at 0545, when I witnessed with Joe Raven the duty engineering watch section lighting off the plant. Now a duty section bridge watch sailed us out of port. I wanted to sit down. The elevated chair on the port side of the pilothouse was the XO's, mine, but I still didn't have guts enough to sit in it yet, and besides, now was not the time. I had to ensure a safe passage out of the harbor, easy though it may be.

A flashing light winked at us from the tender. "From the admiral," shouted our leading signalman. "Interrogative damage."

The captain thought for a moment, then shouted to the signalman, "Send, 'Two bamboo fenders and three egos.'"

"Well said, Captain," I whispered.

He looked at me grinning. "Surface admirals . . . no sweat."

"The landing practice was great, Captain . . . it'd be better if we could do that every day for a week," I said.

He pulled his binoculars from his eyes, looked at me for a second, and said, "Better, XO, is the enemy of good enough."

I went over and stood next to Willie while one of his quartermasters ran himself wild getting visual fixes all by himself as if this were an emergency sortie. Willie's eyes searched out the landmarks as he navigated in his mind. Combat sent up a string of recommendations with only two men running the watch. They did well.

"For four sections, Willie, you're going to need another striker. Got anybody in mind?" Strikers were seamen who were working in a rate trying to qualify for third class petty officer.

"Mr. Sanders told me. Yes, sir, I do . . . young kid in the deck force. Guy named Reeves, been training with me on his own for about a month now. Not too bad, he'll need some work. The deck apes think he's a flake though."

"Is that the one they call Wimpy Reeves?"

"Yes, sir . . . but I think he has potential."

"Shit, that's all I need is a quartermaster who's a fuck-up and cries every time someone tells him to do something."

"It's not that bad, XO, he's got potential . . . it'd be my responsibility."

I looked at Willie, frowning as I said, "Good thought . . . but it'd be my ass . . . you know how it works."

"Yes, sir, I know, but will you give it some thought . . . the kid'd be okay if he were only brought along properly." Willie was a demanding leader, his two third classes were better at celestial navigation than ninety percent of the navy's navigators. His spaces and equipment were immaculate, and his men adored him. He tended to be a little disrespectful to officers, but I could suffer that easily in light of his competence. The officers didn't complain. He'd saved their asses many a time.

"Lemme think about it."

"Thank you, XO."

"Don't thank me just for thinking about it."

"Not anything to do with that, sir," he answered, pointing to a southerly course marked out on his chart of one seven two degrees to skirt San Clemente Island and take us to our exercise area off San Diego.

I nodded assent and whispered, "We'll use Combat's."

I winked at him and walked over to the captain and stood next to him in silence. We passed through the breakwater. The rolling jabbed me in the stomach like a mule's kick, but I managed to keep smiling.

I keyed the 21MC intercom system, the bitch box, to Combat, "XO here, course to our exercise area?"

And almost before I could get my hand off the key, they came back with, "Combat recommends initial course to exercise area one seven zero degrees true."

I asked the captain for permission to secure the special sea and anchor detail. He said yes. I nodded to Lieutenant Sanders, the OOD, who nodded to the boatswain's mate of the watch, who passed the word.

As the navigator, I recommended an initial course of one seven zero to our exercise area. Lieutenant Sanders turned to Lieutenant (jg) Baldachino and repeated the order. Mr. Baldachino ordered left standard rudder and our bow turned south. I overheard the talker to CIC say "My God, Jonesy, the XO took your recommendation."

Lunch was, as a wardroom should be, light and carefree with the junior officers gladly joining in the conversations and kidding the officers who had made the landings and under ways. Just as we sat down, a young seaman came in with the twelve o'clock reports and the captain thanked him, complimenting him on his fine military bearing. The kid floated out of the wardroom.

Occasionally, I had trouble realizing I was truly a naval officer. Wardroom meals reminded me. It went back to when I was a kid and my mother would take my sister and me to Boston by railroad. On these vacation trips we'd eat a few meals in the dining car. It was expensive, but we indulged ourselves. The tables always had white tablecloths and linen napkins and silver sugar bowls and engraved glasses and pitchers. The waiters were always courteous and efficient, catering to our every desire.

Breakfast was the best. Little glasses of thick tomato juice sat in ice bowls rimmed with silver and looking redder than I'd ever seen. The eggs were done expertly, with lots of bacon and sausages, and the toast was cut diagonally, and on the triangles plenty of real butter, not margarine, was spread.

At dinners—we never ate lunch in the dining car, too indulgent, my mother said—the menus listed exotic things I'd never heard of, but tasted like what my mom made. At first I didn't know what to do with the array of silver knives and forks and spoons, but my sister told me to simply use the farthermost one out and work my way in on each dish served. It worked, everyone else was doing that. I felt better, even though I couldn't pronounce the names on the menu.

To me, eating in the dining car was a luxury, eating in the wardroom was a luxury. Officers eat in the wardroom. I am eating in the wardroom, ergo, I am an officer.

The captain thanked each steward by name for every dish they served and for the coffee they poured. *Shit, I hadn't even known all their names yet.* The captain pushed back his chair and lit a cigar. Three junior officers joined him. Coffee was served. "Captain?" Mr. Baldachino asked. "I've always heard submariners get much better training than we do . . . special schools and all, that true?"

The captain looked at him for a second, then said almost reluctantly, "Well, we—I mean submariners, do have sub school, and it's damn hard. They turn out a good product. But I understand destroyer school is up and running, and they too turn out a good product." He looked at the department heads, who were all graduates except for the supply officer, and watched them smile.

I listened to the captain talk, and he allowed that submariners did get more training because they sought it out. "It's the nature of their job," he said, "they have more opportunity to train. Every merchie or warship is a target for us."

I noticed he used the word *us*. *Shit, Captain, I, you're slipping back into your submariner's persona.*

"I don't think surface ships do that . . . though they could if they wanted to; we'll give it a go." The captain's cigar went out. I handed him my Zippo.

He continued, saying that the biggest problem he sees in today's navy is management, raw-assed, men and material management. None of the services seems to do it well, he allowed, leaning his chair back on its hind legs, rocking easily in concert with the sea.

"Management is basically easy," he continued, warmed to his subject. "The XO boils it down into three words: organize, deputize, and supervise. Simple, but it works. The supervise seems to be the most neglected part of the equation." The stewards brought out more coffee as Leading Steward Santos leaned on the sideboard, listening.

The captain was giving a leadership lecture, so smooth, so unassuming, I'm sure none of the officers knew it for what it was. "As I say," he continued, "management is easy. Take care of your men, and your men will take care of you. That's an old saw . . . but it works."

He was right, I concurred, but the problem, as I saw it, was keeping one's ego intact. When one has power, illusions of grandeur can easily get in the way. One had to be honest with his men.

The captain relit his cigar, blowing its blue-gray smoke up into a greedy vent opening. "One more thing, gentlemen, watch the junior officer trap of the 'captain says' when giving an unpopular order. It'll pollute your authority. The captain might have *said,* but to your men, it's *you* who *says.*"

Mr. Baldachino fidgeted with his coffee cup. He opened his mouth several times, but the sounds coming out never formed into words. The captain looked at him, then to me. "What is it, Mr. Baldachino?" he asked.

Baldachino's mouth stayed open, he tried to move his lips, but they wouldn't obey. He coughed, cleared his throat, took a timid sip of coffee, and blurted out, "Well, Captain . . . XO, that all sounds good, but with all the things we have to do like PMS and watches and all the other shitty little jobs we have, there just doesn't seem to be any time to spend with our men managing them. The chiefs have to do it." His frame straightened as he finished, as if he had finally exposed the navy for what it truly was. He smirked as he drew his coffee cup grandly to his mouth.

The captain didn't seem to mind the comment. His slow smile indicated he welcomed it, as if Baldachino were shilling for him. The tip of his cigar glowed brightly as he took a second to suck in a mighty puff. He blew it toward the overhead and said, "That may be true . . . maybe there's another way, a better way. I remember the story of the woodsman thunking his dull ax into a tree with very little result. This guy comes up and sees the dull ax. 'What are you doing?' the man asked the woodsman."

"I'm chopping down these trees!"

"Why don't you sharpen your ax?" the man asked.

"I can't, don't have time, gotta chop down these trees."

The ship took a five-degree roll. Instinctively we all grabbed something on the table to keep it from toppling over.

"What I'm saying, gentlemen, is take a minute, now and then, to sharpen your ax." I wanted to jump up and sing. The captain had hit it on the nose. The other officers nodded in agreement.

I was carefully rolling my napkin into its silver napkin ring with XO engraved upon it, when the captain surprised me again. "Talking about training, I've contacted an old sub driver buddy of mine, and they agreed, condescendingly, to give us services tonight if we're up to it."

I looked at Jeff Hobson, the WEPS officer, and then to Vince Baldachino, the ASW officer. "I don't know, Captain, what do we look like, Jeff?" I asked.

He looked down at the table, then to Vince Baldachino. Baldachino shrugged. "Frankly, XO, under the old captain we—"

"We don't care, Lieutenant Hobson, what used to be . . . how are you now?" I snapped back.

"The sonarmen are gun shy, but damm it, they're good men, and I think we'd do okay."

I turned back to the captain and with a haughty, undeserved confidence replied, "Piece of cake, call 'em in."

With a wry smile the captain turned to me, and in a voice too low for anyone else to hear, said, "Targets, XO, submarines and targets." Then the phone at his left knee buzzed. He picked it up, listened.

"Okay, thank you, Mr. Sanders, I'll tell him." He turned to me. "The OOD says to tell you he's spotted the AO, the fleet oiler, you mentioned heading south to San Diego . . . what's that all about?"

"I read on the Fox schedules she was leaving an exercise off San Francisco and heading south. I'm hoping she'll let us come alongside a couple of times just for practice. With your permission, Captain, I'll make a message to her." He nodded and I excused myself from the pleasant atmosphere of the wardroom.

For the ninth time in four hours the 1MC announced, "We are making our approach port side to, to the oiler. All hands stand by. The smoking lamp is out throughout the ship." For the first three runs the captain stood next to me, monitoring, learning what I was doing. Submarines rarely did this. On the fourth approach he stood nonchalantly to one side as I coached the conning officers on the fine art of going alongside.

If Grif Maxwell had been defeated under the old captain, his manner didn't show it now. "Feel the ship, Grif, let it talk to you," I whispered as he lined up for his second try. His face flushed in near ecstasy over the perfect high-speed approach and alongside seamanship he had just completed and the prospects of making another.

"Take her in to eighty feet, Grif . . . make it easy for your boys to get the lines over. They're your boys; they know you're here. Make 'em look good, Grif," I counseled as the distance line came over. We were right on the white flag. Rub Your Belly With Grease—a memory aid for the red, yellow, blue, white, and green bits of colored cloth on the distance line, each one twenty feet apart. White flag—eighty feet.

"Well done, Mr. Maxwell. Well done," the captain offered, and Grif Maxwell, ex-defeated first lieutenant, beamed in appreciation. "And pass to your men for me, excellent job on the lines." We were just passing a line back and forth on each approach. Our object was to train the officers in coming alongside and breaking away, the hardest and scariest part. For here you were maneuvering close to a gigantic piece of steel, where a mistaken order or a freak sea could smash you violently into the other ship.

Long times alongside would come later. Confidence is what we were building today. The crew didn't seem to mind the hard work it entailed, or the long hours they'd been on high line station and on the bridge. I'd insisted Willie train all his quartermasters on the helm. He watched them intensely; they were his boys, and they'd best not mess up.

I told the captain that everyone had had two times at bat, and requested permission to secure from drill. "I'm getting a little tired," I admitted, surprised at myself for my candor, for admitting a weakness. I trusted him.

"I'm not surprised, XO, you've had a bit of a long day, but one more time, if you please; I'd like to try it once."

One more time I signaled to the oiler as Mr. Maxwell pulled ahead and whipped us back into waiting station one thousand yards astern.

"This is the captain, I've got the conn." The bridge went silent. This one evolution would prove the captain. Word spread throughout the ship. Willie took the wheel after an asking nod from me. The high line detail straightened up as if standing taller would help the captain they'd learned to admire in just a few days.

"Main Control stand by for twenty knots," he ordered, and waited ten seconds as he eased off the base course line for his approach. "All engines ahead full make turns for twenty knots," he ordered in a voice exuding confidence. I knew he had never made an approach before. "Steer course one eight zero."

The afternoon seas grew fresher. The wind, backing a little, increased, causing a chop to ride on top of swells coming in from the west. Conditions could become a little uncomfortable. They'd been building for about an hour and, though both the captain and I acknowledged their earlier presence, we tacitly chose to ignore them. Not the most favorable conditions to go alongside with. We should have turned into the swells before coming alongside, but this was a favor from the oiler, and it wouldn't be quite right to ask her to change her course away from her home port after being gone for some time. Hell, it wasn't that bad yet.

What would I do if the captain made an error? Would I advise him? Of course. Would I take the conn if things got really bad? I doubted it.

I held my breath as he crossed the low pressure area existing one hundred feet out from the oiler's stern, caused from their screws sucking water from just ahead of themselves. He corrected course slightly to compensate and when passed, came back to one eight zero. *Great!* At precisely the right moment he cut speed to fifteen knots and moved into eighty feet, holding her there with rocklike precision. The lines came over. He looked at me and smiled. A natural ship handler.

The CO of the oiler, lifting a power megaphone to his mouth, shouted, "Hey, Frank, you got some shit-hot boys there . . . your guys looked good. Didn't know you tube sailors ever got command of a destroyer . . . standards going to hell, I guess."

A wave of fear shivered through me, the captain has the conn alongside, and the other guy wants to chat over a power megaphone. *Disaster.* "Steer course one eight one . . . add two turns," the captain ordered as Mr. Sanders handed him our loud hailer. "Take the conn, XO," he ordered, taking the megaphone. *Whew!*

"XO here, I have the conn. . . ." The helmsman and lee helm reported their course to steer and speed rung up.

"Hello, Marv, knew you got an oiler . . . yeah, standards are the worst I've ever seen . . . hard as hell to come alongside you airedales when you're steaming all over the bloody ocean . . . don't you guys have any pity on us poor little tin-can sailors?" the captain jibed.

"Hell no, Frank, when'd you take command? I thought you were still in San Diego on staff," the oiler skipper yelled back.

"Tell you all about it next time . . . thanks for your time and patience . . . hey, when do you get your carrier?"

"Well, if hot jockeys like you don't crash into me, in about six months . . . glad to have helped out. Tell Marcy I said hello. Don't scratch my paint limping away from me."

The captains waved good-bye to one another, and Captain Macaby took back the conn. "Tell Main Control to standby for twenty-five knots," he ordered, and I added, "Tell 'em no smoke."

When the twenty-five-knot bell took hold, we leaped ahead, and with fighter-plane-like precision, eased out and heeled over to starboard as the captain cranked on right full rudder for showmanship and dash. He'd won his spurs.

A flashing light message from the oiler followed us out. "Lookin' good, Frank."

Think Like a Fox

After dinner the captain took a long puff on his stubby cigar, pushing his chair back, getting comfortable. He wasn't going to waste this camaraderie, and with no apparent reason told the wardroom that only aviators can command carriers. He added that they don't know very much about seamanship, but it was the law. And with some disdain he said only aviator admirals can command carrier task forces. "The theory, I guess, is that you have to know how an aviator thinks and how airplanes fly to appreciate your responsibility . . . I don't think it's true, but that's current doctrine.

"Screws up opportunity for surface types like you guys . . . us . . . I should say." He glanced at me; I nodded.

"Well, what it does is denies command of our most powerful offensive weapon to the largest segment of our officer pool. It thwarts surface officers on promotion and keeps them from getting task force commands. I don't think it's valid, but the big boys rule. It was different when the battleship guys reigned supreme. Aviators were little better than scum then. What comes around goes around, I guess."

The captain went on to explain that it fouls surface officers in another way too. To get sharp aviators shipboard experience, they give them command of large auxiliary vessels like that oiler. "They do that to teach him shipboard things and a smattering of ship handling. But it's just a pass-through. They have to have a deep draft command, like an oiler or such, before they can become the captain of a carrier. Guess who gets the oilers, ammo ships, and replenishment vessels, the so-called deep drafts?" His eyes went from man to man, all looking at him.

"The aviators, that's who . . . or how could they get their ticket punched for a carrier. So you guys get screwed out of command of them too." Santos poured the captain another cup of coffee and offered the pot around the table. He emptied the ashtrays.

"What's left then?" Grif asked, leaning forward in his chair, soaking up, as were all the other officers, every word the captain was saying.

"Oh, the cruisers, all the destroyers, the big ones and the little ones . . . and the amphibs, I guess."

"What about you, Captain? Submarines?" Al Jellico asked.

The captain explained that that was a little different, that their career path was command of an attack boat . . . then if they didn't screw up too badly, a ballistic missile boat, a boomer. "Then we're beached," he explained. "Staffies. Maybe a squadron command, but hell, commodores are just staffies too that go out on the boats once in a while and get in the captains' way. And unfortunately there are too few flag ranks available, we—"

His phone buzzed. He listened, then looked at me, then, glancing to the OPS officer, said, "We're entering our night steam area, and there's a submarine there . . . reckon they're my old buddies waiting to sink us. C'mon, gentlemen, let's see what we can do."

On the bridge the captain was on the radio as we set the 1-AS team. "Tango Mike, this is Uniform Zebra actual checking in for exercise. Over."

There was a minute's delay, then, "Uniform Zebra, this is Tango Mike actual . . . ready for COMEX, no rules. We'll let you ping for ten minutes, then we'll get serious. Over."

"This is Uniform Zebra, concur. Be advised, you're going up against a crack team of sub killers and we're going to wipe your tubbie butt. Over."

"Yes, sir. Copy all, be advised, this young dog has learned new tricks. We'll put you on the bottom a few times for the sake of all the grief you've ever given me. Be alert for my flares. We'll close to a thousand yards before we fire them. Stay loose. Over." You could hear the laughter in his voice.

"I would hope so, Tango Mike . . . we'll debrief by phone this weekend. Tell Nancy hi. Over."

"Submarines and targets, Uniform Zebra. Out." And the sub went off the air. The captain laughed.

We made a bathythermograph drop, BT, and found a thermocline layer two hundred feet down but breaking up from the choppy seas. Since this was just play for the 1-AS team, the anti-submarine team, we didn't go to GQ. It'd been a hard day for the crew. In combat I watched my team form up. Dropping my guise here as the ship's administrative officer, I became the CIC evaluator, a combat role charged with advising the CO on how to best fight the ship, and during ASW, to fight her myself.

On *Henshaw* I had begrudged the XO this exalted position and wanted to do it myself. I thought I was much better at ASW than he was, though I'd never proved it. Surfacing that whiskey-class submarine in the Formosa Straits hadn't been that great an accomplishment. Now I'd see how good I was under the glaring eye of an ex-submarine skipper.

My constant pipe smoking would have betrayed my apprehension if the crew had known me better. They would, but by that time I'd be okay, my self-confidence would be back. I wanted to impress the captain and his insufferable disdain that all submariners had for destroyers.

In CIC the captain watched our preparation; we were wretchedly slow at it. The captain said he'd talked to the CO of the sub, and they had agreed to no exercise rules. The sub had told the captain he would dive at COMEX and let us track him for ten minutes to get the feel, then he said he'd sink us a few times for old times' sake. "The sub's skipper is my old XO . . . he's damn good."

Shit, that's all I needed.

"To catch a fox, think like a fox, Don," the captain mumbled, telling me he'd just observe and chat about it later. "Your show, XO." He left for the bridge, and I ordered superheaters lowered and secured.

We had the surfaced sub on radar at three and a half miles and a weak, breaking-up sonar signal. I asked if the ASROC was manned and ready.

A talker spoke into his mouthpiece and in ten seconds reported. "ASROC will be up in a few minutes. Sonar ready. Mr. Baldachino says the sonar performance figures are not so good, but he still holds the sub weakly on the surface."

I berated myself for not having visited Sonar. Shit, I didn't even know the leading sonarman's name. I'd let the administrative bullshit take too much of my time. I'd worried more about mess cooks, cleanliness, and properly filled-out forms than I had about torpedoes and sonar.

I puffed continuously on my pipe, now so hot I could hardly hold it. Even so, I sucked in the hot, acrid smoke; it was tasting more and more like dog shit with every puff. But as we manned up at a crawl, I kept on puffing, even though the top of my mouth must have been suffering third-degree burns.

My stomach rebelled at the rolling seas. I didn't like being the XO at this moment with all the responsibilities I couldn't control. I wanted to be back at Monterey, going to school and reading and talking and drinking. *Unfair! Unfair to put me in such a failure-prone situation in front of the new captain. God damn these incompetent sons of bitches of an ASW team. Team? Why aren't they faster?*

"Five minutes to COMEX," came the CIC-to-bridge talker.

"Can we pipe in the sonar speaker?" I asked, fighting to hold my voice under control. It sounded to me as if I were whining. The radarmen fumbled around, trying to figure out how to do it.

"We're looking, sir. Sorry, sir." *I'll fry some ass for this.* Abuse and threats are the last vestige of the incompetent. This is my team; I should have paid attention to their training. *I'm lookin' bad. I can't stand that.*

I keyed the 21MC bitch box to Sonar. "Mr. Baldachino, you guys know how to pipe in your audio to the bridge and Combat?" I asked, my voice testy.

"Give us a minute, XO. I think we found it."

"ASROC manned and ready."

"Four minutes to COMEX," the bridge reported.

Shit, we'll never be ready down here. This'll never happen again. I swear by the mighty sea gods; this will never happen again.

I could hear the ASROC launcher slewing around on the 01 level aft of Combat. At least that was working. The CIC officer whimpered that the DRT won't come on. I just stared at him as I refilled my pipe, burning my fingers on the bowl as I did.

"Three minutes to COMEX."

"Captain, evaluator here," I called over the 21MC, the intercom system to all control points throughout the ship. "I'm simulating all, repeat all, weapons systems manned and ready, request all weapons free. I repeat, Captain, *all* weapons free to include nuclear depth charges. National release authority and authentication assumed complete," I said into the combination speaker-microphone as I held its keying switch down so hard that it hurt my finger. I used my title as evaluator, indicating I was in a combat mode. At least it did to me.

"All weapons, repeat, all weapons free, Evaluator," the captain answered, playing the game. But it was no game to me. It was the killing field; it was high noon again as my mind twisted me back to the heat and the horror of the Mekong Delta.

I felt it. My damaged right arm and side pained terribly from the shrapnel an exploding Vietcong rocket had fired at us a half hour ago. In my mind I could see the makeshift tourniquet stemming the gush of blood from my near-useless limb. I felt myself wiping the blood from my face with a dirty rag I'd found in the bottom of the high-speed gunboat, the PBR, I commanded.

I once more saw the six powerful boats following me astern as we roared in for the attack. The scream from my forward gunner screeched through my mind as a slug tore through his chest. I felt the inferno of the Southeast Asian sun. I heard the sizzle of the gunner's blood pumping out over his hot-barreled twin .50-caliber machine guns. And sweat clogged my eyes again as my mind bellowed

"Commence fire" over the roar of the fourteen screaming engines hurling our guns against the deadly VC 306th Battalion.

I shook myself, trying to dislodge the scene, trying to bring myself back to the present as a detached voice rumbled through a tunnel, "One minute to COMEX."

My mind cleared, but my body still hurt as I ordered, "Director, gun action surface starboard . . . slew out and acquire submarine target bearing one eight nine, range six thousand yards. Mounts fifty-one and fifty-two stand by for guns free. Stand by to fire on my command," I ordered over the 21MC in simulation.

"Aye, aye, sir, understand stand by for guns free," came Mr. Sanders's report from the bridge. He was with me. A loudspeaker announced, "Sonar manned and ready, all communications circuits up." The bridge acknowledged and so did I.

"DRT up, tracking sub."

"Thirty seconds to COMEX."

I lit my pipe again watching the tracking team bend to their task as the Vietnam death scene slammed back into my wayward mind. I was there again as the boat captain hurtled backward, as if hit by a truck, slamming into me as machine-gun bullets ripped him across the stomach. I pushed him aside, jumping to the hot cherry-red M60 machine gun he had just been blown away from.

I heard again the sound of helicopter gunships sweeping in low over us, erupting the riverbank in white smoke and flying tree limbs as they launched their 2.75-inch rockets against the Vietcong.

My exploding head whirled as I clutched the edge of the DRT in *Kramer*'s CIC, where I stood leaning with the wild movement as my gunboat heeled over, banking hard in a panic turn to avoid an incoming rocket.

In the cool, air-conditioned CIC, my body poured gallons of sweat down my shivering skin.

"Twenty seconds to COMEX."

"Combat, director tracking target," Mr. Sanders reported over the 21MC.

"You okay, XO?" someone asked, but I pretended not to hear. You okay, XO?"

"Fire at my command," I stammered.

"Director aye."

"ASROC tracking the target," came for real.

"ASROC, stand by to fire."

"Five seconds to COMEX . . . five, four, three, two, one. COMEX, COMEX, COMEX."

"Director, guns free, commence firing, fire for effect. *Commence fire.*"

I swear I could hear four 5" naval guns blasting out. I could feel the inferno erupting out of their muzzles and smell the harsh cordite punishing my lungs. I could see the first four fifty-four-pound shells slice through the night sky to impact on a half-submerged submarine. This was no game to me; I wanted that submarine dead.

"Cease fire," I ordered as the bridge reported the twelfth round on the way.

"Guns tight. Secured from firing, twelve rounds expended . . . no casualties," Jeff Hobson, the weapons officer, simulated his obligatory report.

The dots on the DRT indicating the last contact position took shape as penciled lines connected them, showing the sub's movements. "ASROC, stand by to fire, nuclear depth charge. Stand by. Break break . . . bridge enable ASROC firing key. I intend to launch a nuclear depth charge. Stand by. Stand by. ASROC, let me know when you have a solution."

"I have a solution."

"Fire." In my mind I watched as if I were the missile itself. I felt my slow acceleration as my booster rocket lifted me off the rails, my nosepiece ripping through the light protective covering on the square pepper-box launcher. I spewed my hot rocket blast over the deck, searing the well-manicured paint as I launched into the cool night air, one hundred ten miles west of San Diego.

I felt my booster push me faster and faster until exhausted, separated, dropping away into the sea. I winced when the parachute deployed, yanking my speed off to lessen the impact. I entered the water sinking as my fuse sat poised waiting, waiting for the sea's pressure to act against it. Waiting to activate the main charge, detonating the nuclear warhead.

Click.

HEAT! HEAT! CATACLYSMIC HEAT.

"Left full rudder make turns for twenty-three knots," I ordered in the standard doctrine of once you fire a nuclear weapon you up-ass and get the hell out of the blast and fallout area. Ass to the blast, ass to the blast. In ten minutes, out of our area now, I ordered all ahead two-thirds and steamed away for another ten minutes.

"Secure the after plant," I told the OPS officer over the 21MC. "It is my intention to disguise our sound signature and sneak up on the bastards. . . . Oh! Excuse me, Captain . . . the submariners."

"The captain says that's okay," Larry, the OPS officer answered, chuckling.

In twenty minutes we were on the way back into the exercise area at eight knots with one screw and every unnecessary pump and piece of machinery secured and our sonar on passive. Even the evaps were shut down. As we approached the exercise area, the faint sound, ever so faint return of a sub running dead slow, blessed our ears. We stayed at eight knots. Sweat from my forehead in the air-conditioned CIC dropped on the flimsy DRT paper.

I hadn't touched my pipe for half an hour. The right side of my body quit hurting from the shrapnel that had shredded me four years ago. Blood no longer streamed down my face. The screaming of the boats and the deafening roar of the guns and cries of the wounded men passed back into the dark caverns of my mind, where I thought I had buried them.

No flares fired up from the submarine to indicate a torpedo launch. Maybe our changed noise signature was working, and it confused them. It wouldn't work for long. Then a transient noise like a dropped tool or something metal showed clear on the sonar screen. "Stand by to launch an MK-46 torpedo," I whispered to the bridge. We all whispered as if the sub could hear our words. "I intend to ping once for range, then launch," I told Mr. Sanders over a sound-powered phone. "Please tell the captain."

Their was a pause, then Mr. Sanders came back with, "He says good idea."

It took an hour for the next three minutes to pass as the subs' steaming noise grew ever so slightly louder. "Stand by for launch of an MK-46 torpedo. Stand by, Sonar, for one ping on the bearing of your passive." The bearing drifted down our starboard side. I counted ten for no good reason and ordered, "Sonar, light him up."

The powerful ping of our low-frequency SQS-23 sonar reverberated throughout the ship. The speaker in Combat echoed out: "Sonar contact bearing two seven eight, range thirteen hundred yards. Echo quality sharp, no doppler, classify as possible submarine. Shallow."

"Range clear," the talker repeated from the bridge.

"Set torpedo firing data, starboard side," I ordered. "Bearing from Sonar . . . I repeat, bearing will be set from Sonar. Range thirteen hundred yards. Set Mark-46, starboard side, to circular search: floor three hundred feet, ceiling seventy-five. Report when ready to launch."

In five insufferable seconds, "Mark-46, starboard side ready."

"Sonar, set bearing . . . fire . . . MK-46. Starboard side."

In my mind I heard the whooshing sound of high-pressure air violently escape its imprisoning flask. I smelled its greasy sweetness. I heard it embrace the torpedo, nudging, launching it on its way. I saw the eight-and-a-half-foot, near thirteen-inch-diameter torpedo leap thirty feet out of our starboard launcher. I felt it ease into and accept the wetness where her mission lay. I saw her propellers start in anticipation and heard the active sonar in its nose ping, reaching out, cooing for its mate, searching. And I saw its five-hundred-pound mass fishtail through the water as it sought its contact.

A good launch for us, hydrophone effects for them.

I saw it hesitate, as if thinking: Is that a target? Then yes, run straight in for the rendezvous at forty-five knots, ramming its hundred-pound, high-explosive warhead into the hapless, fear-struck submarine's hull.

Very few subs could escape an MK-46 hot on its ass at short range. Another kill. Three, but, of course, they wouldn't know that unless the captain told them. I'm sure he would, this weekend, by phone. But the crew would know and that was good enough.

In three minutes two white flares burst into the sky out of the water, simulating two torpedoes fired from the submarine. I turned into them as doctrine demanded and laughed. Dead men can't shoot torpedoes.

Chapter 4

The Captain

"Night orders, Captain. And as you wanted, Maxwell has the mid watch and Baldachino has the four-to-eight. Jeff Hobson and Joe Raven standing backup watch in CIC. I think it's a good move, both guys did okay today. I've talked to both of them, and they'll call you if a sea gull shits within a thousand yards."

"I've briefed them too, XO," he said as we went into his sea cabin to read the night orders with me. It was 2145 as he settled in his desk chair, and I sat on the already made up bed that became a couch in the daytime. "Cigarette?" he offered, handing the signed night orders back to me. I nodded no, my mouth still feeling as if a cock-fight had taken place in it. "How do you think we did on the ASW thing, XO?"

"Poorly, sir, a lot of rough edges, but the guys tried."

"You know how the sub got you?"

"No, sir, I guess he figured out the ruse, I'd like to know . . . can you find out?"

"Yes, I will . . . it certainly confused him in the beginning, or he would have fired sooner. I'm sure he made an ident by putting up his ESM, his electronic search measures, antenna for a few seconds. He probably detected our SPS-10 radar," the captain mused, thinking over the actions of his old XO on the sub. "In hindsight I guess we should have secured it . . . I'm afraid I wasn't much help to you, Don. I just didn't think we could do it. Too many years of sub

training and indoctrination, I'm sorry," he finished, his tone indicating he was taking responsibility for the sub's attack on us.

"It was me, Captain, I just didn't think about the radar," I answered, deflated over my blunder.

"You did okay, Don, you did great, as a matter of fact . . . I've rarely
seen such aggressiveness. You had a lousy team, but you pulled it
off well," he said, lighting a cigarette and blowing the smoke away
from me.

"Yes, sir, I know, we've got a lot of work to do. Training's not too
good on this ship, Captain, we've got a long way to go, and if I may
say so, you've made a big difference in the short time you've been
here. In six months we'll be the sharpest tin can in the fleet."

"I'm sure we will, Don. Go get some sleep."

As we finished breakfast, Lieutenant (jg) Baldachino came into
the wardroom from his four-to-eight watch on the bridge. "Mr.
Maxwell has the deck, sir, weather's fine," he said, taking a chair next
to Mr. Sanders at the *big* end of table, thus demonstrating a
subtle shift in self-esteem. After all, he was standing OOD watches,
wasn't he? I smiled, recalling my first watches and the self-importance
they gave to me. "Sorry I called you so many times last night, Captain. I was a little nervous at first."

Larry Sanders spoke up immediately. "Mr. Baldachino, it is *im-
possible* for you to call the captain too many times. Remember our
conversation, *when in doubt, call.*"

"Yes, sir," he answered, sick of hearing that instruction. But he
smiled nonetheless as the steward put his breakfast in front of him.
"Everybody told me that, even Willie. He was up there half the watch
with me. I guess he wanted to make sure I didn't damage his precious
bridge."

"Willie's quite a man," the captain chuckled. "Are you tired,
Vince? You didn't get much sleep last night what with the ASW drill.
How do you feel about the drill?"

"Surprisingly, no, I'm not tired, sir. I guess the excitement of the
exercise and my first OOD watch," Vince answered, taking a sip of
coffee. "We weren't very good last night. The XO carried the day
with his attacks, but Sonar didn't really do anything but detect the
sub for a few moments on passive, and I figure that was because

of the XO's ploy with the engines. No, Captain, we weren't very good. If it hadn't been for the transient, we'd never have acquired the sub. He screwed up . . . and the XO nailed his ass . . . excuse me, sir, got him."

Captain Macaby looked at me, smiling. "The XO and I came to about the same conclusion, Vince, but I'm pleased you gave me an honest answer." Vince Baldachino flushed in embarrassment, holding his coffee cup midway between the table and his lips. "What can we do about it, son?" *Son?* My mind flashed back to my first CO, Commander Baker, and the heavy influence his leadership had on me. He called me son when he was pleased. I liked it.

"We need sonar time against a submarine, ping time, and exercises. I've got a second class down there who's never heard a real submarine on sonar . . . do you know, Captain, every sonarman was down there last night to watch. They were jazzed, sir, jazzed."

The captain turned back to me. "XO, call a meeting of the sonar gang and Mr. Sanders and Mr. Hobson for 0930. I want to talk to them. Also, Mr. Sanders, I want a meeting here as soon as you can with Mr. Baldachino and Mr. Maxwell, you, Mr. Hobson, Mr. Raven, and the XO."

"Mr. Maxwell has the watch, sir."

"Relieve him, Mr. Sanders," the captain answered bitingly as he stood to leave.

"Captain, if Hobson and Raven are here, we don't have any OODs to relieve him."

The captain pondered that for a few moments, then said, "XO . . . I'll be strolling about the deck."

At 0820 I had my fifth cup of coffee as Santos placed the coffee server on the table. We had the JOOD standing the OOD watch in observance of the captain's earlier dictum that if you had the watch, you had the duty. I backed it up by asking Willie to be on the bridge, just, I told him, to keep an eye on things. He understood.

We stood as the captain entered. Mr. Maxwell spoke first. "I've been temporarily relieved by the JOOD, sir. No vessels in sight." The captain looked at me with a sly smile. We'd done the right thing.

"Gentlemen, I'm here to talk about being a CDO," the captain started to say. "It's not a position to be taken lightly. Comments please."

Silence followed as we looked at one another, wondering what the captain was up to, he wasn't usually this oblique. I pondered what comments we could make from his brief statement. "Well . . ." Mr. Sanders began. The captain cut him off. "Not you, Mr. Sanders . . . Mr. Baldachino?"

Baldachino cleared his throat and looked around at his mates, hoping for a clue on what to say. None came. I realized then the captain could be a real ballbuster when he wanted to be. I saw he was forcing the officers to come up with their own concepts, their own plans of action—a nice leadership technique. I hoped I'd never see him pissed off. You don't become an attack boat skipper by being a nice guy all the time. I could see now that he had conned me with his little help-me help-me act when he first came aboard. It had worked.

"Well, sir, I'm not quite sure I follow what kind of comment you're looking for, Captain," Baldachino said between sips of coffee. "But the CDO is responsible for the ship when the CO and XO or officers senior to himself are ashore. He has the duty of command and in an emergency must take action as the situation demands."

"Fine textbook answer, Vince. Boil it down for me."

In a few seconds and with hesitation Vince blurted out, "When the shit hits the fan, kick her in the ass and get her under way."

The three department heads winced at the flippant statement, first looking at one another, then to the skipper, who amplified with "Damn fine answer, gentlemen, too many lost opportunities and damaged ships have taken place while a CDO waits for the captain or the XO. When we get back to Long Beach, the XO and I and will keep you, as we always do, informed of our movements ashore. I would appreciate you department heads doing the same thing, if you would.

"If you're the CDO and can't get hold of any of us, and you feel the situation demands it, get under way."

The three department heads looked at one another nodding their assent as the captain continued. "Every time I leave the ship or go to sleep, my career is in your hands. I thank you for taking care of it." He paused for a moment, pouring himself another cup of coffee.

"I strolled around the ship this morning and the men greeted me with respect. I owe you guys for this. When we arrive in Long Beach, they'll be in four sections, and you guys will be in five . . . you've earned it. I realize we still have a few holes in the manning, but I'm sure you'll get them filled.

"At 1500, Vince, Grif, I want you two to brief me and the other CDOs on SOPA regs for Long Beach. I would like the senior officer of each of the four new duty sections to attend . . . questions?" There were none.

What a crafty bastard the old man was by briefing the CO and the other CDOs, and by having the watch section officers attend, he ensured they'd know the SOPA regs, the regulations of the port put out by the senior officer present afloat. By assuming they already knew them, which they probably did not, he was sure they'd study them with a fervor. He thanked us for our time, stood up, and left. The meeting had been brief and powerful.

At 0930 the sonarmen sat fidgeting in the wardroom. This was officers' country, a place not within their status boundaries. They weren't comfortable in this bastion of pampered commissioned incompetence, as most enlisted men thought their leaders to be. Even though their officers, Mr. Baldachino and Mr. Hobson, assured them nothing bad was in the wind, that the skipper just wants to talk with them, they were not convinced. They remembered the tyranny of the old captain. Sonarmen by selection were in the top percentiles of the navy's IQ spectrum.

"Sit down, men," the captain said as he poured himself a cup of coffee from the ubiquitous hot plate. The stewards never showed up when there were enlisted men in the wardroom. "As you probably know, I was the captain of a nuclear attack submarine. I've been in subs most of my career, and in subs, sonarmen are one of our most cherished assets. I fully realize destroyers have several missions while the attack submarines I'm used to have only two: destroying surface ships and destroying submarines.

"Help yourself to coffee, men," He interrupted himself, waving his arm to the hot plate. "Smoke if you'd like." He lit a cigar. Turned to me. "XO."

I cleared my throat, the skipper wanted me to brief, wanted the sonarmen to hear it from a surface officer, not a submariner, whom they might not trust.

"One of our main missions," I started to say, "is to kill submarines, like we did last night. I reckon we made three good kills, not due to a crack sonar team, but, rather, more to unorthodox thinking and aggressiveness.

"Even though much of the blame for the ineffectiveness of destroyer ASW is blamed on surface vessels being poor sonar platforms, which is for the most part true, I think it's because of our mindset on how disadvantaged we are going up against a submarine." Feet shuffled and coughs interrupted the soft purr of ventilation fans.

"Additionally, I don't think surface-ship sonarmen think very much of themselves. Sonar detection is almost a mystical thing, a feeling in the gut, an amalgamation of science and occult.

"The captain knows that." I swept my eyes across the faces staring at me. "Many years ago, and I'm not bragging, just making a point, I detected one of the first Russian nuclear subs off our East Coast running at forty knots because of a gut feeling I had while flying in the back of an S2F.

"My last destroyer surfaced a Whiskey in the Formosa Strait a few years back, and though some say the initial contact might have been luck, I didn't think so. Our lead sonarman had a feeling . . . luck?"

All faces were on me, like red-robed inquisitors waiting to find a flaw in my words. Blood rushed to my face, painting it, I'm sure, crimson. I felt the heat, grunted, and went on.

"Luck. I don't define it quite the same way as the dictionary when it comes to sonar contacts. It's in your gut; it's a little voice, a tingle telling you a sub is there. But it's soft . . . you've got to listen; you've got to know the feeling. You can do it."

I stood up into the silence, poured myself another cup of coffee, and tried to light my unfilled pipe.

"Until you feel that way, gentlemen, you'll never be good sub fighters . . . most submarine sonarmen feel it, and so must you. Your ears and your mind will overcome convergent zone effects, bottom bounce, and layer promulgation. Your mind, gentlemen, listen to that inner voice . . . that inner voice." I sat down. "Any questions?"

No one spoke, no one looked at anyone else. The captain leaned his chair back on its rear legs, adding: "Belief is a muscle of will; it must be constantly exercised if it is to remain healthy and strong.

Never, and I repeat, *never* fail to call out a contact you think may be valid. *Kramer* will prosecute every contact you get. I know there are subs transiting these areas every day and destroyers never make contact. I'll set up a visit to a SOSUS station so you can see. I know the speed we crank on makes it difficult to detect anything. I realize it's hard, but I want you to know I'm part of your team. I'm part of the solution. Talk to me."

We stood as he left, none of us willing to break the silence till First Class Sonarman James said, "Hot shit." And we left the wardroom, no one saying another word. He'd summed it up.

For the next two days we trained at everything we could think of, the captain not taking an active part in any of it. He watched without comment. We scrounged services from any ship we could. We ran AAW, antiair warfare, tracking attacks on airliners leaving San Diego International Airport and on the navy jets taking off and landing at the naval air station at Coronado. We laid in wait to track subs coming out of the harbor, maintaining contact on them as far as we could and for much longer than we used to be able to do.

We exercised our gun tracking against merchies and other naval ships we came upon. When nothing was available, we ran engineering control drills and damage control exercises. Our dragging asses went to GQ so many times that we could do it in our sleep. The captain gave free reign to the OODs to run man-overboard drills and time to "play" with the ship's controls to get a feel for them. The sea gods cooperated, giving us calm seas and warm November sunshine.

At 0923 Thursday morning, our asses dragging, the OOD, Lt. (jg) Griffith H. Maxwell, USN, NROTC, came alongside a sister destroyer at our assigned berth at the U.S. naval station, Long Beach. As the first line went over, "Moored" echoed throughout the ship. Lieutenant (jg) Vincent D. Baldachino assumed the CDO duties and sounded liberty call at 0937. Only one-fourth of the crew stayed aboard. White hats left the ship with only a salute to the colors and the quarterdeck.

At 0953 the 1MC announced, *"Kramer,* departing." And the black and white absentee pennant unfurled into the morning's breeze. We were a U.S. Navy ship of the line again.

Nuclear Capable

Several months passed, it was coming on winter 1970, and things were going well. And we were looking good as we got under way to onload nuclear depth charges for our ASROC, anti-submarine rocket launcher. We'd offloaded our previous ones when the ship came back from WESTPAC. Four sections and a most generous liberty policy had worked magic as the now-empowered officers, and by extension their men, took greater pride in their responsibility.

Our sense of well-being, the beautiful day, and the calm seas settled a veil of euphoria over us as we steamed out of Long Beach Harbor, heading for the destroyer tender that held our nucs, and the required lectures at San Diego.

On the tender we sat on hard straight-back chairs in a small office as we tried to listen to the lectures that all nuclear weapons capable ships had to endure once a year. We again saw all the old movies of nuclear destruction and fallout. Nagasaki and Hiroshima horror clips flashed in front of us to remind us of the awesome power our ship would soon possess.

Responsibility, security, and safety pounded our temples with the constant drone of speakers we didn't want to listen to and movies we didn't want to see.

The stuffy room and the monotoned speakers dwindled my mind to indifference. *For Christ's sake, we know our responsibilities.* The veil of boredom eased through my body, shutting down my systems, weighting down my eyes, forcing a yawn. My eyes closed. I snapped them open.

Pay attention!

I tried, but my recalcitrant mind wandered, then focused on a horrifying vision of nuclear destruction. I could feel the sweat dampening my freshly starched khakis as the terrorizing scene played itself once again through my wayward thoughts. I could hear the sputtering port engine of our P2V patrol aircraft trying to maintain altitude through the sun-washed sky of the South Pacific Ocean as we headed for Eniwetok Island. The starboard engine had died forty-five minutes earlier.

We were going down, losing precious height with each mile flown. Parachutes, pens, pencils, anything, everything we could unbolt or chop away, had gone out the bomb bay doors in our attempt to get weight off the plane.

The pilot had dumped fuel when he estimated Eniwetok one hundred miles away. We continued sinking, barely maintaining a few knots faster than stall speed.

Our squadron of P2Vs patrolled and kept other aircraft and ships away from the site of the first hydrogen bomb drop called Operation Ivy, in 1953. We were in the Marshall Islands, ten miles away from the small island of Eniwetok, ten degrees north of the equator.

Hundreds of old World War II ships, only tethered hulks now, waited to be ignobly destroyed by the hydrogen blast and later studied like cadavers in a medical school. We were the last aircraft out of the area after making one more sweep to ensure no stray merchies had shown up.

The port engine coughed, stopped for a second, and caught again, costing us one hundred ninety feet of altitude. In ten minutes Eniwetok came into sight about five degrees to port; we gently swung left, lining up for the approach.

The port engine sputtered again, dropping us fifty more feet. The tiny island dot of Eniwetok loomed larger but still looked too far away. Breathing came hard as I fought for each breath of sodden air. There was nothing left for me to do but wait impotently as panic penetrated my defenses. I glanced at the altimeter dancing around six hundred fifty feet. Shit!

We lumbered down to six hundred feet above the calm, and, I was sure, shark-infested waters. I couldn't control my shaking.

I heard Captain Macaby's words yank me back to reality. "You okay, XO?"

"Yeah . . . yes, sir, just the stuffiness, I guess," I answered, turning away in embarrassment. But my thoughts slammed me back uncontrollably to the failing aircraft the second I tried to concentrate on the droning lecture.

I saw us come across the runway's threshold at twenty feet, smashing down hard, tires screeching in protest to the jammed-on brakes. We veered to the right as the faltering port engine slewed us around. The pilot reversed the pitch, but before it took hold, the engine died. The plane careened side to side.

The narrow runway disappeared fast behind us until finally our starboard wheel caught a mound of coral just off the strip. It twisted us to a jolting halt, collapsing the starboard landing gear.

We bolted through the emergency exits to a racing pickup truck braking hard to a swaying halt next to us. *"Hurry, hurry!"* screamed the driver. *"Get in, get in, for Christ sake. We only got five minutes!"* The six of us jammed into the truck bed as we sped away through the profusion of swaying palms.

"Get behind the berm there," he shouted. *"Keep down."* We crouched, hugging the hard coral. Scared. We should have been three hundred miles away from there.

The blinding flash passed over us: the heat singeing my hair and burning my face, and the noise deafening my ears. In a daze I stood just as the shock wave bulldozed the beach. I took it full in the chest; its power yanking me as if I were a child: lifting me, throwing me ruthlessly ten feet backward. My flight suit shredded as I rolled and tumbled while the sharp, deadly coral tore my flesh in a thousand places.

And it was over. The first hydrogen bomb had just exploded nine miles away, and I had been stupid enough to stand up before the shock wave hit.

My body still shook as the briefing officer's final remarks brought me back to the lecture. "Well, I hope what I've discussed with you is taken well to heart . . . be safe, be secure, and," he added with a smirk, "I hope you never have to see one go off."

So do I, I murmured under by breath.

Mr. DeLeon

"Nucs loaded, XO, and the security watch set . . . and this is Jim DeLeon, my relief," Mr. Hobson reported, standing awkwardly outside my stateroom. I stood offering my hand to the tall, brown-haired lieutenant, whose smile spread easily over his classically chiseled face.

"Don Sheppard . . . Mr. DeLeon, welcome aboard. Captain's still on the tender. Don't stand at attention. Have a seat," I said, moving away from my desk so they could slip by. DeLeon's bull neck and bulging arms swelled his khaki blouse, flaring in sharp contrast to Mr. Hobson's body, which had been let go. "Didn't expect you for a couple more weeks. You're early," I added, ringing for a steward to bring in three coffees.

"Yes, sir, I cut my destroyer school leave short so I get here earlier," he answered, looking around my stateroom as if he were sizing it up for his own. On every swing of his head, his eyes rested on my khaki blouse hanging on a bulkhead peg. He stared at the rows of ribbons over the upper-left pocket and the command button over the right.

With the advent of destroyer school, the professionalism of destroyer officers grew considerably. No longer could a young officer advance to a department head billet without first attending. A far cry from my early days, when the captain and executive officer had to train the department heads themselves.

The old system wasn't very good, especially if the CO and XO had taken the same career path, which was usually operations, and most of them had. Now a young officer on his first tour aboard destroyers had to prove himself and volunteer and be recommended by his captain in order to attend the school. And he had to be qualified at the least as an OOD(I), independent steaming, or better yet as an OOD(F), fast carrier task force.

The officers, by the time they graduated, were usually full lieutenants and came aboard with a firm knowledge of every department and every weapons system. A quantum leap forward, we were now on par with the aviators and submariners.

"Where did you get all the medals, sir, Vietnam?" Mr. DeLeon asked with a respect he hadn't demonstrated when he first entered my stateroom. He did not have that degree of subservience in his voice and manner that a junior officer should have when first meeting his new XO, a man who could ruin his career with the stroke of a pen. He seemed to have a rebellious streak, which could easily get him in trouble unless he was good, damn good.

"Yes, river gunboats in the Delta," I answered, trying, as I always did, to minimize any conversation about it.

"Been to the hill and seen the elephants, eh?" he remarked almost silently. I looked at him, amazed; not many men could quote the saying of Roman soldiers in reference to going to the Alps to fight Hannibal and his invading elephant corps.

"The silver star, eh? Legion of Merit . . . three Bronze Stars, two Purple Hearts—"

"Enough, Mr. DeLeon, I know what medals I have. Mr. Hobson

will get you checked in," I said, cutting him off. *Trouble here, I hope he's good, if he has talent we can refine him.* In a masochistic sort of way, I liked him.

"What was your last duty assignment before destroyer school, Mr. DeLeon?" the captain asked at lunch.

"XO of a minesweeper, I served two years on a destroyer before that," he answered with a haughty look at me as if we were equals because he had once been an XO. An XO is an XO, I guess, even though a minesweeper had only three officers compared to our fifteen and a crew of about ten men to our two hundred fifty.

"Well done, Jim," the captain answered. "We're getting under way early tomorrow morning. Will that give you any problem with a car or anything?"

"No, sir, my wife dropped me off and drove herself back to Long Beach. I'm ready!" The captain glanced at me, suppressing a grin as if he expected DeLeon to jump up and march around the wardroom table.

He'd shared my feelings about DeLeon after they'd met and when we talked about him earlier. "May I take the ship out, Captain?" Mr. DeLeon asked with unheard-of audacity. The captain glanced at Mr. Sanders and received an astonished shrug of his shoulders. Mr. DeLeon had either gigantic balls or incredible bad taste asking to take the ship to sea with less than half a day aboard.

The captain looked at me. I paused, also shrugging my shoulders. "We'll talk about it, Mr. DeLeon," I answered, trying to end the conversation as the other department heads stared at him in disbelief of his faux pas.

The captain, seemingly unfazed, asked him, "Why'd you choose the weapons department . . . you obviously had your choice, graduating first in your class. Not that the weapons department is bad, I just thought surface officers all went for Operations if they could."

"Why, Captain," he answered as if the question insulted his intelligence. "That's where the guns are."

We were the innermost ship moored to the tender in a nest of four destroyers. DeLeon had the conn. "Main engines test satisfactorily," he reported too loudly. With this final input, I reported all departments ready for sea. Mr. DeLeon ordered all lines, except those on the bow, slackened and taken in.

Before backing, we had to take a line from the remaining ships in the nest and pass it to the tender so the other ships would not drift free. We waited patiently. You couldn't hurry it, but Mr. DeLeon paced back and forth as if it were a personal affront that it wasn't be done faster.

"This'll change," I heard him mutter on one of his frequent quick-walking passes by me at the chart table. "What's the current, Quartermaster?"

For the third time in as many minutes, Willie said in the monotone he used to answer stupid questions from officers, "Still flooding, sir, still an hour before slack water, sir." I gave him a reproving look. He smiled, and turned away.

Mr. DeLeon asked the phone talker to the fo'c's'le—the forecastle, the head of the ship—what the hell was taking so long. I walked over to him and said softly, "Take it easy, Jim, we're in no hurry. You can see they're doing okay . . . Don't fuck over their minds . . . They're doing okay. You're doing okay. Take a strain."

He flushed over my use of the word *fuck*. I'd gotten his attention, he smiled, and a wave of relief passed across his sweating face. "Bridge, fo'c's'le, other ship's forward line secured to the tender."

"Request permission to get under way, Captain," Mr. DeLeon asked in a calm, normal tone.

"Permission granted," came an even calmer reply.

"Lee helm, tell Main Control to stand by to answer all bells," Mr. DeLeon ordered.

Instantly the lee helm answered, "Main Control still standing by to answer all bells." Mr. DeLeon had given the order twice already.

"All engines back one-third," Mr. DeLeon ordered, and as our backwash rushed forward, the nest drifted out to port, leaving us a clear wedge of water to back down into. "Let go and take in all forward lines," he told the talker, and ordered all stop as the rest of the destroyers in the nest settled away from us out about ten feet. "All clear," came the fo'c's'le, "All lines taken in."

"Under way."

"All clear astern," Mr. Maxwell, the first lieutenant, who was in charge of the deck force, reported from the fantail. We moved back slowly with our backwash pushing the nest even farther apart. I could see heaving lines from the next ship in the nest snaking their way over to the tender as a yard tugboat pushed on their sterns. Everything was okay.

"All engines back one-third," Mr. DeLeon ordered, glancing astern.

"Whistle signals, Jim?" I whispered.

His tense face grew white in anger as he rushed into the pilothouse, shouting, "Sound one long blast and three shorts." The long blast would indicate to other ships we were changing status, that is, from moored to under way. The three shorts said we were backing.

The flooding tide, a tide coming in, had the nest laying up harbor, the way we wanted to go. All we had to do was back down, twist a little to head fair of the nest, then steam around them and head for sea, in this case with a stop at the refueling dock at Point Loma. Mr. DeLeon, despite his initial first-time jitters, did it in textbook fashion.

I shuddered at the thought of the refueling docks, remembering my first attempt, so long ago, and how I had bungled it so badly. The incident had humbled me for years. And thinking about it now hacked at my confidence, which flittered away in small pieces as we drew closer.

The sharp morning breeze and our forward motion tousled Mr. DeLeon's just-a-little-too-long dark-brown hair as he stood on the conning platform on the starboard wing. Every inch of him personified the recruiting-poster image of the destroyer man. The Gallic warrior riding to battle. I walked over to him. "You familiar with the fueling pier here, Mr. DeLeon?"

"Yes, sir, brought our minesweeper in here many a time," he answered as if fending off an insult.

"You know about the sudden winds, then?"

"Yes, I do . . . XO," he answered as if I were a retarded child having a hard time understanding. The wind roared down the cliffs at thirty knots as he started his approach. I stood behind him, ready to take over if he fumbled. Coming in sharp against the wind to minimize their effect, he pushed the bow almost straight in, perpendicular to the pier. The captain's left eye twitched and his eyebrows pulled lower, stretching the skin of his forehead.

Mr. DeLeon ordered number one line over while still fifty feet out and closing. *Too soon.* A heaving line went over. Missed. Another line went over. A better toss and it made it to the pier, barely. Sailors in the line-handling party grabbed it up and pulled in the small heaving line attached to a one-inch line, then finally to our five-inch manila mooring line. They made the mooring line fast to the bollard quickly so as not to lose it by the ship blowing away. It was a mean, thankless job.

"Moored."

He ordered another line out through the bull nose, and when made fast, let out thirty feet of slack and passed it to Mr. Maxwell on the stern to put the waiting MIKE boat just forward of the port screw guard and push. "Left full rudder, port engine back two-thirds, starboard engine ahead two-thirds." The stern slowly moved toward the pier as the doubled number-one line took the strain against the twisting stern.

We inched ahead as the more efficient ahead engine took over. "You might want to ease that forward bell a bit, Mr. DeLeon, just for a minute," I counseled softly into his ear.

"Starboard engine ahead one third," he ordered, compensating. About thirty seconds passed, then he increased the starboard engine to ahead two-thirds again.

The howling winds screeched unabated, but in four more minutes a heaving line went over aft, and in another three minutes, number six line was made fast to a bollard. Mr. DeLeon reduced his twist to one-third bells. The strain on number one eased, and he ordered it taken to the windlass and hauled about.

"Over all lines." And four heaving lines arched to the pier. Number six kept a steady strain as the boatswain's mates took up the slack as we drew closer. Only twenty feet to the pier. "All stop." The push of the MIKE boat astern and the windlass on the bow brought us the last few feet into a perfect parallel landing. "Double up all lines, sir?" Mr. DeLeon asked, looking at me with a smirk. I nodded my head toward the captain.

"Double up, Mr. DeLeon, double up . . . outstanding bit of sea-manship, young man, outstanding," the captain answered, walking back into the pilothouse. "Secure the sea detail, XO. Give the men a rest," he added, plopping heavily in his chair with a sigh. Maybe his cool exterior extorted a higher toll than I imagined.

"The smoking lamp is out throughout the ship," the boatswain's mate passed over the 1MC.

The fueling hoses mated our trunks like an elephant's in heat as the pungent, flammable petroleum smell irritated our nostrils and stung our eyes, its odor permeating the ship. There was nothing to do but wait. I yearned for a pipe, as I did every time the smoking lamp was out.

The smoking-lamp tradition dated back to the sailing ship days when seamen didn't have matches. The only way they could light their pipes and cigars was from a small oil lamp in the galley kept for just such a purpose. When the captain didn't want the men to smoke, he ordered the "smoking lamp out" just as we do today. But now it's an order, not a physical thing. We all have Zippo lighters.

"Jim, you did a fine job here. The first and only time I conned in here, it took me close to two hours to make fast . . . beautiful work, beautiful."

"Not for a good ship handler like me," he answered with a wide grin, then, breaking out in laughter, said, "Not really, XO. At de-stroyer school this was one of our classic shitty-places-to-go problems, and the whole class worked it out. I just replayed my mental tapes of the bull sessions," he finished with a modesty I didn't think he could muster.

The Martial Arts

Days later, back in Long Beach, there was a knock on my open door. A voice said: "It's Mr. DeLeon, sir."

I looked up. "What's he doing now, Chief?"

"He's back on the fantail in a black-belted, karate outfit or some-thing, with most of the duty section. He's breaking boards with the side of his hand," the chief master at arms said, sitting on my couch. The chief master at arms (CMAA) headed the XO's private police force. Each division furnished one man to be on the master-at-arms force, and they in turn reported to the chief and he to the XO.

The masters at arms dated back to the olden days as a force to control the ship's seamen. But it continued in use to enforce ship's regulations like not wasting water, or not smoking when the smoking lamp was out, or ensuring taps and reveille were properly observed, or helping drunks get aboard and into their racks, or anything that had to be done to preserve order. Best of all, however, the CMAA was a direct link from the crew to the XO.

"How's he doing otherwise, Chief?" It was 1700, we'd knocked off ship's work an hour ago, and most of the off-duty crew waited for dinner before going ashore.

"The men like him and he runs a fair show . . . but he can be a bit overbearing and bullies the men at times. But he's got his shit together. He's okay, XO. He gets a little weird sometimes, like now, and I thought you might like to know."

The hidden meaning from these watered-down complaints was damning. The chief, always on guard when talking to officers, laced his words with modifiers, lessening the true intent of the problem. I knew that by the time the CMAA felt urged to talk to me, things were bad.

The CMAA was, as was usual, the chief boatswain's mate in charge of First Division, the deck apes, under the first lieutenant. "Got another bit of a problem with Seaman Reeves, XO. He stands around crying like a baby quite a bit . . . unnerving to the men, can't you get rid of him?"

I didn't address the Reeves problem, as the chief meant for me to do. I came back to DeLeon. "Are you saying Mr. DeLeon is a problem, Chief?"

"No, XO, not a problem at all, just keeping you informed, sir," he chuckled sarcastically. *Yeah, Chief, yeah.*

"About Reeves, I can't foist him off on anyone else. That's how we got him; another ship dumped him on us when they deployed. Maybe he just needs some talking to?"

"Tried that, didn't do any good."

"What's he want?"

"Out of the navy and back to his mother."

"What does Mr. DeLeon say about it?"

"I've told both him and Mr. Maxwell, but they don't seem to want to address the problem. They just said let the weenie go over the hill.

Don't seem right, XO," he answered, looking away as if he'd gone too far.

"Thanks, Chief, anything else?"

"Mess cooks, XO, we're changing out again in a week or so, and we keep getting the screw-ups all the time. The cooks get pissed off because they get shit from the crew on the lousy service . . . it isn't their fault if their help is so bad. Can you kick some commissioned ass on this?"

I had failed. It was one of my first orders. I'd made the mistake of not following up, and here the problem remained because of my poor management. I took a breath, trying to shed off the smashing effect of failure. I fought a silent inner battle for calmness.

Organize, deputize, and supervise. I had neglected the last step—the most important step.

Can you kick some commissioned ass on this? he'd said, but really meant, can we kick *your* ass on this.

The chiefs took liberties with me that they could never have done to a non-mustang. Chiefs always tried to push the envelope of authority with officers. I did it myself when I was a chief. I let my chiefs get away with it, and my power base grew because of it. We had a tacit understanding on how far they could go, and never in front of the men or the officers. It was a good arrangement.

I scratched in brilliant red on a notepad: *Mess cooks . . . kick ass,* and dismissed the chief with: "Thank you, Chief Master at Arms, I'll take care of it."

On the fantail, sure enough, there was Jim DeLeon doing a slow kung-fu dance. He was sucking in his breath, slowly flailing his arms and feet about, and shouting in some esoteric language, sounding like *tongues* at a revival meeting.

I stood watching along with the several men circling him. Noticing me, he twisted and lunged with his feet flying up, his distorted mouth yelling a bloodcurdling cry as his stiffened hand flashed down, stopping an inch from my neck. It frightened me, and I fought not to take defensive action.

I winced even though I knew from watching him that he had control enough to stop the blow before it struck. He jumped back, smiling as if he were a second grader having just successfully recited a simple poem to his classmates. He bowed, sweeping his hands to his attentive audience. They clapped and shouted for him.

"Mr. DeLeon," I said, keeping a smile on my face, and in a voice low enough that only a few could hear. "Get into the uniform of the day *immediately* and report to my stateroom on the double. Do you understand that order, Mister?"

He looked at me, his face twisting into a sardonic grin, his arm theatrically sweeping up as he bowed to his audience and walked off. Exit stage left.

In six minutes he stood outside my door in freshly pressed khakis with the sweat from his karate exertions staining through them. Around him, the pungent odor of a cheap New York fighter's gym combined with an expensive aftershave lotion, withered my nostrils.

"Sit down, Mr. DeLeon," I said, not looking at him as I shuffled a few more papers. Then, standing up, I closed my door just as a duty steward asked me if I was going to eat aboard tonight. I didn't usually leave the ship until about 2000 and often ate dinner with the duty officers. "Save me something if you would. Thank you."

Mr. DeLeon sat on my couch, grinning disrespectfully, as if he had a secret joke but wasn't going to share it with me because I wasn't worthy. I kept all anger out of my voice, as if we were having a friendly chat, and thanked him for coming to see me so promptly. His breathing settled in at normal; he sighed and lit a cigarette.

With a sweep of my hand I removed it from his mouth and snuffed it out in the ashtray. His eyes widened. He coughed an indecisive cough and stared at me.

Deliberately I stepped over to my hanging blouse and using a pencil, tapped a ribbon as I spoke in a slow, considered voice.

"See these three Bronze Star Medals, Jim, all with combat V's for valor? You're always asking me how I got them. One of 'em I got for putting out a fire at a rocketed air force base. Not much to that. Another, Jim, I got for going in with machine guns and grenades and destroying maybe fifty sampans filled with women, old men, and children. At the time I thought it had to be done." My voice stayed coolly modulated though my gut boiled to kick the shit out of him.

I went on, telling him that another of the Bronze Stars was for going into an opposing village and destroying it with flamethrowers and grenades after we pounded them with helo gunships and heavy machine guns for several hours.

I told him I figured it had to be done, and I considered myself an avenging angel sent by God to make the world right. The Presidential Unit Citation came to us because my boys played the same stupid game I did.

His wide, expressionless eyes never left the pencil, as if by staring, the adventures would transfer to him.

He looked at the Silver Star Medal, a drop of spittle easing out of the left side of his mouth. I told him I got it for disobeying an order by being someplace I had been forbidden to go, and while there, destroying three or four junks carrying maybe thirty or forty Vietcong each.

I let him stare at the Vietnamese Honor Medal, some called it a medal of honor. I didn't remember why I got that. I must have done something stupid. The Vietnamese Cross of Gallantry was the only medal I felt I deserved, and I got it for saving a village under attack.

The Purple Hearts came because I was stupid, and still, three years later, no day went by that I didn't hurt from the shrapnel embedded in my body. They couldn't dig it all out. Actually, I mentioned, I'd been wounded five times but didn't report any more than two because Saigon would have kicked me out of the country. Most of my officers and men did the same thing, and we comshawed treatment and confiscated and destroyed medical records. We believed in what we were doing. Enlisted men were transferred out after two wounds, officers three.

The eyes of his slack-jawed face were a marvel of hero-worship.

I continued my little tongue-in-cheek lecture, telling him that the legion of merit came as an "atta boy" culminating a short and bloody year killing Commies for Christ and preserving the Western concept of democracy in Southeast Asia.

Citations for the medals rarely indicated what really happened, and all they did was heap praise for heroic actions *allegedly* performed. Citations were usually written by staffies who knew little of what really happened, and they were ninety percent bullshit. My legion of merit citation used the word *perspicaciousness*. I'd never heard it until the admiral from Yokosuka presented the medal and read the citation. But at the time I was getting the medals, I was convinced I was carrying the banner of God and the United States, and I saw a job to do and I did it. No half-assed measures.

"XO, I . . ."

"Shut your fucking mouth!" I snarled, snapping the pencil in two and throwing the pieces hard unto my desk. His eyes followed their journey. I sat down, staring at the bulkhead, then, rotating my chair toward him, said, "You may wonder why I'm telling you all this, Jim. Simple, if you intend to do something, you do it. If you draw your gun, you fire. If you unsheathe your knife, you jam it home."

I was well familiar with the martial arts, but not the showtime presentations DeLeon danced on the fantail. Mine was taught for killing, not for bullshit. My lessons emphasized that if you attack a man, you kill or cripple him, whatever your goal. I did not play with half-assed theatrical displays of self-control.

"If it ever happens again, Mr. DeLeon, I will assume you're trying to kill me and react as necessary. I watched you. You could probably put me down. You're good, damn good, and I'm over forty and have lost my edge. What are you, maybe twenty-seven? You'd have to go for the kill, Jim."

"XO, I didn't—"

I yelled at him to shut up and told him he was goddamned lucky that I wasn't going to charge him with assault on a senior officer with a deadly weapon. He always bragged how lethal his hands were. I hesitated for a minute, letting my words clank through his mind. I lit my pipe and told him I was not taking official notice of his conduct or how foolish he made me look in front of the men. "But what I am going to do," I said, my eyes burning into him, "is give you five days in hack. Do you understand that, Mr. DeLeon?"

His face blanched with the prospect of staying aboard, confined to his stateroom, for five days unless he had the watch or duty or had to perform bodily functions. Meals would be brought to him.

"XO, I—"

"You do know, Mr. DeLeon, that I do not have the authority to put you in hack. Only the captain can do that after he awards you a captain's mast, under the Uniform Code of Military Justice, the UCMJ, Article 15, nonjudicial punishment. You do know that, don't you, Jim, you were an XO."

"Yes, yes, sir. I know that."

"Would it make you more comfortable if I have the captain do it so you wouldn't get the impression that your ol' XO doesn't always obey the rules."

He was shrewd enough to know the captain could only take official notice of things, and the matter would, perforce, appear on his fitness report. "I understand, XO," he answered, no gusto, no bravado left, sweat pouring from his face and body, adding new sweat stains to very recently fresh khakis.

And in a parting shot I suggested since he'd be aboard anyway, and that he'd probably not want to sit in his stateroom all the time, maybe it would be a grand gesture to take the duties for his fellow CDOs for the five days.

He paused, looking at me, hate in his eyes. "Yes, sir. Good idea, XO. I understand."

"Great, Jim, let's go have some dinner. And unless you want to, we'll speak no more of this, nor will anyone else know of this conversation. And one more thing, I don't like the sounds I'm getting about you bullying the men . . . that shit will never happen again or you're off the ship, no matter where we are . . . do you know what I'm talking about, Jim?" I received a feeble "yes, sir" as I turned on the fan and opened the door to ventilate out the stench of his body odor.

"Larry, I'm staying aboard tonight. I'll take your duty if you want me to," Jim said to Lieutenant Sanders as he sat down at the wardroom table. I joined them, apologizing to the steward for having to prepare two more rations.

Early the next morning I joined the captain for our early morning meeting. "Captain, we got an OPNAV, action message, from CNO entitled 'Z-gram,' you ever hear of them?"

"Yeah, at the club with a few other COs yesterday. I heard Admiral Zumwalt, the Chief of Naval Operations, thought life aboard ship was too austere, and he was going to do something about it. I guess the Z-gram is the start. What does it say?"

Palace Revolt

And the Z-grams came forth like tablets from the Mount in a heroic attempt to restore seagoing sailors to dignified human beings and give them a life as normal as possible when in port. Civilian clothes were allowed onboard, and sailors could go ashore in "proper" attire.

Unfortunately, what is proper to a nineteen-year-old lad from Texas is not usually proper to the more senior captains commanding the squadrons or the admirals commanding the flotillas or the more stodgy commanding officers aboard ships and their bewildered XOs.

Besides, they lamented, there was no place aboard a small ship to store civilian clothes. A preposterous idea. Not authorized in this command! No way.

Six-section liberty, come on, they shouted. How can we possibly get the ship under way and steam it with only a sixth of the crew aboard? Quite right, I concurred, remembering the problems we had adjusting to four sections.

Properly trimmed beards could be worn if the sailors desired, and their hair could be longer in the style of the day. Nonsense, screamed the commanders. What's the navy coming to with that upstart hippie in Washington? Thus came the not-too-subtle guidance from above, and Z-grams became more honored in the breech than in the letter.

We did the best we could under the constraints of our squadron commander and whoever gave him his orders. In trying to comply, we went to five sections with trepidation. Trepidation like you might have if your sixteen-year-old daughter were going to the junior year hayride with the leader of the Hell's Angels.

We found it worked okay with little hardship except for getting under way—we still demanded the duty section make all preparations for going to sea. And some of the CDOs in the squadron were that in name only, qualified OODs on paper only.

Fleet morale plummeted as the sailors saw the Z-grams suffer the flagrant disobedience of their senior officers. Most junior officers lauded Admiral Zumwalt. Z-grams were OPNAVs (all navy messages from the CNO). They didn't end with the statement "If you disagree with this order, sorry, just don't obey." "They were OPNAVs, god-dammit, direct orders from the CNO." They loudly lamented. "And if the fuckin' senior officers don't have to obey orders, why the hell do we," came mutinous talk, spreading throughout the fleet like the black plague.

The captain and I strolled the deck bemoaning the vagaries of higher command. Rust streaks showed, fire hoses dangled sloppily, damage control equipment hung, improperly stowed. The first signs of the insidious cancer of low morale. Pride was gone.

As we approached the quarterdeck still hidden by the super-structure, we both jerked to a halt. His anger whipped through me, adding exponentially to mine. He stretched his arm and pointed, un-able to speak. On the haze-gray bulkhead in front of us, a three-foot red Z had been painted.

We looked at each other, both furious, both afraid to speak, afraid of what might come out. "I . . . I'll be on the flagship . . . be, be back in an hour, XO," he stammered.

"*Kramer*, departing."

I called for the chief master at arms.

Each Z-gram carried within it the requirement that it be posted for the crew. Even this fell to violation as some ship captains at-tempted to hide their existence. This mendacity only enraged the already-angered sailors. It was foolish, because radiomen around the world had first access to all incoming telex traffic. That's how Z-grams came in, and the radiomen ensured each had maximum circulation, even risking their careers to pass the word. Young officers in O-clubs discussed the Z-grams in hot debate as the pros and the cons fought it out; and there were damn few cons.

I really didn't know what was going on, we lowly lieutenant com-manders didn't offer much advice when the big boys got into it. Only fools question when admirals bellow.

The captain and I stood by, perplexed as we watched our navy melt down like birthday cake candles. Due for a WESTPAC tour in six months, we could only hope we'd hold together till then.

A problem endemic to the Z-grams was the built-in modifiers to let commanding officers remain in charge. Words such as *when fea-*

sible, when appropriate, make every effort to, and so forth, actually created a tremendous loophole in the Z-grams, and the local top brass took every advantage of it.

And then the hit teams.

Another OPNAV rocked the communication system with its terse assertion that CNO was displeased with *some* of the senior officers in the fleet. He was displeased with those who failed to fully grasp the intent, and through this misunderstood the point and therefore failed to implement the Z-grams with the vigor they demanded. A few three-starred heads rolled.

An advisory board was convened to *advise* the CNO on ways to increase the navy's morale and help to get the word out to the fleet. Junior officers, no greater in rank than lieutenant junior grade, and enlisted men, second class petty and below, were to be chosen. These anointed ones—those who were to sit at the foot of the king— were ordered to Washington immediately.

The senior enlisted man in each command was to be designated as a senior enlisted adviser, the SEA. He was to have direct access to the CO, direct access to the SEA of the command directly above his CO, and the one next senior to him. And by tenacity the SEAs had direct, *unquestionable* access to the master chief petty officer of the navy, who was CNO's senior enlisted adviser, and sat next to the throne in the five-sided castle of Admiral Elmo "Bud" Zumwalt, USN, a destroyer man's destroyer man.

The SEAs had been in place for quite a while, but the CNO breathed new life into their previously sinecurial duties and responsibilities.

It got everyone's attention. Word soon came from Washington that ships in port no longer had the requirement to get under way and fight their ship in an emergency. Captain Macaby called the commodore and was told to stand by. We imagined the commodore called the flotilla commander, and guessed the flotilla commander called the type commander while we waited.

At 1600, five-sixths of the crew went ashore while one-sixth stayed aboard hoping to Christ nothing would happen. The captain left the ship at 2200. I left at midnight.

In the morning the ship was still there.

The turbulent times subsided and Admiral Zumwalt had his way. The navy grew for it and reenlistments increased, and we settled down to a more efficient and humane navy. "Thank you, Bud."

Please Call Me Julie

She sat in my stateroom. The door was closed.

"Tommy said you called him a wimp . . . do you think that was very nice, XO Sheppard?"

"Please, ma'am . . . Mrs. Reeves, call me Mr. Sheppard or XO, but you can't combine the titles," I said to the dark-haired woman sitting on my couch.

"Miss," she corrected me, her moist eyes widening as she looked at me. She was obviously here to plead for her son's survival in the navy. He *was* a wimp, moping around crying at the simplest things. His brother seamen had lost tolerance for him, and he had become the butt of every joke, and his petty officers gave him every shit detail. He failed on every one. I'd talked to him several times but to no avail.

The base psychiatrist recommend he be given a general discharge. A serious matter.

"Miss Reeves, the crew calls him a wimp . . . not me." A slight tear came to her eyes. A general discharge, even under honorable conditions, would blight his record for life, not a step we take lightly.

It meant he hadn't cut it in the navy. Not bad in itself, but there were too many people out there in the civilian world who had made it through the service, and put up with the bullshit, and got an honorable discharge. A general discharge was a flag of incompetence, or wrongdoing, or he just couldn't cut it.

She sat with her legs crossed under her short skirt. Her black hose showed to her thighs. I fought the testosterone surging through me as I tried not to glance down at them. I wasn't doing well.

"He says you sent him to see a shrink, and the guy didn't like him so they're going to kick him out of the navy."

I wished I'd left my stateroom door open after Mr. DeLeon brought her to me. Her hand reached out lightly, touching my knee. She left it there. Her breasts fought to break out of the skimpy lace topped bra she wore under a loose-fitting red silk blouse. Her fingers stayed on my knee, casually squeezing and rubbing lightly. "Actually, Mrs. Reeves . . . ah . . . Miss Reeves, I've had many talks with Seaman Reeves, and I do not concur with the base psychiatrist . . . I . . ."

"Please call me Julie, Mr. XO."

"Yes, ma'am . . . Julie . . . and you can call me XO. I think he can make it if we give him a little extra attention. We—"

"Oh, thank you, Mr. XO," she cooed, slinking herself off the couch, entwining her arms around me, kissing me wetly on my cheek.

With my hands firmly on each of her shoulders, I pushed her gently aside as if this were some grade B movie. Her long black hair flashed across her face as she twirled her head, letting me guide her back to the couch. The couch, which turned into a bed, entered my thoughts with more than the utilitarian aspect of it in mind.

I stood over her as she docilely sat with a sly smile forming on her face. I couldn't help but look down as I stood over her. "There now, Miss Reeves, Seaman Reeves is a member of my crew . . . on *Kramer* we take care of our own," I said, hoping it didn't sound too corny.

"You mean, XO Sheppard, you're not going to kick him out . . . he's such a good boy and just wants to do well. . . . I'd be so *very* pleased, sir."

"It's no longer your problem, Mrs. . . . Miss Reeves. . . . It's the navy's concern. Everything will be okay," I said, thinking what a whoosh I must sound like. "Now, if you'll excuse me, ma'am, I've got a meeting scheduled in five minutes. I stood, opening my door as I extended my hand to assist her up.

She gently pushed the door closed, putting her arms around me in a motherly embrace and kissed me on the lips. "Oh, thank you, Don." *Don? How'd she know my name?* "You won't regret it," she said, pulling back from me as she took a lipstick out of her purse. She glanced to the closed door in the forward end of my stateroom. "Is that a rest room?" she asked, her hand still holding mine.

She came out in a minute, fresh lipstick applied as I wiped her old lipstick off my lips. "Oh! Sorry," she giggled. I escorted her through the wardroom, where Mr. DeLeon, the CDO, and Ensign John Fuller, the disbursing officer, sat finishing their supper. They both stood as we passed through. DeLeon winked, smirked.

At the gangway I took her arm. She placed her hand firmly over mine, exciting a tingle as I escorted her down the brow, a slippery walkway with side rails from the ship to the pier. On the pier she took my hand as if to shake good-bye. "In high school Tommy had the same problem," she said with her deep black eyes not leaving mine. "I talked to his vice principal, and we reached an understanding, and my dear little Tommy made it through. . . . He's a good boy, Don, and I thank you for your time."

"Thank you for coming, Miss Reeves"

"Yes," she interrupted, "that would be nice." She winked.

"I, ah, meant to the ship . . ."

"Why, of course, so did I . . . Donald." *Donald?*

"I understand how hard it must have been for you."

"Yes, hard . . . hard. Do you understand?"

"Yes, ma'am, I understand."

Turning to leave, she took my hand, rubbing her fingers across it as softly as a little girl might caress her furry Easter bunny. Her smile redirected my blood. I swiftly placed the sheafs of paper I carried in front of myself.

She released my hand with a squeeze, pursed her lips in invitation, turned, and walked down the pier. I stared at her wiggling little butt as did the turning heads of every sailor she passed. I looked down into my hand; she'd slipped me a note. It contained a local telephone number. Is that how Tommy made it through high school? I tore the paper in half and threw it over the side as I walked up the gangway. Then wished I hadn't, then glad I did. Well, sorta.

In my private head, the same number was written in her lipstick on the mirrored door of my medicine cabinet.

I'd have to do something about Seaman Reeves. Maybe assign him to Willie; he wanted him.

Settling In. V-Neck/Crew Neck

Commander First Fleet's Quarterly Deployment Schedule showed us under way for WESTPAC in two months and slotted us to undergo an operational readiness inspection, an ORI, in three weeks. Had I already been aboard more than a year?

An operational readiness inspection tested every facet of a ship's ability to go to war and survive. It tested everything mechanical, every pump, every fitting. Tested every man. It exercised the crew at every evolution, every skill. It examined every piece of paper, every instruction, every doctrine.

It made us review our procedures. It made us aware, sometimes painfully, of our shortcomings. Administrative death awaited the poor CO and XO who came up UNSAT.

I had fallen into my job well, and the captain and I made a good team. He was content to let me run the ship, and I ensured his confidence by meticulously reporting everything to him. That's all he wanted; he was a patient man, and if I asked for advice on how to handle a situation, he gave his opinion without sarcasm or rancor.

At sea, unlike many COs, he included me in the bridge routine. Sometimes this was just too much. The bridge was his domain, and I had far too much administrative work to do running the ship to worry about operations and the training of the OODs. Each day I marveled at the XO I had on *Henshaw*. Things went smoothly on *Henshaw* and I thought it just happened that way, not realizing my old XO's firm hand guided it. Well, I realized it now, *Henshaw's* XO worked his ass off keeping it that way. And so did I.

But it was okay with me to be involved intimately in operations. I couldn't stand not being in the middle of everything, and anyway, running our Thursday planning board for training demanded my active participation. And it was a break from worrying about mundane reports, and mess cooks, and indebtedness letters from jewelry stores that conned our men into overbuying cheap jewelry, or car dealers that suckered our sailors into paying too much for junk automobiles. I made the division officers and department heads write the letters and counsel their men.

Morale once more stood high, the ship was lookin' good, and we had very few problems since we could properly implement the Z-grams.

The captain, though not as flamboyant as my first CO, Commander Baker, was more personable—a good man who trusted and listened to his officers and men, and they responded. On the social occasions we had, he seemed withdrawn and a bit stodgy, but his attempts at good humor and his willingness to join in made up for it.

He'd confessed to me on one of the rare occasions when he drank too much that all he wanted to do was get another submarine command, a missile boat. Submariners seemed to have this weird obsession. He was afraid he was getting too senior and bemoaned that being CO of *Kramer* was delaying him.

Then another shaker hit us: open-collared short-sleeve shirts. The uniform regs were changed; no longer did we have to wear long-sleeve shirts with a tie. A huge leap forward for the stodgy naval establishment. A good thing, more comfortable. We bought and wore them—then the argument. Our T-shirts showed at the collar. My God, officers and chiefs with their underwear showing? John Paul Jones thumped his casket trying to turn over in it.

Then the enlisted troops were authorized to wear short-sleeve white shirts. The entire navy had their underwear showing in public. Senior officers sputtered, aghast in disapproval.

The navy polarized. V-neck, crew neck—most didn't give a damn. Polls were taken in true democratic fashion. We had to vote. Rumor said the vote leaned on the crew neck. Economics? Navy men owned tens of thousands of crew-neck T-shirts. If the navy went V-neck, they'd have to spend a lot of money restocking their sea bags.

They voted no to the V-necks, but I guess the senior officers had more votes. We went V-neck with one concession to economic reality: You didn't have to comply for six months. Once more our seniors saved us, saved us from the ignobility of walking around with our underwear showing.

Seaman Reeves

It was late on a Sunday morning, I was in my stateroom cleaning up some paperwork for the ORI. A knock on the door. I turned, looked up. "What is it, Willie?" I snapped.

"My striker, sir, I'm going to need one for WESTPAC," he asked in his competent tone. Sometimes I wished he'd screw up so I could yell at him, chew his ass out. But he never did.

"I'll let you know," I answered, dismissing him with a casual wave of my hand, angry that this hadn't been taken care of already, then angrier with myself for treating Willie in such an offhand, cavalier manner. I was getting that contagious XO syndrome that manifested itself with the firm knowledge that no one on the whole goddamned ship did anything unless I gave them a firm, unequivocal order. *Why do I have to be here on a Sunday morning?* Even my stapler had betrayed me. It ran out of staples. I hated that.

I picked up the phone to the quarterdeck. "Pass the word for Mr. Maxwell to report to my stateroom." Mr. Maxwell was the CDO.

In three minutes his six-foot frame filled the doorway. "What's the word on Reeves, Mr. Maxwell?"

He told me Mr. DeLeon was going to transfer him to OPS in a couple of weeks, that they'd had a few long talks with him and he seemed to be okay. "He's quit crying at everything now, well, almost everything, and I think he may be able to hack it with Willie's smooth hand."

"Should we dump him? He could be a liability in WESTPAC."

"No, sir, Mr. DeLeon has been working with him on building a little self-confidence, and he's not doing too badly. He—" My incredulous look stopped him midsentence. "No, just a little karate over at the gym . . . nothing on the ship. No, sir, nothing on the ship, and he seems to be responding."

"Transfer him to Willie after quarters tomorrow. I don't have time for this shit."

"But, XO . . ."

"Do it, goddammit, Maxwell, and send him in to see me straight away if he's aboard."

I barely heard the timid knock on the bulkhead next to my open door. There was a slight pause and another knock. "Ah . . . sir, XO, Seaman Reeves reporting as ordered, sir, XO."

"Just XO, Reeves, sit down please," I answered, scootching my chair up so he could get past.

"Whaddaya want to do in the navy, Reeves?" I asked, trying to affect my most pleasant, fatherly tone.

He didn't answer, didn't move except for his head. It swung up and down, hinged from the neck, as if he were a swivel-headed plastic dog in the rear window of a car.

I waited an intolerable time. A tear started down his left cheek. "Well, whaddaya want, Reeves . . . what can the navy do for you," I asked too testily.

"The navy, XO, sir, I just want out. . . . I don't like it. They want me to work too hard, and the men make fun of me."

"Have you talked to your chief?"

"He just says to get out of his face and start working before he kicks my ass and feeds me to the sharks. . . . He frightens me so much. He's so mean." My mind flew back in cold consternation to my seaman days on the dry docks and the chief. Even now I hated that sadistic sonofabitch that treated us seamen like shit.

I looked at Reeves in silence before answering, letting my anger subside. The chief boatswain's mate and I would have a little chat. Mr. DeLeon was supposed to have taken care of this.

"You know, don't you, that the naval station psychiatrist recommended that you get a general discharge. I stopped it, thinking you'd be okay. Do you still want it? Do you know what it means?"

"Yes, sir, but I don't care. I just want out of the navy," he answered, confidence in his tone. "I want to go home."

"Would you like to be in the quartermaster gang?" I asked, ignoring his statement.

He started to cry. I sat there, fidgeting, waiting for him to stop. His wails shrilled in intensity, pissing me off more every second. I grew angry at his crying; I grew angry at DeLeon. I grew angry at Lieutenant (jg) Maxwell, his division officer, and most of all I grew angry at myself for not addressing this situation sooner. I was failing my prime responsibility to the ship: taking care of the men. *Fuck all this paperwork. . . . Why didn't the captain help me with some of it anyway?*

"YEAH!" he bellowed, superimposed over his shrieking cries. "You're just doing this . . . doing this, just so you can fuck my mom. You're doing it now . . . well, I want out . . . want out . . . want out . . . " He screeched a pathetic wail.

My left hand flashed to his collar, yanking him up off the couch. My right hand slapped him hard across his face. And then again. He tried to twist free, his face contorted in pain and surprise. Fear. I swung him around over my chair, propelling him into the passageway. He flew out of my hand, smashing into the bulkhead on the other side. I was on him in a flash, pulling him up by his collar, my face inches from his. I heard scrambled chairs pushing back in the wardroom.

"You pussy little bastard. . . . You ain't worth shit to yourself or the navy. . . . You're out, out. You understand that, you crybaby . . . you're out, fuckin' out."

I drew back to slap him again as I felt a restraining hand grab my arm. I flashed around to attack when the stern, horror-strained face of Lieutenant (jg) Maxwell stood there with an iron grip on my arm.

"XO! XO! It's okay, XO," he yelled, dragging me away from the crumpled frame of Tommy Reeves lying stunned, sobbing, on the deck.

I sat in my chair, staring at Reeves as my sanity fought its way back. He shouldn't have accused me about his mother. He shouldn't have done it. "Whaddaya want me to do, XO?" Mr. Maxwell asked in a soft tone barely heard over Reeves's sobs.

"Get him off the ship to the hospital right now. . . . Maybe he'll kill himself on the way," I blurted out, not sufficiently recovered to choose my words with greater care.

Mr. Maxwell led him away. I sat filling my pipe, my shaking hands spilling most of the tobacco over the desk.

In what seemed like only seconds, Maxwell burst into my room shouting, "XO! XO! He's gone. . . . He's gone. Here, this was on his rack." He handed me the bottle. *Oh, my God.* The label said Valium. The bottle was empty. There was no cap on it. "I just sent him below to pack his sea bag, and I was only two or three minutes behind him. Oh, my God, XO."

My veins opened wide, letting blood cool my skin as I shouted, "Search the ship while I send a party ashore to look for him. I'll call the base for help." Fear slammed through my body as I dialed security.

I ran back to the quarterdeck. "Yes, sir, I saw Reeves a few minutes ago. He looked sorta strange, but he's such an asshole, you know. Looked sorta drunk . . . staggered a bit as he walked down the pier. But who gives a shit about Reeves, XO?" the petty officer of the watch on the quarterdeck aft said without concern.

"Well, I fuckin' do, goddammit. . . . Get some men ashore to look for him. . . . Pass the word for Mr. Maxwell. Tell him the same thing. On the double, boy, on the double," I shouted, hurrying down the gangway. "Is the corpsman aboard?" I yelled as I stepped onto the pier. A nod answered me. Halfway to the foot of the pier I looked back to see Mr. Maxwell running toward me with about twenty sailors.

We spread out, trying not to be too conspicuous in our search. A security vehicle, its siren screaming, raced down the pier approach road toward me. I waved it to a halt. "Hey! Hey! You guys . . . let up. Shut off that goddamned siren. We got a sailor wandering around here . . . that's all, a short, dumpy-looking guy with thick glasses and about fifty pounds overweight. He's a little sick. We're just looking for him. Just drive around and look, okay? I'm his XO," I explained, getting into the pickup truck's cab.

We hadn't driven more than fifty feet before Mr. Maxwell and two sailors supporting Reeves walked from around a building. I motioned them into the back of the security truck.

The corpsman met us at the foot of the gangway, his arms reaching out to help the groggy Reeves get out of the truck. He all but carried him up the gangway and into sick bay. "Not to worry, XO, I gave him that Valium myself over a week ago, only ten, and even if he took all of them at once, he'd just sleep for a week or so. I'm going to pump his stomach anyway," the corpsman said as if I were an anxious parent. I was.

"We'll let you know, XO," Mr. Maxwell said, guiding me out the sick bay door. "I'll give the doc a hand." He closed the door behind me, and I wandered about the ship in a daze as I contemplated the end of my naval career. Finally, I forced myself back to my stateroom to work on the ORI, the reason I was aboard.

In about a half an hour the growling phone pulled me away from the huge preparation package I was desultorily working on. "Maxwell, sir, can you come back to sick bay?"

Willie was there. "Reeves wants to talk to you, XO," the corpsman said, holding him up by the shoulders amid the putrid stench of vomit and the opposing sting of antiseptics.

"XO, sir . . . I'm sorry, I'm sorry I caused you so . . . so many problems. I'll be a . . . good sailor . . . a good . . . from now on. You won't be sorr—" He paused, trying to keep his eyes open, slumping against the corpsman and Willie, who was helping to hold him up.

The corpsman winked at me, nodding his head up and down. "Mr. Maxwell . . . he . . . he says you saved my life. He says . . . I'm lucky . . . not dead. Don't tell Mother, okay, XO, sir, I . . . sorry. Don't tell mother . . ." And his eyes closed.

I looked at Maxwell, who was trying to conceal an angelic smile. He said nothing. Willie and the corpsman lay Reeves back on the narrow operating table, and the corpsman strapped him down. "I'll stay with him, XO, and clean things up, and clean him up," the corpsman said.

Willie walked forward with me as we left. "Gosh, XO, you sure gotta go through a lotta shit to get a striker on this ship."

"Fuck you, Willie."

Chapter 5

TARGETS

The grizzled old salts who knew their business gave us our ORI in San Diego. We barely passed, but passing was all that counted. The type commander's inspectors were so intense and professional that even the captain was addressing the chiefs as sir. Once inspected, we knew our weak spots and our strong, the purpose of the inspection. It was worth the heartbreaking effort just to know. *Well, maybe.*

Before leaving Long Beach for San Diego, I briefed the captain on the entire Reeves matter. He stared at me in silence for a moment, then his face curled into a smile. He laughed, saying next time send her to him. "Is he all right now?" he asked as I attempted to go on to the next subject.

"Yes, he is. I'm sorry, Captain."

"You didn't do much wrong, probably did good for the guy."

"I should have acted sooner, before the problem got out of hand."

"Well, it's done. . . . Let's get to the ORI."

On the way down to San Diego for the ORI, Reeves stood instructional watches under the fine eye of Willie. He walked with difficulty, obviously in pain. "You okay, Reeves?" I asked. He looked at me sheepishly, avoiding my eyes as he nodded yes.

"Willie, what's with Reeves, he seems to be hurting," I asked when Reeves walked away. "How's he doing, you seem to be working his ass off."

"Could you come out on the wing, sir?" he whispered.

"What's going on?"

"Well, XO, you know that forty bucks you gave me to take him out and see that he had a nice time and to get him laid?"

"Yeah?"

"He's got the clap."

Three weeks later the hint of a sun just clearing the horizon over San Diego gave its gray cast to the sky as the USS *Burton*, three thousand yards of the starboard bow, exchanged flashing light signals with us as she and another destroyer cleared the sea buoy. On this Sunday morning we stood off Point Loma, waiting for them. We were on our way to WESTPAC. Captain Frank L. Macaby, USN, who to this point lived his professional life in stealth and surprise, was the senior CO, and therefore the officer in tactical command, the OTC. "Bridge, this is Sonar," came the terse voice over the 29MC from way down in the bowels of the ship close to the precious sonar dome. "Slight indication on passive of a submarine contact bearing to the west. Very hazy, request permission to go active."

The captain looked at me, shaking his head no. He keyed the 29MC to Sonar and CIC, then he told them to wait on going active, and that we were going to condition 1-AS.

"Gather 'em up, Mr. Sanders," the captain ordered, sweeping his arms to the approaching destroyers.

Lieutenant Sanders picked up the microphone and read his prepared message. "Alpha Echo, Mike Fox, Tango Lima, this is Lima Whiskey. Kilo romeo one. Bravo tango ten. Charlie two two five. Sierra one five," he sent over the ship-to-ship short-range UHF transceiver, telling the two sleek gray ships that we were in tactical command and to form up in a column behind us at one thousand yards in the order of the radio call signs. Course 225 speed fifteen knots. They acknowledged.

"Bridge, this is Sonar, contact's signal strength slightly increasing."

"Combat manned and ready." I passed the word up to the bridge from my 1-AS station at the DRT. "Sonar, you read okay?"

"Read you five squared, XO." Readability was measured from one to five for loudness and clarity with five being the best. To be read "five by five" was perfect. The hot shots would say "five square" or "five by" or just "five" to show they were old salts.

The hours we spent in the ASW tactical trainer were paying off. We had a good ASW team and could afford to be informal. It sped things up.

"Captain, whaddaya think?" I asked over the open phone line between the bridge and combat. "Should we tell the other two ships to go passive?"

"Probably one of ours; they sit out here practicing their intercepts. We'd surprise the hell outta him if we prosecuted. . . . Let's do it. Those submariners are just too damned cocky," he answered.

"Yes, sir, I've noticed that, Captain. But on a Sunday morning?"

He ignored the dig and said, "But let's not change anything or we might spook him," the captain answered back over the sound-powered phone system.

The captain picked up the ship-to-ship microphone. "Tango Whiskey, this is Lima Whiskey actual, we have what looks like a sub at about two seven zero, range unknown. I'm going to come to two seven five and close it. Follow me but do not actively search for this contact. We are on passive. When we get closer, we'll hit him hard with a single ping. I'm almost sure it's one of ours, but let's not take a chance. We took a bathy about a half hour ago, and there's a medium layer at two hundred feet and scatter layers around, but they're breaking up. Not so good for submarines. Commence lowering superheat. Over."

The ships answered in turn as they adjusted to join up on our new course. Tango Whiskey was the day's code for all ships in the sailing, and Lima Whiskey was the call sign of the OTC. When the captain said "actual," he meant it was he himself talking.

"Combat, this is Sonar, signal getting a little better, he's got to be about six thousand yards away. Recommend active when about two thousand."

"Sonar, this is the bridge. Captain says to wait; he's coming down. XO, Captain says for you to shift to the bridge."

It felt good to see the captain taking an active interest. I guess my bugging him to go to the attack trainer with us was paying off. He was thinking more like a destroyer captain now instead of a beached submariner.

As the OTC, we had responsibility for all the other ships and had to keep track of them and worry about them. Normally, a commodore's staff would do this but now it was only us.

I guess the captain wanted me on the bridge because we were joining up, and we weren't used to each other yet. It would be a long trip for the captain.

"Bridge, this is the captain in Sonar. He sounds a bit like one of ours, but the signal is too weak to really tell. He's in the submarine-approach lanes. We gotta get closer. XO, if you don't mind, I'd like to take this one; it sounds a little like my old boat." I could almost hear the smile in his voice.

"Understand, Captain, and superheat is coming down quite nicely. You want me to get some helos from Zummy Heaven if I can?" I referred to the naval air station, North Island, in Coronado.

He didn't reply, I asked again, wondering what he might be thinking. I doubted he'd go for it, but he answered, "Affirm, XO. Maybe we can humble this mother."

"Tsk-tsk, Captain," I answered. A laugh came back.

It took ten minutes to raise the duty officer of an ASW helo squadron stationed at North Island, and it was through a patch from the air station comm center. "That's a rog, Lima Whiskey," he answered in his best aviator flippancy. "It's Sunday, you know, but we've got two birds, Cherry flight, warming up at this time for fam hops."

"You might wanna hurry, could be interesting," I came back with equal flippancy.

"Okay, Lima Whiskey, we'll kick the tire, light the fire, and brief on guard. Be advised, no ordnance onboard. They'll report to you five miles from your location. Overhead your location estimate two zero on fleet common. . . . Good luck. Out." Fleet common was a frequency all ships and nearby aircraft monitored so they could talk to each other when they needed to.

The captain's voice came over the amplified sound-powered phone circuit clear and commanding. Comforting.

"Maintain course of two seven zero, XO; this guy is getting better defined. It's a sub all right, and I'm not sure he's one of ours. He might be getting a little nervous with us heading for him. How long before the others join?" I told him three minutes.

"Okay. Start running some tactical maneuvers at five hundred yards. Use a lot of turns and wheels and work us toward the west for about fifteen minutes. Have everyone go passive. When we get into the right position, all three of us will light him up."

We turned and wheeled and did all the destroyer things in columns and lines abreast as we slowly made our way west. The two helos, ASW SH-3s, showed up and I gave them the plan. They remained low and behind us to the east, out of sight if the sub raised its scope.

"We've snookered him, XO; he's sitting fat, dumb, and happy maneuvering very slow and very quiet. I've got the mother," the captain's calm voice announced. He tried to play it cool, but the joy rippling over the speaker was unmistakable. My stomach muscles relaxed, coming back to normal after the wrenching blow they took when the captain told me to start tactical maneuvers on three seconds' notice.

Lieutenants Sanders and DeLeon jumped to the task, handling it beautifully as we overcame the shock of being responsible for more than one ship. I tentatively gave them their head but watched like a buzzard waiting for its supper. Actually it was quite simple when you were the guide. You just had to ensure one maneuver was completed before another was started.

Often, various commodores' staffs, due to lack of destroyer experience, gave the orders too fast, and the formation disintegrated in confusion as the COs broke away for safety. We did it nice and simple at ten knots, always easing west.

"Okay, XO, get 'em in a line abreast five hundred yards apart heading two six eight. When I figure we're almost on him, we'll all torch off together and give that sonofabitch a roaring headache," the man who just wanted to be a missile boat driver passed up over the phone.

"Careful, Captain, I'm recording all this. You may get kicked out of the tubie fraternity if I ever passed it to SUBPAC," I chided.

His chuckle preceded his exclamation. "My God, I didn't think I'd ever be doing this, but it's sorta fun—in a docile way, of course."

"Of course," I answered.

"Tango Whiskey, this is Lima Whiskey, stand by my count for active. One ping," came the captain's deep voice over the loudspeakers on the bridge. "All ships prepare to drop grenades on my command. Helos on the way, overhead zero five. Stand by for active, one ping: five, four, three; he can't be more than five hundred yards in front of us, two, one, light off!"

Three high-power, low-frequency AN/SQS-23 sonars triggered one searchlight blast simultaneously, the ocean screeching for the intrusion. Sonar contact reports filled the radios, and all of us plotted each other's as bearings and distances came in from each ship. They plotted all the same. "Designate Sierra One, datum one. Wait. Stand by for grenades, three, two, one, drop, drop, drop. The roar of explosions smashed into the speakers from the passive sonars and across the quiet early morning.

Before the reverberations died, the captain was on the gertrude, the underwater phone. "Uncle Joe, Uncle Joe, authenticate ALPHA BRAVO, over?" No answer.

"XO, disburse the starboard wing ships to five thousand yards north and south. Tell Burton to ease out to three thousand to the west and go active, where are those helos? Slow to five knots and come around. She hasn't moved yet."

"Captain, helos overhead requesting instruction," I answered.

"We'll move out, XO, let 'em play" he said, then gave the universal surface-to-sub identification call again, "Uncle Joe, Uncle Joe." The captain, who was now a sub killer, kept calling. "Authenticate ALPHA BRAVO!"

Nothing!

The captain's clipped voice took on an ominous urgency as he ordered *his* three ships to general quarters. The SH-3A, anti-submarine helicopters, roared in, screeched to a hover, and dropped their dipping sonar balls. Almost instantaneously they came back with "Lima Whiskey, this is Cherry Two, Two, and Five hot. They seem to be heading west at three knots. We'll track. Thanks for the invite. Out."

"XO, get on the horn to SUBPAC and tell them the situation. . . . I don't like this silence. Man the torpedo tubes. I don't like it, XO; he should have come right back on the Uncle Joe. I've briefed the other ships on CIC common. Do it now, XO."

COMSUBPAC at San Diego came back with a "wait one" while they went to wake up the duty officer on a peaceful Sunday morning at 0630.

"Lima Whiskey, this is Cherry One, we have a stray P-3 Orion, call sign Daddy One Three, who wants to play, any objection? He's coming up this freq. Over."

"Roger Cherry One, break break, Daddy One Three, this is Lima Whiskey. Over." I radioed after a fast talk with the captain.

"Rog, LW, been following your game. Can we join? Over?"

I asked the captain who gave instructions for me to clear the helos and let him get some MAD returns.

"Daddy One Three, permission granted. Welcome aboard. We'll break the Cherrys off for you to run some MAD in there. . . . Interrogative, do you have ordnance aboard? Over."

"That's a negative. But why?"

"We've been on this hummer for at least fifteen minutes, and he won't answer our Uncle Joe authentication calls," I answered. "Cherrys are nude. Don't know what this guy is, except he's a little too close to the coast and a little too quiet." I briefed the P-3. "Also, Daddy, call COMNAVAIRPAC and brief him, will you? We can't raise him. Over."

"Copy all, LW; we'll stay on this mother. Out."

The captain handed me a message as he stepped onto the bridge. "Mr. Sanders, put the destroyers on a fence at five thousand yards and keep the helos and P-3 prosecuting the contact in the center. We'll move the fence along the path of the sub." He turned to me. "Whaddaya think of this message, XO?"

"Sounds good, Captain. I can't raise COMCRUDESPAC. COM-FIRSTFLT said for us to 'wait one' ten minutes ago."

"Does my message say it all, XO?"

I looked again at the message he had handed me. Addressed to all EASTPAC staff including CINCPACFLT, the Commander in Chief Pacific Fleet. It detailed everything that happened and requested instructions. It ended with "will prosecute to exhaustion." I loved that kind of talk.

A lot of phlegmatic staff duty officers would be shittin' and a gettin' in several minutes when the operational immediate message got to them. The only higher priority message was a *flash,* and that was used only when you were actually under attack or imminently so. Several senior officers, commodores, and so forth, grandiosely used messages with high-priority designators to show how important they were. Woe be onto any destroyer captain who did the same.

For the next twenty minutes our force worked itself generally west at five knots, keeping up with the sub. The warming San Diego sun deteriorated the sonar conditions and our near bathy drop showed layers forming, which would cause poorer and poorer contact on the sub.

The P-3's constant MADMAN reports gave us confidence. "Lima Whiskey, this is Daddy One Three. Be advised stay time down to three zero. . . . Be advised Daddy One Six will relieve us in one five. Word from the big air boss finally came through saying for us to prosecute as directed by you. I hereby officially CHOP. Interrogative, you got any word?"

Sanders glanced at the captain, who shook his head no. "Negative One Three, thanks for your help. Out."

"That's a rog, LW. Hope I don't miss the big one."

Two more helos called in. A busy Sunday for the fly boys. "Lima Whiskey, this is Cherry One and Ten. Will be overhead in one five to join. Be advised we're packing iron. Over."

The captain picked up the microphone. "Roger, Cherry One, this is Lima Whiskey actual. Interrogative, you cherry actual?"

"That's affirm, Lima Whiskey, my orders are to CHOP to you and prosecute at your discretion. . . . I hereby CHOP. I understand you're an ex-tubie . . . over." CHOP meant to change operational control; in this case, Cherry One shifted to the captain's tactical command.

"That's affirm, One. Here's the situation—"

"Roger, copy all. The boys at Tubie Town say they're gettin' some paper to you."

"Roger, understand . . . break break . . . Cherry flight, Daddy flight, Tango Whiskey, this is Lima Whiskey. Will send Alpha Echo"—USS *Burton*—"in for one more Uncle Joe, then resume fence at five thousand. Cherry One take command of air element. Be advised no passive joy on surface sonars. Over."

All units answered in sequence, and there we sat slowly moving west. Burton had no luck with her Uncle Joe. Thirty minutes later, two hours after our early dawn's messages to the big boys, we received a reply: "Prosecute contact at your discretion. Avoid all hostile acts. Standard rules of engagement apply." A mealy mouthed message, shit! The standard white-hatted code of the West: Don't fire until fired upon.

My stomach growled its message. It was getting late and I realized we'd been at general quarters since before the crew had been fed. I released the cooks and mess cooks to get a quick breakfast together.

The tantalizing smell of frying bacon wafted up to the bridge as the captain came up from Combat. I asked him if we could go in for some ping time; either us, or the other destroyers.

His head kept shaking no almost imperceptibly as he kept staring out to the sea, where he knew the submarine was lurking. "I think we got us a live one," he muttered. "Sure is different from this end, XO. But, no, I don't think we should go in and ping. If he breaks out, I want all quadrants covered," he answered without emotion. *What is he thinking?* He used the word "he" referring to the sub. In our navy we used the word "she." The Russians used "he."

My admiration for him soared during these past three hours. He'd always seemed so indifferent to things; but now, here, in a real-live situation, I saw his face harden, taking on purpose as he easily slipped on the mantle of the warrior as if it were an old and favorite jacket.

Cherry One rotated his helos in over the target, getting firm contact each time. He interspersed the P-3 in every ten minutes to verify the contact with his magnetic anomaly detection, MAD, gear. Another P-3 was on its way, along with two S2Fs. Someone thought this was serious.

The captain's quizzical stare left me uneasy. He was supposed to know all this sub stuff. Maybe they weren't supermen after all. "I don't understand it, XO; doesn't make sense. If it were one of ours, he should have answered our Uncle Joe. Even if it were damaged, he could have shot flares or sent a beacon up. If it's a Soviet, he could have bugged out in the beginning, and none of us would be the wiser, unless, of course, he's damaged. If it's friendly, SUBPAC would know its location and tell us, or call us off. I just don't know, goddammit! I just don't know," he moaned, his normal cherubic face plowed with heavy lines of concern.

"BRIDGE, RADIO SHACK," the 21MC blasted out, causing both of us to wince. "OPS immediate, top secret message coming in. Need someone down here."

All messages in the fleet came in coded, and our computers decoded everything automatically. A far cry from my early days, when we had to decode by hand every classified message coming in using a baffling little machine, in a small, musty, seasick-generating crypto room three feet long by three feet wide. Nowadays, when a top secret message came in, the automatic decoding machine just showed a series of five character groups. One had to activate another decoding computer to decipher the already, once-coded message.

These computer code cards resided in a small safe in the crypto room of the radio shack and only the CO, OPS officer, and I had access. It sat right next to our double-combination nuclear-release data safe.

The captain handed the decoded message to me. We were told to break off, repeat break contact, and proceed on mission assigned. All air assets were to be detached and for us to remain on station for fifteen minutes after they left. And a personal for Comdr. Frank J. Macaby, which made the message top secret: "Two of your buddies on the way. Hurry home; we miss you."

Twenty-two minutes later we turned south from west and headed for the Naval Station, Pearl Harbor, 2,228 nautical miles away in Hawaii. "Set condition Yoke, XO," a voice basted in disappointment mumbled to me then trailed off into a disturbed silence. Then he whispered to himself, "I should be down there, god damn that sonofabitch, I should be down there." I could only guess who "that sonofabitch" could be.

"Now set condition Yoke throughout the ship," the 1MC announced. In ten minutes condition Zebra gave way to Yoke's easier access, and the 1MC's deep-throated command blared, "Now secure from general quarters. Secure from general quarters set the normal under way watch, on deck section two. Breakfast for the crew. Now set holiday routine."

Gun Line

Our trip across the Pacific proved uneventful except for the strain of being the OTC. But we got used to it, got used to the heady opium of power. After a week in Yokosuka we operated with a carrier group for twenty-one days while waiting to get to Vietnam and assume our gun-line duties: firing shells at targets designated by U.S. Army spotters. At least it was something to do beyond digging holes in the ocean.

We were ten miles off the west coast of South Vietnam. A battered U.S. Army UH-1, Huey helicopter, hovered precariously over our minuscule flight deck. His call sign, Rammer Two Eight. His voice squeaked over the radio in high-pitched excitement. "This is Two Eight, Navy. Okay, okay, we're getting fuel now, Navy. Thank God, we're getting it. We owe you big-time. Over."

"Rog, Rammer Two Eight, but you don't owe me shit. Sorry we can't pump any faster," I yelled over the whipping monsoon wind and rain into a microphone at the helo refueling station on our never-used postage-stamp-size flight deck.

"I'll take just enough to keep airborne while One Nine orbits and comes in, comes in after me. You're saving us a long walk, or swim, copy?"

"We copy, Eight. Sorry can't take you aboard. We're not stressed for a Huey, especially with grunts onboard. You'd sink right on through. Sorry. We're pumping to the max. Hang in there, boy."

The Huey slick bounced unmercifully, trying to maintain a decent hover over our flight deck designed to hold only a drone ASW helo, which never worked out. The heavy monsoon winds and vicious rain bashed the helo into constant gyrations, up and down, sideways, back and forth like a drunken gymnast staggering across the balance beam. The grim face of the pilot only thirty feet above me glared ashen white.

The warrant officer looked young, a high school graduate whom the army trained by the hundreds. His clipped words over the radio betrayed his nervousness. He was obviously new, but doing a hell of a fine job keeping his wily helo above our flight deck and not letting the savage wind toss him away.

Minutes before they had arrived we'd received an emergency call for refueling from two helos who had extended themselves to extract a group of soldiers from a hot LZ. They'd had trouble finding them, and when they did they had to lift off far above their maximum gross takeoff weight. The wind and torrential rain hindered them even more.

Our HIFR, our helo in-flight refueling gear, pumped to its pitiful maximum. When the helo came to a hover above us, it dropped a line, and we just tied the diesel hose to it. They'd hooked it up some-how and were now taking on fuel.

Gaunt, frightened faces of the soldiers gaping out the helo's side doors made me ashamed that I was safe in this turbulently vicious monsoon, and they weren't. The violent bumper-car bouncing of their rescue helos assaulted their stomachs and vomit spewed out of their mouths. The wind blew it back in their faces.

I deliberately stood at the pumping station with a fascinated Jim DeLeon at my side. He had begged to be with me as I stood just off the hangar door, exposed to the groaning helo to instill a modicum of confidence in them. It was probably stupid.

It was stupid. The rain ripping into the open rear doors drenched the pathetic grunts. Ripples of water-soaked blood ran down their grimaced faces through the frighteningly soiled battle dressings they wore. Their pale, surrealistic faces looked awfully like the pic-tures of the survivors of the Nazi death camps. With locked feet they held several body bags in place from being tossed into the sea.

"Listen to me, Two Eight, are you the flight leader?"

"Yes, yes, sir," came back a voice just on the edge of panic, all the brash aviator bravado gone. Christ, the guy couldn't be more than nineteen years old.

"I'm Lieutenant Commander Sheppard, the XO, and I've got a lot of time in Hueys, okay? Listen to me, Two Eight, you're doing great, but you're not going to make it if you don't get rid of some weight. You're coming within two feet of crashing into our deck. You gotta dump some weight."

"Yes, yes, sir!" the wind-distorted voice whispered from the speaker next to me.

"Two Eight, dump the body bags. Dump 'em, Two Eight. They're dead; save the live ones. You've got a responsibility to the living. Dump your weapons, dump your ammo, dump everything you can, or you're going to die," I ordered with all the confidence I could muster.

"I can't, Navy, I can't."

"DO IT! GODDAMMIT, MAN, DO IT FUCKING NOW," I shouted over the microphone as his left skid banged into the fight deck, flash-ing sparks into the rain as it instantly bounced away.

Another terse, equally stress-ridden voice from the other helo broke in. "Two Eight, this is One Nine. Be advised I'm jettisoning at this time." Five large bundles dropped out a thousand yards off our port quarter. The monsoon cartwheeled them like stringless kites until they splashed seconds later into the tossing gray-green waters of the Gulf of Thailand two miles off the Cau Mau Peninsula, the infamous U-Minh forest of the Mekong Delta.

"They'll float. We'll pick 'em up when you guys are on your way home," I broadcasted, lying, knowing the seas would toss them to pieces. "Good work, One Nine. DO IT, TWO EIGHT. DO IT NOW!"

Four body bags tumbled out of the tethered helo, one landing on the lifelines bending over at the stomach before falling into the sea. Another hung up on our port screw guard, twisting grotesquely, hanging there until a wave yanked it off, dumping it into our thrashing screws. Even over the wail of the storm I could hear the crunching. The other two splashed and disappeared.

The helo's control smoothed out as rifles and ammo boxes and helmets spewed out the side doors. Luckily the helo had been pushed to the side and none of the weapons or ammo cases landed on our decks. "We got enough, ah, juice for now, Navy. Let's bring in One Nine. Okay?"

They lowered the hose and moved off. The confused winds steadied, now blowing just east of south. The rain drove almost horizontally across the ship, reducing visibility to no more than one hundred yards. We put the wind fifteen degrees off the port side and called in the other helo. It held beautifully steady in the constant wind and came off station in fifteen minutes, and the first helo hooked up again. In an hour of jockeying, both helos had just enough fuel to return to their base.

Before they lightened their birds, we could pump only enough fuel to cover their consumption—now their thirsty tanks went into the green. But our diesel fuel was getting low now, and my engineering mind concerned itself with the emergency diesel generators and the worry of having enough fuel for ourselves if we had to use them, which hadn't ever happened before.

"We gotta enough, Navy. Put it on the army's bill, and next time, please, will you check under the hood?" Two Eight radioed to us, his aviator's jauntiness returning now that he had control of the situation again. "And, Navy, ah, thanks. See you back in the world. Out." And with the whoop! whoop! whoop! of their rotor blades cutting deep into the rain-ripped skies, they disappeared to the east over the U Minh forest, back into the shit.

The "world," anyplace not Vietnam. I thought of the clean white sheets on my bunk and the ice cream we'd have tonight and the movie and the popcorn served in sterling silver bowls.

I thought of the Bassac River and my boats and the screaming and the wounded and the mutilated bodies and the dead and I cried, glad the pelting rain mixed so heavily with my tears.

Mr. DeLeon stared at me in wonderment. "XO, that was something, XO. I. . . . How was it over there? You know, in the jungle. I want to go over there."

"You don't want to know, Jim. It's a piece of shit. Forget it. Your job is to lob shells into where they tell you to. That's good enough; that's close enough."

"God damn, XO, dumping the body bags. . . . You saved their lives," DeLeon, the tall weapons officer who wanted to be a warrior, said, his voice exuding respect.

"The living . . ." I murmured, walking away from this bellicose man who talked as if he were a consummate killer but had never seen a bullet tear open a man's body.

He grabbed my arm, pleading for me to arrange a trip ashore so he could see for himself, experience it himself, test himself. He had to; he swore. The war would be over soon. He'd never know. I understood.

I told him I'd see what I could do, and pulled my arm away and headed up to the bridge.

"Now hear this, now hear this, secure the 'hyfur' refueling detail. XO, please call the bridge. Away the motor whale boat." The 1MC announced its words slurred by the screeching wind.

The captain looked at me as I approached his chair. His eyes, heavy with sadness, looked at me as if we'd never met. He said he'd marked the spots of the dumps but didn't think we'd find them, not in this wind.

"Thanks, Captain, I know, but I said we'd try."

He said I'd done a good thing and that he wondered if he could have done the same. He put his arm around my shoulder as if he were comforting a child.

Five futile hours of searching left us drained and exhausted. The captain shook his head in disappointment, looked at me, and shrugged. "Let's go back to work, XO."

I turned to the OPS officer, Lieutenant Sanders, his melancholy face sludge gray in the storm-dimmed daylight even though it was barely past 1500. "Tell Panther Three Six, Cannon One mission ready," I ordered.

Lieutenant Sanders hesitated, looking back and forth across the bridge before saying that maybe we should look a little longer. His voice pleaded as if we had been searching for a lifeboat full of live women and children. The bridge watch nodded their silent concurrence.

I lost it. "*God damn you people. They were dead. Don't you understand? They were bloody well fucking dead. . . . Snap out of it; we've got live ones to support!* Gimme that goddamned microphone," I screamed, yanking it out of Sanders's hand.

"Panther Three Six, this is Cannon One. Emergency mission complete ready for call fire mission. My posit four miles due west Point Zulu. I say again, ready for call fire mission. Over."

"Roger, Cannon One, be advised Two Eight and One Nine recovered without incident. Thanks, Navy."

We'd been on the gun line, firing support missions for three weeks and had settled down into a vapid routine of lobbing shells into geographical locations that a disembodied voice asked for over a radio circuit called the "gun-line net." We knew them only as a call sign, and we were nothing more to them.

At first, on opening night, we excitedly manned up at general quarters to fire our 5"/38 guns. But that didn't last long. Call fire had to be available twenty-four hours a day, and we fired only about three shells an hour, mostly just harassing and interdicting, H&I, fire. This meant just put a shell out there somewhere to keep the Vietcong shook up.

We couldn't stay at GQ for very long, and exhaustion forced us to a modified "ready fire team." Either the captain or I remained on the bridge at all times along with either Sanders or DeLeon as OODs and firecontrol officers.

In the gun mounts, where it normally took twenty-seven men to service the mount, we went to nine and fired only one barrel. From three men in the director, we went to two. In the fire control computer room we went from five to two. One repair party was manned.

We rotated the mounts to keep gun wear constant. The rest of the crew went about their normal steaming and housekeeping duties, but no one was allowed on the weather decks anywhere near the firing mount. It was a constant worry that someone might inadvertently walk by a firing gun. His last walk.

After ten minutes the loudspeaker on the gun fire net crackled once, hissed, and voiced, "Request you move up the coast about three miles and stand by. . . . We may have a mission for you, Cannon One. Out."

We reset the ready fire team. The captain had the control watch; it was daylight. I had the nights because, as the captain so cogently pointed out, he was the captain. It was okay because I could sleep in my chair on the port side of the bridge, being awakened only to verify the line of shot and the coordinates. I finally got used to it, even comfortable sitting in *my* chair.

I sat in it now, thinking of the jungle and the men dying in it. Tiny slivers of shrapnel still lay resident in my body from a Vietcong grenade, tossed at me four years ago. They must be enjoying the heat and humidity. Did they realize how close to Vietnam they were? Did they want to go home? I felt two of them pricking at my shirt-sleeve. It hurt when they did that. I picked the small chunks of steel from my forearm. I always carried a set of tweezers.

Years, the doctor had told me, it would take years before they all worked their way out. They gave me pain, pain when the weather was good, and worse when it changed.

Sitting in my chair, staring out into the rain-whipped sea, my mind played back the grenade's explosion. It happened less than eighty miles from here. I heard myself scream again. I saw myself lying in the mud. I felt the arms around me, pulling me behind a fallen tree. I heard their shouts.

"XO! XO? You okay?" came Willie's voice, penetrating my fog of memory. I bolted from my chair, grabbing for an imaginary rifle. Willie's arms went to my shoulders, stopping me, steadying me.

"Yeah . . . yeah. Okay. Okay."

I walked out to the port wing of the bridge, letting the rain wash down on me, letting it wash away the nightmare. *How foolish of DeLeon to want to be there.*

I put my binoculars on the coast two miles away; nothing showed but the jungle. I thought about the Vietcong and the grunts huddled in their crude base camps where the constant lash of the rain sapped their initiative and any pretense of life beyond survival. I thought about myself and the blood and the torn bodies.

A half hour passed. The captain looked at me every several minutes as if trying to fathom my feelings, but said nothing. The loudspeaker crackled, hissed: "Cannon One, this is Panther Three Six, be advised we have a fire mission for you at this time. Over."

I was still on the bridge, checking our position, when the coordinates came in. Combat plotted them against our position where we thought—hoped—we were. The almost straight coastline of the southern part of Vietnam and the absence of suitable landmarks for radar navigation made us uneasy about firing our guns onto the beach. We really didn't know our position all that well.

Naval shore bombardment is a highly skilled art, and we took great pride in laying the shells where they were wanted. The gun system, after all, was designed to sink moving ships, but accuracy depended on knowing where you are and where the target is. We didn't know exactly where we were, and we cringed each time we fired. Sometimes we'd get an army aircraft to spot our fire, but most of the time not.

Panther Three Six, our fire control coordinator, knew this and made the necessary correction, which meant we fired quite a bit away from our troops, which made us somewhat ineffective.

"Whaddaya think, Reeves?" I said. "How does it look?"

"Here, sir," he answered with confidence. "It looks good. See this spit of land, the little outcrop." He pointed to the chart on the nav table. "It shows up well. I'm sure we're right here," he said, banging his finger on the chart.

I glanced at Willie. He nodded his head yes and lipped the words, "He's one of my boys."

"Did you verify with Combat, Reeves?" He looked at me with a pout, telling, of course, he had. The kid whose mother had big tits was doing okay.

"Set mark position," I yelled to the gunfire control team, thereby inadvertently taking over the captain's job. He nodded acknowledgment. I guess he figured I needed to do something. The talker passed it to Combat. The fire controlman in the computer room in the bowels of the ship came back with "set position" after we called down the target coordinates just received from Panther Three Six.

Lieutenant Sanders shouted that he was ready to fire as Mount 51 completed its swing around toward the beach. The 3,995-pound, radially expanded steel barrels moved up and down, but in reality they were gyro-controlled and held steady as the ship rolled under them.

"Guns free," I said, and Mr. Sanders shouted, "Fire."

The fifty-four-pound projectile packed with trinitrotoluene, TNT, flashed out of the starboard barrel at 1,800 miles per hour. Mach 2.5. The shell would be there long before the sound.

The noise smashed against our eardrums, driving pain into the back of our necks. Its pyrocellulose flash tortured our eyes, quickly constricting in defense. The acrid smell of cordite jammed into our nostrils and filled our heads with the overpowering smell of death.

I followed the shell as it arched up and away to an unseen target in the jungle seven miles away. We didn't hear the explosion or see the flames. We had two more miles of range if they had wanted it.

Panther Three Six relayed from the airborne spotter, Spyglass Nine, for us to drop a half klick, half a kilometer, and come left a quarter. He ordered us to fire. And advised there were friendly troops in the vicinity.

"Roger, Three Six, do you want more barrels? Over," Captain Macaby asked over the gun-fire net.

"Wait, Cannon."

In thirty seconds Panther's controlled, monotonic voice came back, "Rog, Cannon One, he says the shit's going down . . . no arty available. Ceilings too low for the fast movers, and he can't get anyone to help the snake eaters but you. Can you provide?"

In the middle of the conversation the captain turned to me and mouthed, "General quarters."

"That's affirmative," he answered. "Tell him to give me five minutes, and he'll have four five-inch tubes at his call." Mount 51 was swinging back into battery as the fire control computer cranked in the additional elevation needed to compensate for the eating away of the chromium-plated bore.

Each round fired took a little of the bore with it, and naval guns had to be adjusted, reaimed, after each shot. We looked at the chart marking the Green Beret outposts, the snake eater's camps. It was six miles inland from our position one mile off the coast. And the coordinates showed the impact point not more than five hundred yards from the camp.

As the crew leaped to obey the call to arms, the captain keyed the 1MC. "This is the captain speaking—a Green Beret outfit is under fire and in deep shit 'bout six miles inland. They're up to their elbows and need us to save their ass. We'll wipe out the fuckers. Let's do it."

My mouth gaped open as he spoke. I used language like that, but had never heard him talk so crudely before. He winked at me as he sat back down in his chair. What an enigmatic man.

In four minutes the captain announced, "Ready for fire mission to Panther Three Six." Fire a round, we were told. Spotted. Adjusted. Fire. Spotted. Adjusted. "You got it, Cannon One. Fire for effect, blow those motherfuckers back to hell!"

Four guns blasted simultaneously through the rain and wind. We couldn't see the beach; the radars painted only confused orange pictures, useless except for psychedelic delights. We didn't care, we had a spotter and a trusty firecontrol computer that told the guns our course and speed, the temperature, and the relative humidity. Receiving this data, it constantly adjusted automatically in elevation and train to keep their hot tubes on target as they continuously recomputed for bore wear and barrel temperature.

Every minute, thirty-two five-inch rounds blasted out, arching high into the sodden sky. They whistled up, passing through the rain and wind into the brilliant sun. At apogee, they gently dipped ballistically down, diving, exploding in the jungle, fifty feet above the ground, spewing their shrapnel over the luckless enemy beneath them.

Deep down in the magazines, so low in the ship the rounded hull formed its sides, cursing, sweating men who could barely breathe from the choking heat and humidity wrestled fifty-four pound projectiles into the lower projectile hoists. Swift conveyors sent the heavy rounds up to the next deck to the handling rooms, where they were placed in ready service racks, just below the guns.

Here, other sweat-laden men kept the upper projectile hoist to the turrets filled from the service racks. Next to them, more glistening-skinned men sent twenty-eight-pound cartridge cases up on an adjacent hoist.

Each round fired spewed hot, biting gases into the confined three-quarter-inch steel, armor-plated turret. Men coughed and spat blood as the cordite and the pounding explosions ran pains of nausea and headache through them as they serviced the demanding guns. Except for physical layout, a replay of Nelson at Trafalgar.

When the breech block slams home, like a bull elephant mating, a red light appears in Fire Control Central. A quick finger on a permanently mounted trigger pulls back, and a pulse of electricity flashes the igniter, detonating the fifteen-pound powder charge in the cartridge—exploding it, driving the twisting shell out of the barrel.

"Cannon One, Spyglass says you're right on, keep it up. He's only got fifteen minutes till bingo time, when his fuel state demands he leaves. He says your rounds are stone-aging the place. Wait! Wait!"

In seconds he came back on the air. "Adjust two klicks left. They're bugging out to the north. They're running . . . blast away, Cannon One. Ease north slowly . . . each couple of rounds. . . . Out."

The steady stream of shells swept their inferno of noise into the steel of the ship and air around us. Noise, so deafening as to be the only focus, demanding, eclipsing, every other sense. "Cease fire . . . Cease fire!" Panther Three Six shouted over the gun-line net. "Spyglass Nine bingo at this time. Out."

"CEASE FIRE . . . CEASE FIRE." A heavy sigh rippled throughout the ship. The bridge crew rubbed their ears as if that would stop the drums still pounding against their skulls.

In ten seconds Jim DeLeon turned to the captain. He saluted and reported the firing complete with three hundred three rounds expended. He said no casualties, and requested permission to strike ready-locker ammo below to the magazines, and could he secure gun mounts for maintenance.

After his terse report, DeLeon's shoulders slumped, his midsection undulated ever so slightly, his eyes glazed, and his breathing came deep and satisfying like he'd just had an orgasm. He lit a cigarette and gazed out to sea as he puffed it, and smiled.

"Now hear this, set condition Yoke throughout the ship." Ventilation fans came on. The ship opened up. Weary, fatigue-ridden gun crews, near dehydration from sweating, crawled out of the mounts and up from the stifling magazines as we secured from general quarters.

The men lay motionless on the rain-soaked deck, their shirt-sleeves under their arms caked white with salt from the tablets they'd taken. The more they sweated, the more water they drank, and the more water they drank, the more salt tablets they took. And the more they sweated, the more the salt forced its way out to decorate their wet clothes with patches of white like tiny desert salt flats.

The sizzle of boiling rain striking the still-blistering barrels became a soothing melody in contrast to the pounding guns.

A small Cessna O-2 forward air control aircraft, with its push-pull engines and twin boomed tail, headed toward us from the beach, low to the water. She lifted just as she passed over us, wiggling her wings in salute. She pulled high and whipped down our starboard side. Her pilot waved at us. "Cannon One, Panther, Spyglass Nine says great job, and he takes back every mean, nasty thing he's ever said about you squids. Over."

The captain picked up the microphone, "Tell him we're here to serve. Over."

"Cannon One, Panther, he says, 'Roger that.' And he loves you guys."

Tears and Ears

The hell's crucible of the blazing sun toasted the metal of our rust-streaked destroyer as we meandered north and south waiting for another call fire mission. We hadn't fired a round in thirty-six hours. Our heroic air conditioners fought valiantly to ward off the heat, but failed. Inside the five-inch gun mounts and down deep in the magazines, no attempt at air-conditioning existed, and the hapless men lay in soundless stupor.

In the engineering spaces, temperatures sweltered in at one hundred fifteen degrees. I forced myself to visit them daily just for appearance's sake. Afterward, I'd rush back to my stateroom and stand in front of my whirling fan, begging it for relief and glad I wasn't an engineer anymore.

Lieutenant DeLeon, "the impotent man of the lion," as he referred to himself when particularly morose, continually bugged me to get him ashore to liaise with the grunts. He insisted we needed it to ensure proper procedures and coordination. It wasn't true, but he pleaded anyway, his faraway eyes always looking over at the late French Indochinese armpit of Vietnam. His persistence impressed me even though I told him each time it was bullshit. But I recognized the zeal burning in him.

I had often asked the captain to let me arrange something, but he answered no each time except the last. Yesterday afternoon, he said with a conspiratorial smile, that the impotent man of the lion should show a little Marconian initiative.

The next day I was standing in for the captain on his gun watch while he took a tour of the ship and got some exercise. Jim called my name as he walked toward me. I turned to the sound of his voice, brushing the metal bulwark as I did. I yanked my hand back, but not quickly enough. "Shit," I yelled, angry with myself for the stupidity of touching any sun-exposed portion of the ship as my right index finger turned red from the burn.

Jim asked again to go ashore; this time with a new set of reasons. "Goddammit, Jim, quit asking. Do you spend all your time thinking of ways to ruin the old man's career. I'm not going to ask him again. What if you got shot? What could he say in justification? His ass'd be grass and you bloody well know it. Look at my finger! I got it burned because of you. Stay away from me."

Jim's face equaled that of a little kid whose mean and nasty stepfather had forbidden him from riding his new bike. I wasn't going to tell Jim what the captain said to my last request, but he wore me down, even though I knew his going ashore was both stupid and unwarranted. He just wanted to shoot somebody.

"Mr. DeLeon, when I asked the captain, for the tenth time last night, he said you should use some Marconian initiative."

"Marconian initiative? What the hell does that mean?"

"Marconi had a great deal to do with the invention of radio wave transmissions," I answered, walking away. He'd have to figure the rest out for himself. As I turned away his face lit up, and I swear I saw a lightbulb appear over his head. He'd gotten it. If the army called us and asked for a visit from a liaison officer, the captain surely couldn't refuse. *DeLeon could handle that.* He walked away, heading for Combat and the administrative frequency to Panther Three Six, and I returned to my stateroom to battle the paperwork.

"AWAY THE GUNFIRE PARTY TO THE BRIDGE. PROVIDE." Thundered over the 1MC. Four gunner's mates, the gunfire party, rushed to the small arms locker to draw rifles while two others ran to the bridge to man our two mounted .50-caliber, heavy machine guns. Provide meant to bring their weapons.

The gunfire party was part of the ship's landing party, that luckless group of seamen designated to go ashore to fight for flag and country whenever the captain deemed it prudent. The fleet still used the old World War II M-1 Garands. The navy hadn't seen fit yet to issue the fast-firing small-caliber M-16s or the 9.62mm M-60 machine guns. But hell, we'd never have to go ashore anyway. Would we? We hoped not, all of us except Mr. DeLeon, who prayed for the chance.

I quickly spun the combination of my desk safe, my hurrying fingers screwing it up. I tried again, this time more slowly. It opened, and I took out my Colt Model 1911A1 .45-caliber automatic pistol. I slipped a loaded clip up into the butt and pocketed another.

I kept only three rounds in the clips so as not to weaken the feed spring by keeping it compressed. I grabbed a box of .45 rounds and loaded the spare clip to its maximum as I scampered to the bridge, my shins colliding with every watertight door coaming as I went. "Shit!"

"Over there." Lieutenant Sanders pointed, his finger indicating a dilapidated fifty-foot boat one thousand yards off our port beam. Its small sail hung limp from its broken main mast, and I saw through my binoculars an emaciated young man attempting to wave a large white piece of cloth. Perhaps ten to fifteen Vietnamese huddled on the small open deck. The boat had no superstructure, only cracks and torn supports showing it had been violently yanked off.

I heard the double cock of the port side .50-caliber heavy machine gun, indicating it was ready.

"Fishermen?" asked the captain. I answered that it could be a ruse, could be pirates looking helpless but under deck armed to the teeth and ready to kill us if we take them alongside. I didn't believe it though.

At two hundred yards I saw the women with children cuddled in their arms, their skinny bodies accentuating their bloated stomachs. Three old men looked at us with indifference, as if their souls had already died. The five younger men stared without expression, except the one who sloppily waved the white cloth. He forced a grin, pleading in words we couldn't hear. An old woman stood reaching a child out to us, her eyes begging acceptance.

"Captain, I don't think they're a threat. Can we take 'em alongside? I'll question them."

"You speak Vietnamese, XO?" he asked.

"*Ti thoi*, a little, sir, *chut chut*."

"Who do you think they are?" the captain asked.

I said most likely fishermen who probably got hit by that storm that just passed through. But I knew damn well that that many people didn't go out in small fishing boats. He nodded for me to bring them alongside.

I cleared the open deck of sightseers, and with Mr. Would-be-warrior DeLeon in tow, along with two seamen volunteers, took the shattered junk along our port side. Lieutenant Sanders and four riflemen kept the boat covered, and I could see the .50-caliber machine gun pointing right at the chest of the rag waver. *Steady, boy.*

My .45, with the safety off, nestled in my right hand behind me in the small of my back. I kept a wary eye for signs of betrayal. "My God, a .45, I shoulda brought one too, goddammit, goddammit," DeLeon murmured.

* * *

An hour later I briefed in the captain's sea cabin, telling him they've been under way for four weeks. The old men were politicians, and the Vietcong were putting pressure on them to come over and support their cause. They figured Saigon was going to fall soon and the ARVN soldiers protecting them would disappear, so they figured they'd best leave.

The captain raised his eyebrows, nodding his head to the left.

They said they were heading for Bangkok, until their fuel ran out. That was three weeks ago. They tried to sail, but the winds were negligible. They drifted more than made headway toward Thailand and then the monsoons hit and pushed them all the way back down to here.

I paused, sipping a cold cup of coffee. My adrenaline seeping back into its glands left me weak, uncertain. My coffee cup shook in my hand as I related the story, my mind playing over the hundreds of sampans and junks I'd searched on the Bassac. And those that greeted us with a shotgun as we stepped aboard. It all came back when I was on the boat. How long would it take to go away?

I sucked in hot air and continued the story. All but a half kilo of their rice gave out a week ago, and their water gave out three days ago. They tried to flag down several merchies, but none would stop for them. Four people had already died.

They decided to save the rice for the only baby onboard. The mother chewed the rice as much as she could and then fed it to the baby. No one else ate anything. They were in bad shape, and when I told them they were back to Vietnam only a few miles from the coast, they went to pieces.

We fed them, but they couldn't eat much, only soft stuff. Doc treated those he could and gave them medicine. We filled their tanks with about a hundred gallons of diesel fuel, and the boatswain's mates sewed up their sail. The engineers cleaned their filters and injectors and did a little tuning on their dilapidated engine . . . not much they could do though. We filled their small water tanks and gave them four bags of rice. The stewards weren't happy about that, but we should be in Subic Bay in a couple of weeks anyway.

"That's about it—oh! They tried to offer us money, but I refused.

Jim, you have anything to add?" He shook his head sullenly, turning his face away from me. *He probably wanted to shoot them.*

"Will they make it, XO?"

"I doubt it, sir, about four hundred fifty miles in an open boat with an antiquated, faltering engine with no repair parts and only make-do sails and with no real sailors or engineers aboard and with the monsoons starting . . . I don't give 'em one chance in hell."

He nodded and looked away.

The next day the captain seemed in ill sorts as he relieved me of the gun watch duty. It was 0645, the sun already burning our gray steel heat sink to a simmering boil. The chief engineer walked up to the captain and me as we stood on the port wing of the bridge, the still air permeated by the hydrocarbon stench of our stack gas.

"Water's getting critical, sir," he reported, "seawater temperatures are just too high for us to maintain a decent vacuum in the evaps, and crew use is very high. Our main condensers are providing only twenty-six to twenty-seven inches of vacuum, and fuel is getting low."

"Well, Mr. Raven, we knew this would happen," the captain answered curtly, seemingly disturbed about being briefed by the chief engineer on something he already knew. Turning to me he snapped, "XO, go on water hours . . . no showers at all!"

"Yes, sir," I answered as a radioman handed me a message. I looked at it and handed it to the captain. It ordered us detached and to a rendezvous at first light tomorrow with an oiler and ammo ship off the eastern coast of the Cau Mau peninsula about forty miles up from the southern tip.

"Umph, it's about time," the captain said, walking into the pilot-house. "Here, Reeves, plot this and let me know the distance." It seemed Reeves was always on watch.

The ubiquitous Willie appeared as if on cue and took the message from Reeves. He read it and gave it back, murmuring it's about two-hundred fifty miles. In five minutes Reeves had it plotted and reported the distance to be two hundred forty-nine miles. Combat reported two hundred fifty-three.

"Cannon One, this is Panther Three Six, have administrative traffic for you. Over," the gun line net speaker called out, disturbing the still air.

Lieutenant DeLeon, who had been loitering around the pilot-house, grabbed the microphone, answering in a most commanding voice, "Roger, Three Six, this is Cannon One, send your traffic. Over."

"One, this is Three Six, break break, if feasible, request a liaison officer at your command to be assigned this location for a few days to brief on naval gun-fire procedures. We will provide helo. Over."

The captain smiled at me. "Whaddaya think, XO?" he asked innocently, as if the subject were news to him.

"I don't know, Captain, what with a big replenishment coming up, we'll need all our officers here," I answered, winking at the captain, my back turned to a frothing-at-the-mouth weapons officer.

"I'll volunteer, Captain," DeLeon blurted out, not hearing what I'd said.

"Did you hear the XO?"

"Oh! No, sir?"

"He asked about the replenishment. Maybe we can send the chief gunner's mate. He's well qualified. XO, whaddaya think?"

"The chief's good, he can handle it, and Mr. DeLeon won't miss a replenishment," I answered, looking at the crestfallen face of the man of the lion, who had just been told he couldn't search for the Holy Grail.

"No," the captain said, "send Mr. DeLeon, him being a volunteer and all. You can fill in for him on the UNREP if you would." The captain and I had already discussed this and agreed if Panther Three Six called, we'd send *Sir* DeLeon ashore.

"Certainly, Captain," I answered. Then, turning to a cloud-nine naval lieutenant who grinned like a small kid on Christmas, I said, "Make the arrangements, Mr. DeLeon."

The Huey slick hovered one foot over our flight deck as Mr. DeLeon and a seaman loaded four cases of beer aboard. All naval ships carried a hundred or so cases locked up tight in a storeroom for those occasions when we were at sea a long time. We could then—for morale purposes—lower a boat over the side with ice cold beer in it and rotate the thirsty sailors in and out. No drinking allowed on a U.S. naval vessel.

Next, ice cream and ice wrapped in huge insulated bags went into the helo. Finally, wearing fresh khakis and a web belt holding a leather holster containing a .45 automatic pistol, a canteen, and three .45-clip holders, Lieutenant DeLeon stood to attention, saluted, and climbed aboard. The helo rose, dipped, and flew off. And at long last, the imagined mighty man of the French aristocracy, of the heritage of Charlemagne himself, was whisked off to war.

"Recommend initial course to rendezvous, 189 degrees true," the talker to Combat announced flatly the second the helo lifted free and we secured from flight quarters.

"Quartermaster?" I asked.

"Quartermaster recommends initial course, 187 degrees true, sir."

"OOD, Navigator here, initial course to rendezvous 188 degrees true," I announced, splitting the difference.

I saw First Class Petty Officer Wilhelmson squeeze Seaman, quartermaster striker, Tommy Reeves's arm so tightly that a tear came to the kid's eyes as his usually benevolent boss hissed venomously, "Quartermasters are always first with their recommendations. . . . Don't you ever forget it, you motherfucker, or I'll have your miserable fat ass scraping paint with the deck apes again. You understand that. . . . You made me look bad. You made me look bad."

"You shouldn't call me that, Mr. Willie, it ain't right, I never did that," the chubby quartermaster striker said, his face twisted in anguish.

"What ain't right, Reeves?" Willie snapped back.

"Calling me a motherfucker. . . . I never did that, I just . . . ? I walked away, not wanting to hear the conversation as Lieutenant Sanders spoke into the microphone of the gun-line net. "Panther Three Six, this is Cannon One, as previously stated, Cannon One reports, I shackle, 'Bravo Sierra, Victor Uniform.' Acknowledge." Lieutenant Sanders had just told the U.S. Army major in charge of the gun-fire support unit three miles inland from the coast that we'd be off station for three days for replenishment.

Modified GQ was secured and the ship dropped into an easy lethargy as we headed south. The crew ate the last of the steak and lobster for dinner and watched again the least boring of the films we had onboard. The captain opened up the showers. If we didn't make the UNREP, we'd run out of water. Engineering suicide. He was taking a chance for his men—the mark of a superb leader. They deserved it; they deserved him.

From my stateroom I listened to the muted tones over the 1MC. "Now taps. Taps; lights out. Keep silence about the decks. The smoking lamp is out in all berthing compartments. Now taps . . ."

This used to be silly to me. Why such an elaborate ceremony to tell the off-watch crew to go to sleep? But I knew now: tradition. Tradition gives men something to identify with, an anchor, something they can depend upon. It's a familiar warm teddy bear that brings mental comfort. Although on the intellectual level we know it to be foolish, sometimes it's all the stability we have. We know where we stand; we know the game. Even if we're living in chaos, we can handle it.

Two and a half days later, at first light, we reported in to Panther Three Six. No answer came back over the speaker. The boatswain's mate of the watch, with his finger on the 1MC switch, looked at the clock on the after bulkhead and raised his boatswain's pipe to the microphone. At the instant of 0600 he clicked on the switch and took a deep breath, then piped "all hands." As the shrill of it reverberated throughout the ship and drifted out to sea, he broadcasted, "Now reveille. Reveille all hands heave out and thrice up. Set material condition Yoke throughout the ship. The smoking lamp is lighted in all authorized spaces. Now reveille."

The UNREP had gone well in spite of the monsoonal storm, and we were back early fully replenished with fuel, water, food, movies, and ammo.

We called Panther Three Six again. Again no answer. We tried again and again while we waited and watched smoke rise through the rain from the jungle about three miles in from the coast. We closed to one mile, then to a half. Nothing. It appeared as if an air strike were going in near Panther Three Six's location. The driving rain pelted our sides like machine-gun fire. Visibility deteriorated. We called again. No answer.

By 0800 both the captain and I were in near panic as we hopelessly stared at the jungle and the smoke. Where was DeLeon? The starboard lookout reported a light plane over the coast. It flew toward us for a minute, then banked around, heading back over the jungle. We couldn't communicate with these spotter planes; we didn't have the equipment. Only static sounded out of the gun-line net speaker. Then a garbled: "Can . . . Can . . . non . . . ?"

The captain grabbed for the microphone, yanking it off its hook. "Panther Three Six, this is Cannon One. Over?" He bent his ear close to the speaker as if that would help.

"Cannon, we're in the shit"—he faded— "call fire mission . . ." He faded. It sounded like DeLeon.

"General quarters, XO," the captain ordered.

"Coordinates, follow." The voice from the beach faded for a few seconds, then came in once, slightly garbled, with a string of coordinate numbers. In Combat I plotted the position. At the nav table Willie plotted the position. The CIC officer plotted the position. The leading radarman plotted the position. We all concurred.

"Hold fire," I shouted into the sound-powered phones hooked up to speakers on the bridge. "Captain, these coordinates are only five hundred yards north of Panther's position. Request retransmission."

"Batteries weak . . . shot up"—fade—"shoot on coordinates given"—fade—static—"we know . . . fire for God's sake"—fade—static—"gooks coming through . . . wire. No spot just fire . . . fire." It was DeLeon's voice.

"Fire control central manned and ready. Mount 51, ready. Mount 52, ready. Combat, ready."

Nothing further came over the gun-line net as I called to the bridge. "We have a solution. Request guns free. Captain, you think . . ."

"Guns free!" was his answer.

Four five-inch rounds blasted out simultaneously. We waited for a spot. Nothing. Four more rounds went out on the coordinates DeLeon's voice had given us. "Drop . . . one." Fade. Static. " . . . Thousand . . . left five . . . five, eh, hundred . . ." came over the anemic net. It still sounded like DeLeon's voice. Four more rounds burned through the rain. Then eight, then sixteen, then thirty-two. "Good! Good! Left." Fade. "Left five . . ." Fade.

"Left five fucking what." I heard the captain's anguished plea over his open phone.

"Let's try five hundred, Captain," I answered with more calm than I felt.

"Yeah! Five hundred," he called out, and eight more rounds smashed into the jungle, left five hundred yards from something. Eight more of our shells exploded somewhere in the rain-filled jungle.

The spotter plane came in low down our starboard side, wiggling his wings. He turned one thousand yards in front of us, heading back down our port side, our firing side, his wings wiggling even more violently. "Cease fire! He wants us to cease fire. Depress the barrels. Show him we understand," the captain ordered Lieutenant (jg) Maxwell, who stood in for DeLeon as gun control officer on the bridge. Halfway down the ship, the light plane banked and headed straight in for the coast. We both had the message. "Damned courageous fool," I heard the captain say over his live microphone.

The rain quit. Visibility cleared. Two F-4 Phantom jets, the fast movers, screamed low over our mast, heading for the shore. Another message. Seconds later the eerie, phantasmagoric flash of napalm lit the sky over Panther Three Six's location. Another two fast movers came in from the south, followed by the deep, thunderous roll of five-hundred-pound bombs tearing up the jungle.

We waited; there was nothing we could do. Two Phantoms came at us from the beach. They silently shot over our masts, wiggling their wings, clearing us by inches as the roar of their engines followed them out, smashing us broadside. More strikes went in, each one appearing a little farther to the north. In ten minutes a flight of eight slicks and four gunships whoop-whooped in from the south and dropped down over Panther Three Six's location.

In five minutes, seeming like hours, the gun-fire net speaker boomed out from its maximum volume settings. "CANNON ONE, THIS IS PANTHER THREE SIX, VISITOR, GOT NEW RADIOS FROM GRUNTS JUST ARRIVED. HOW DO YOU READ ME? OVER."

Now on the bridge, I reached for the phone with the captain's nod. "Panther Three Six, read you five by five, interrogative situation? Over."

"Fine fine, XO, ah . . . Cannon, stand by for call fire mission co-ordinates follow; be advised I will pass spots from Spyglass Nine. Thanks for the assist."

For another half hour we pumped shells into the jungle swamps, each four rounds respotted to the north and each round taking a little longer to get out of the barrel as the physically fatigued and heat-prostrated gun crews tried their best to keep the guns firing at their maximum rate of fifteen rounds per minute per mount.

But despite their heroic efforts, each mount soon slowed to two rounds per minute. I could just imagine the hellish conditions down in the sweltering magazines and the blinding, bitter smoke filling the hacking interiors of the mounts.

"Cease fire, Cannon, Spyglass Nine says great job. You saved some ass today. Stand by; I'll be leaving for home in half an hour, Dad," DeLeon's smart-ass voice graced our bridge.

As the noon sun threatened to blind any fool looking very close at it, the army slick let down easily over our flight deck hovering at twelve inches above our slightly rolling ship. A muddy, athletically trim man wearing a camouflage-covered helmet jumped out of the helo onto the deck, turning to wave to the pilots who were already lifting off.

He wore filthy tiger greens and muddy combat boots and a web pistol belt weighted down by a .45 automatic in a soiled leather holster. His gaunt, wide-eyed stare and slumped body belied the smile he tried to project through the rain-streaked distortion of the smeared, green and black camo paint covering his face.

"Hi, XO."

"Jim."

Jim DeLeon

The next day, Lieutenant DeLeon stood hesitantly at my door. "XO . . . ah . . . can I talk to you?"

His war stories had regaled the wardroom for three meals, but he never met my eyes when he bragged about them. His biggest story was about going out on a patrol with the Green Berets. By the fourth time through, his stories turned wearisome to his fellow officers. They couldn't relate; they treated him as if he were merely describing a movie. I listened. I knew it was important for him to get it out of his system.

I could see the captain's eyes narrow every time DeLeon mentioned going on patrol. DeLeon had disobeyed his order to not leave the compound.

I asked him curtly what he wanted. I was not in the mood to address the problem right then. He furtively looked around as if to ensure no one else was listening. He said he wasn't doing well, not well at all, and needed my advice. I motioned him in. *More DeLeon bullshit.* I kicked the door shut. I listened to the hum of the ventilators trying to cool my stateroom as I filled my pipe.

I reminded him that he called in an air strike mighty close to his position and that was certainly doing well.

He scootched around nervously on my couch. I lit my pipe, waiting for his answer. He told me he didn't have a choice, the grunts were there shooting, and the major ordered him to call in the fire.

"Seeing the VC charging us made me so scared, I was no more than a robot reacting to his orders," he said barely above a whisper, so much so, I had to move my chair closer to listen.

The driving rain pelted the outside bulkhead of my stateroom as I waited. I knew it best not to question. "Wanna tell me about it, Jim?" I asked. He paused for a few minutes as I refilled and lit my pipe. I scowled as I gave a come-here sweep with my right arm. "Well?"

He told me he went out on this ambush with some of the grunts, Green Berets.

I was still pissed from when he talked about it at lunch, but I had held my temper. I had emphatically told him not to leave the base camp, not to go out on any patrols. I was pissed, but more at myself for giving an order I knew would be disobeyed. A prime leadership failure on my part. I knew he'd be under a lot of pressure from the grunts to prove himself, and I knew how much he wanted to get into combat. *Shit! Now what do I do about it?*

He told me he wanted to do real well in front of those guys, but he was scared. The waiting, he said, the waiting was awful. He outlined the sequence: He was in the lead position and was supposed to let the VC all go through, then attack the last one in the column while the grunts would get all who passed by him. "I knew I could do it, XO, my mind played it back over and over. I had every step planned and rehearsed in the two hours we waited out there in the rain. You know what I mean?"

"Yes, go ahead, Jim."

He went on to relate that at about midnight, the first one came through, and there were supposed to be four. He said he panicked, too scared to wait, and opened fire as soon as he saw the first VC. Then shooting started all over the place, and he just hunkered down. And by the time things got quiet, two of the berets were bleeding, one from his arm, the other from his head.

Jim DeLeon, now the bloodied warrior, stopped and lit a cigarette. I made no comment. He remained silent for a minute. The rain stopped. The ship took on a slight roll. We both knew his premature firing blew the ambush and caused two of the Berets to be wounded. His fault.

"Christ, Jim. How in God's name did you convince them to take you along? They don't usually take untrained people. What did you tell them?"

"That I was a SEAL."

"Stupid!"

"Yes, sir," he answered, then told me that there was something else. It was dark, he couldn't see well, and that the person he killed was small, and he reminded me that all Vietnamese were small. He stopped, his eyes constricting as if his mind conjured a vision that his eyes didn't want to see.

"What, dammit, Jim, what is it?"

He said it was a girl, then cast his eyes to the deck, rubbing his hands together rapidly as if he were trying to cleanse them. "It was a girl, XO. She couldn't have been more than fifteen years old. It bothers me, you know, killing a young girl. I know she was the enemy and it was okay, but a girl?"

I didn't say anything, I didn't know what answer he expected as his blank face turned to me. He obviously wanted validation of his actions; of course, anyone would. I'd gone through it. I let him wait for thirty seconds. "You know what bothers me, Jim?"

"No, sir."

I waited another ten seconds before answering. He fought it; the guy was good, but he couldn't stop his pleading face from slowly transforming into a smirk as if he'd just conned me into buying a used car from him.

When I figured he thought he had me, I whispered, "What bothers me, Mr. DeLeon, is that you don't give a shit. You're putting on this big act of concern, but in reality you're quite proud of yourself."

"But XO? I . . ."

He reared back as my fist smashed down on my desk.

"Don't give me that unmitigated bullshit, Mr. DeLeon. You're a fucking rabid killer, and you loved every minute of it. Who the fuck do you think you're talking to, some goggle-eyed staffie on COM-CRUDSEPAC's floating hotel?"

"XO?"

"I see the orgasmic look on your face when you fire the guns. I saw it when you left on the helo. I detect it in your speech, your eyes. You're a dangerous man, Jim."

"XO?" he whimpered. "I . . ."

"Shut the fuck up, Lieutenant DeLeon. I'm in enough shit about you with the captain already."

"But, XO."

"I said shut up. The captain didn't want you to go. He didn't trust you. I did. I talked him into it. He said you'd run off into the boonies, and he was right and I was wrong. I told him you'd obey my order, his order, to stay at the base camp. You didn't, you sonofabitch. You put him in great jeopardy. You let him down. You let me down."

"XO?"

"And now you come in here and want me to give you my blessings on telling the world you killed a young girl. Why didn't you cut off her tits to show us, were they too small? Wouldn't that have been the manly thing to do?"

He didn't answer as he unconsciously reached into his pocket for a cigarette. I yanked it out of his hand and threw it to the deck. He squirmed on my couch but remained silent. "I'm putting you in hack, Mr. DeLeon, for the first five days in Subic." He winced but said nothing.

My muscles released their death grip on my face, which now softened. He slowly stood up, and I reached over and touched his bowed shoulders. "Jim," I said, stopping him from leaving. "It's different out there. No one aboard understands that except me, and now you. The first kill is the hardest. What you did was foolish. Don't talk about it anymore. If you're really concerned, the thoughts will eventually go away. Mine did." I lied.

My arm went around his shoulders. "You should've just kept your mouth shut."

"But, XO, why are you putting me in hack?"

"Because, Jim, you should be court-martialed for disobeying orders. I begged the old man to let me slap you on the wrist. Don't push it. Get out of here."

Chapter 6

Bambi

Four days later, with our gun-line duty behind us, we euphorically turned the tip of the U Minh forest, passing out of the Gulf of Thailand into the South China Sea. In several more hours Con Son island, the federal prison island of Vietnam, passed down our port side as we steamed away from Vietnam, heading 045 degrees true for Subic Bay, the Philippines. Straight ahead lay two weeks of rest, sex, cheap booze, and ship repairs.

We glided in, landing softly against the camels, those long floating logs that kept the hull from tearing up the pilings. We doubled up the lines and secured the engineering plant as the engineers dragged steam hoses and electric cables from the pier. We were going cold iron, the first time in three months.

I wanted to get off the ship and walk on land again. Liberty call sounded, sailors swarmed ashore—money filling their pockets, desire jamming their loins. On the pier, Mr. DeLeon and I walked the length of the ship, inspecting for damage. The murky water, flecked with landside scum, carried a thin oil slick forming shimmering rainbows from the morning's low sun.

"Smells like stale urine here, XO," Jim said, squeezing up his nose.

"Yeah, you're right, get some fresh urine out here," I replied. He looked at me, not knowing to smile or not.

Green crud covered the brass of the lifelines like a living fungus. Great streaks of rust violated the ship's corrugated sides, corrugated from the decades of seas hammering in her thin steel sides between the ribs and stringers.

True to their reputation, the legionnaires of the Naval Repair Facility swarmed aboard to do our bidding. "The best and the cheapest," they promised. We gave max liberty even though the ship's sides looked disgraceful. We'd be in Hong Kong in six weeks and Mary Soo would paint us in exchange for our garbage. No need to work the exhausted crew. So we looked bad, so what, there were no fleet staffs here?

The evening O-club scene provided the only decent entertainment: shabby nightclub acts, drinking and eating and watching round-eyed women dancing with their husbands and friends. Boring. Neither the captain nor I played golf. It was too hot for tennis, and I sure as hell wasn't going to go boar hunting in the jungle again as I had when *Henshaw* was here some ten years ago. So we went to the O-club; it was the best we had. On our sixth night there, the captain drank four beers. Three more than his usual.

He slurred out that he had a buddy from Rutgers who came over here on deployment and met a Filipino girl. A beautiful Filipino girl. A great woman. I tried not to give a so-what gesture. He ordered another beer, gulped a third of it, and looked around at the young waitresses. His eyes sparkled.

"Let's go into Olangapo," he suggested, his breath coming in measured gasps.

Jim DeLeon, now off hack, and Larry Sanders led the way through the squalid streets, followed demurely by the captain and me.

"He left his wife. Married that Filipino girl."

"Who left his wife, Cap'n?"

"My friend, a guy named Larry from Rutgers. You remember, aren't you listening, Don? I was just telling you about him."

Yeah, Captain, half an hour ago.

"Never figured out why he did it until I met his wife. Carlita. Nice name. Great woman. They're living happily ever after, every man's dream, an enchanting woman. He's got everything a man could want."

The captain had never been in Olangapo, few submariners had. Young, white-hatted shore patrolmen inundated the town. They were everywhere. The repair facility CO didn't think much of sin. He couldn't do much about it by fiat, but he sure could fill the town up with shore patrol and make life difficult for the sailors on liberty.

We chose a bar that seemed less tawdry than the others and whose raucous music was ten decibels lower. The captain looked around as if expecting his wife to appear, gulped once, and led us in. His eyes all but exploded at the debaucherous scene. His head swiveled to every woman on every man's lap. He looked at me, then to Mr. DeLeon. He shrugged and followed the hostess in.

"HEY, CAPTAIN, WELCOME ABOARD." Willie's voice roared over the din as he stood, dragging his quartermasters up with him. Reeves, a lot thinner than when we had left Long Beach, tried to hide his girl behind him.

"You guys doing okay?" the captain asked, shaking each of their hands.

Yes-sirs came from each of the four men, each one holding a San Miguel out to the captain in toast. All but Willie, who was trying to shrink into a gnome.

The captain threw a twenty-dollar bill on their table. "Have one for old *Kramer*, gentlemen!"

We sat in a curtained-off room, as was the custom for the more *mature* patrons. Jim, after a few drinks, was off again on his tales of being ashore. Incountry, he called it. No mention though of leaving the compound. I'd gotten that message through to his egotistical mind. The stories seemed to grow more daring and exciting in the telling.

He asked how old I was when I first came under fire. I couldn't figure out what obscure point he was trying to make in his liquor-laden mind. I ignored him, swigging down a delicious San Miguel beer and eating small pieces of fried pork. He asked again.

"Goddammit, Jim, you're such an asshole. What difference does it make. But if you have to know, lemme see, yeah, fifteen years old."

His face dropped into the hang-dog look he got when frustrated. "*Fifteen!* Come on?"

I told him I grew up in Nameoki, Illinois, across the Mississippi from St. Louis. I related the story of how my buddies and I were sitting in a sleazy restaurant on the second deck of a small hotel in East

St. Louis. I said we were trying to hustle some girls, when all of a sudden the window shatters and a .45 slug comes sauntering into the room and pretty as you please dropped onto the middle of the table.

He answered that it didn't count. It wasn't fired at me. It was just a stray that ran out of energy and dropped on our table.

"So what," I answered. "You wanted to know. Whaddaya mean, it doesn't count. Who's counting."

He said he was trying to determine if I was younger than him when I first got shot at.

The captain laughed, saying for me to send him home, that he was cracking under the pressure of having an XO with medals. He gave DeLeon a good-natured hit on the shoulder and ordered another round of San Miguels.

DeLeon waited a while, downing long swigs of beer from his fourth bottle. Then he started again, his words now slurring. "You know, XO, if my last name was Sheppard, what I would do?"

I allowed I didn't know.

"Well, sir, I'd have a son and give him the first name of *Dalord* and the second name *Ismy*." He burst out laughing, the captain smiled, not really understanding. Mr. Sanders opened his mouth and pointed his finger down his throat. I sorta liked it. "Get it?" Jim slobbered. "Dalord Ismy Sheppard?"

I told him to shut up as the curtains slowly parted and four beautiful young ladies smiled in at us. And with no invitation, they sidled up to each one of us. "Welcome, brave officers of U.S. navy ship, we are here to see you be happy," the oldest-looking one greeted us as she took a seat next to mine, rubbing her breasts across the back of my head as she did.

The captain's was the most beautiful, the youngest, and I swear she couldn't have been more sixteen. She sat in his lap. "My name is Bambi," she cooed as her hand innocently rubbed his chest. He winced and smiled. DeLeon wasted no time becoming acquainted with his girl and Mr. Sanders affected a cool, disinterested demeanor. I told the girl, next to me that I had no interest and she'd be wasting her time with me. She smiled and left, but four whiskeys for the ladies were delivered by a hulk of a man, half brother to a gorilla.

I sat there chatting with Lieutenant Sanders, and after five minutes his ignored girl left. I objected when four more whiskies arrived for just two girls and the scowling keeper-of-the-curtain grabbed them and begrudgingly took them away.

Lieutenant DeLeon staggered out with his girl. Lieutenant Sanders and I excused ourselves to a grateful captain. "So beautiful," we heard him mutter as we left to go back to the ship through the noisy streets, the heat, and the staggering sailors.

The next morning the captain didn't come aboard until nearly lunchtime. He was uninterested in my brief of ship events last night or for today. He left at 1430 saying he'd be in touch. At 1600 he called saying he'd taken a room in the senior officers BOQ, the bachelor officer's quarters, and gave me a phone number. He showed up the next day at 1130 and called Ensign John Fuller, the disbursing officer, to his in-port cabin.

I waited until the disbursing officer left, knocked once, and entered. He looked at me with the woeful eyes of a teenager in love as he snapped a suitcase closed. "Isn't it beautiful here, XO, I'm going to retire here, you know . . . so peaceful, so beautiful," he crooned, sweeping his arm to the open porthole.

I agreed that it was and said we'd received the op order for the carrier ops week after next, and would he like to see a copy?"

He said that that was nice; but no, he'd read it when we got under way.

I told him the admiral wanted a meeting of all COs on the carrier at Cubi Point tomorrow. There was a helo laid on to fly him and the CO's of *Shanning* and *Fairfax* to the briefing. They were in the exercise with us.

"Oh, XO, I can't make it. . . . You go, make an excuse for me. I'm on very important business. Thanks, XO," he said, dismissing me as the disbursing officer returned with a large envelope.

Repairs are going okay, I managed to get out as the door started to shut in my face. I heard his voice saying, "That's nice, take care of it, XO," and the disbursing officer saying, "Sign here, sir," before the door fully closed. *Oh, shit! Not the captain?*

Three minutes later: "*Kramer* departing."

I called Mr. Fuller to come up and see me. In three minutes he appeared. I rarely spoke to him professionally, relying mostly on his boss, Lieutenant (jg) Jellico, the supply officer, to keep me informed. I closed the door. "What were you and the captain talking about, John?" I asked casually, offering him a cigarette.

He said he wasn't supposed to tell anyone. I replied I wasn't anyone; I was his XO. He remained hesitant. I was pissed. For effect, I smashed my fist down on my desk. He jumped up, tripping and falling against me. I tossed him back down on my couch, yelling, "GODDAMMIT, MR. FULLER! If you don't tell me, I'm going to rip your fucking heart out and court-martial your ass for bleeding on the carpet. DO YOU UNDERSTAND THAT, MISTER?" And with a swing, I smashed my fist down on my desk again, scowling my most ferocious XO look.

His face paled, his eyes widened as he stammered out that it was only an allotment request to the finance center. "That's all, really, Mr. XO."

Bingo! "And who, Mr. Fuller, is required to initial all allotment requests on this ship?"

"The XO, sir, you, sir." I felt disgusted with myself for muscling this poor kid. I asked him where it was for me to initial, and then asked him if he was planning to violate naval regulations. I told him to go get the allotment request and I'd cover for him. This time.

I lied. It was my own verbal order that all allotments came to me for initialing. It was one way I kept an eye on what my men were doing. Initialing wasn't necessary, but it gave me a great source of information.

He returned in two minutes. "Thanks, John, I'll take care of it. I gotta send some papers in anyway," I said as he handed it to me while I stood outside my door. I initialed it, smiled, and threw it into my out basket. I didn't want to give the impression of having too much interest in a simple allotment request, but probably had already.

"And, John, *everyone* else is who the captain meant by *anyone,* so don't mention any of this, okay? And I mean it, Mr. Fuller, not even to Mr. Jellico. You understand that, John?" He did.

I read it. Damn! "Amelia J. Santos, Olangapo City, the Philippines, $400 per month. Relationship: sister."

Amelia J. Santos, aka Bambi, got the captain good. He even lied, perjuring himself by swearing on the request that she was his sister. The navy wouldn't send an allotment to a nonrelative. And they would surely question a sister living in Olangapo City.

The Naval Finance Center received hundreds of allotment requests from this port, usually from very young sailors wanting to send money to their *sisters*. I put his signed request into my safe.

We didn't see the captain on Wednesday or Thursday, and on Friday afternoon he showed up just long enough to draw advanced special pay from the disbursing officer. While we waited, he asked me how the meeting on the carrier went. He really didn't seem interested. His biggest concern was if anyone made a point of his not being there. I stretched the truth by telling him no, even though the COs of both destroyers, *Shanning* and *Fairfax,* seemed concerned that he'd sent his XO for a meeting with the admiral.

What's a Naval Officer to Do?

The ship moved smartly away from the pier as the sun shone through the tall palms and a light breeze rustled their fronds in a farewell wave. In half an hour we joined *Shanning* and *Fairfax*. Mr. Baldachino brought us in smartly to station in a line astern and held us there as we settled in to do destroyer things again. The captain sat morosely in his chair, watching but not commenting. He seemed to take only a cursory interest in the evolutions around him. He walked aft to the signal bridge and watched, hump shouldered, as the Philippine islands sank down into the sea behind us.

He sent for lunch and ate it in his sea cabin. He sat in his chair all afternoon and acted like he was reading the op order, but too often his eyes shifted out to sea. He came to supper and attempted several times to join the conversation but failed. He took eight o'clock reports in his sea cabin, but didn't comment. As I closed the sea cabin door behind me, I heard him mutter, "How stupid could I be?"

In the morning, as he came out of his sea cabin, he looked at me, eyes heavy, and said, "I screwed up, XO." I knew what he meant. *Good, his brains have shifted from his genitalia back to his head.* Suddenly his fist smashed into the back of his chair. "SHIT!"

The bridge crew jumped, exclaiming a collective "OH!" as they moved to put maximum distance between him and them. Sailors get very jumpy when their captain acts nervous. Already the story of his fist against the chair and his outbreak was spreading rapidly about the ship via the ubiquitous sound-powered phone circuits.

"Can I help, sir?" I asked, trotting after him as he hurried toward his sea cabin.

As he opened the door to go in, he sighed, his eyes downcast, his hands rubbing each other. He looked back at the sea, his eyes blurry, wandering, as if something horrible existed out there and if he could avoid focusing on it, it would go away. Something like sharks circling, all too ready to devour a naval career. "Oh, maybe yes. Get the ship ready for a change of command ceremony." It looked like a tear was forming in his right eye as he closed the door in my face.

It was time. I was back at his door in two minutes with the envelope containing his request for allotment to Amelia J. Santos, Olangapo City, the Philippines. I knocked and entered, as was his practice.

He asked me what I wanted, his elbows leaning on his desk, his hands holding his head.

"Sir, late tomorrow the skippers are to helo over to the carrier. This envelope missed the mail, could you leave it with them for a COD flight back to Cubi Point?"

He asked what was so important about it.

"I don't know, sir, I haven't read it; my ship's office just screwed up."

I handed him the sealed envelope addressed to the Navy Finance Center. He gave it little attention as he slowly, unconsciously, tore open the flap and took the typed form out. He glanced at it indifferently, extending his hand to give it back to me. I didn't take it. He looked at me. I nodded to the form. With disgust he looked at the paper again. His eyes snapped to attention. His back straightened. The sides of his mouth tried to reach his ears. He grabbed the sides of his desk to support himself. "XO . . . Don, I . . ."

"I'm sorry, Captain, we screwed up, appreciate you taking care of it."

"Well, yes, okay, Don, okay, but . . . but don't let it happen again."

He rarely called me Don. I heard him whistling "Anchors Aweigh" as I left, closing the door, noticing him dancing a jig.

"Foxtrot closed up, sir, flight ops commencing," the OOD reported, keeping his binoculars on the carrier. She'd just turned into the wind, and we cranked on twenty-seven knots to take us to a picket station three thousand yards off her port beam.

For three days we steamed the tedious routine, relieved only when on plane guard station. I wished we'd play ASW, at least that was fun. We had a nuclear attack boat attached to the task group, but we weren't involved in its use, none of the destroyers were. Our only duty was to screen the carrier against submarine attack—what a joke.

I sat in my stateroom looking at the forty-two request forms for marrying a foreign national scattered across my desk. I couldn't blame my guys, the Filipino women were deliciously sexy, and dressed the part.

The experience most of our young men had consisted of blundering attempts to feel up some American girl in the backseat of a car, girls taught by their mothers not to mess around until they were married. Then, once the man was hooked, endure. "Whine a lot and he won't bother you as much. Tell him you have a headache, that always works."

The sailors come to Subic and find the girls are not only beautiful, but are willing—albeit for a price—to indulge in all manner of sexual fantasies and treat *their man* like he was a king and cater to his every wish and whim. It was an unbeatable combination of low price and availability of a much-sought-after commodity. And actually, it was much cheaper than taking an American girl out for a date. Thousands of American sailors had Filipino wives.

Three days later the blinking light from the carrier detached us to proceed on duties assigned—Hong Kong and R&R. Willie had a course recommendation laid out before the light stopped blinking. We'd taken the noon sight together, and he chided me for being two miles away from where we were, that is, his sight. "Better than the old guys," I answered.

"Old guys?"

And I told him Sir Francis Drake, Ferdinand Magellan, Vasco da Gama, Columbus. Those old guys, I said, all they could tell for sure was their latitude by measuring the North Star in the Northern Hemisphere. On longitude they knew nothing.

I mentioned that a decent clock, the chronometer, hadn't shown up till sometime late in the eighteenth century, invented by a guy named John Harrison in 1734. The old guys just headed in the general direction, and when they saw land tried to guess if they wanted to go north or south. "Hell, Willie, they didn't even have any charts worth a damn, but they could sense where they were; they felt it. They just knew in their bones. That's what makes you so good; you've got the feel."

"Whaddaya talking about, XO, I don't have any feel. I use our instruments," Willie said, scrunching up his face.

"No, Willie, you got the feel, just like a good sonarman can feel a sub around, or a helmsman can feel which way to put his rudder to maintain his course in an angry sea. The ship talks to you guys."

The ship had talked to me in the beginning, but I had lost it in the quagmire of paperwork and administration. "I envy you," I said, trying to keep the sadness out of my voice.

Willie moved closer to me, his eyes searching every face to ensure no one was close enough to hear his words. "I know exactly where we are, even in my sleep I know where we are. I never mentioned it to anyone. They'd think I was nuts. And all my fixes end up close to where my mind tells me we are. That's why I'm so fast."

"I know, Willie, and I'm damn glad to have you with me. You've done wonders with Reeves, and I appreciate that."

"Oh, thanks, XO. His mother wrote me, thanking me. Says she'd like to meet me when we get back, you know, come over for dinner or something. How about that?"

"Good, well done, Willie. I'm sure you'll enjoy it," I answered, concealing my smile as I turned, walking away, sad that I didn't have the *feel* aboard *Kramer*.

Hong Kong

The mountaintops of Victoria Island appeared first on the surface search radar at forty miles; then the hills and the craggy coast of mainland China. Six days of Hong Kong liberty, with no external responsibilities, no typhoon, just rest and recreation.

Victoria Island was named in honor of the young British queen who took the throne of Britain four years before Hong Kong became a crown colony in 1842. My mind played through the sordid, drug-based history of the colony. In the early days its entire economy hinged on the insidious opium trade and the taipans reveled and grew rich with it. And the peak, atop the mountain, was the high-bastion playing grounds of the wealthy and powerful. Each brick traced itself back, somehow, to someone who smoked his brains out in some dream house, somewhere.

That was long ago and now the colony flourished in tourism, small manufacturing, and international trade, and offered, reluctantly or not, the economic doorway to Communist China. The Red Giant lay just beyond the bustling Kowloon Peninsula, past the pretentious expanse of the New Territories to the pointed ranges of Kwangtung Province with its well-guarded twenty-two-mile-long border.

Mary Soo painted the ship, a different Mary Soo from when I was here before on my first ship in the early sixties, when we fought the vicious Typhoon Mary. As before, young girls came aboard, when invited, to inspect the bosun's locker and offer negotiated-price lessons in Asian love among the manila hemp and nylon lines and other tools of the trade the hearty deck apes used.

The enchanting Asian girls piqued my libido; it had been a long time and the sight of them stirred an all too familiar tingle in my groin. But I resisted, slightly over the moral and macho issue of being with a prostitute, but more so in the fear of being compromised as one of the senior officers of a nuclear-weapons-loaded ship.

We granted max liberty. Those sailors who had money left over from their stay in Subic rushed ashore, ate well, and drank well. They bought clothes and shoes and Asian bric-a-brac. But the favorite, the most sought after by the young, were tailor-made blues to prove that they belonged, even if vicariously, to the fraternity of the China sailor.

Tailor-made blues showed you were a China sailor, the last of the fiery breed. They were made of a soft black gabardine, not the rough melton cloth that called itself navy blue. They had a greater flare on the back collar, it stood a little higher, rakish. And the flap with the thirteen buttons molded beautifully to the stomach and accentuated one's maleness like a U.S. government sanctioned codpiece, whose meaning wasn't lost on the young ladies.

The trousers had a greater cut to the bell bottoms, which swished, like a musketeer's cape, when you walked, and sailors always walked straighter, more jauntily, when they wore their tailor-mades.

And the crowning touch—existing in blazon splendor and brilliant color—was the embroidered dragons on the inside of each cuff. If some dullard hadn't gotten the message by the material and the cut, a simple roll up of the cuffs, exposing the awesome, flame-breathing dragons, shouted the message to all but the most simple-minded.

You couldn't wear tailor-mades for a captain's inspection, but you sure as hell could wear them ashore.

Orders

At breakfast the last day in port, the captain asked me if I'd read last night's Fox scheds.

The Fox scheds, the scheds standing for schedules, were the continuously chattering teletype machines that broadcasted all messages to all ships, to all comm centers. The theory being that if all messages were put on the air without regard to where the ships were located, the enemy wouldn't know our fleet movements.

It seemed a decent plan, but more important, it offered an electronic bulletin board telling every ship about every other ship. By reading the Fox scheds, one could snoop into what the fleet was doing and the problems they were having. You weren't, of course, supposed to read any traffic not addressed to you. Sure. Tactical messages were rarely put on the Fox scheds.

In the old days, before our crypto machines became computerized, classified messages were sent out in five-letter groups that had to be manually decoded. A tedious chore that plagued junior officers by robbing them of their sleep and entrapping them in a claustrophobically small room with no ventilation and the insidious foulness of dried vomit reeking the deck and bulkheads. Now, thank God, only top secret came in coded in five-letter groups.

All good naval officers read the Fox scheds; ideally, before the captain and XO. Embarrassed that I had not, I answered the captain with a sheepish no. He handed me a multipage message. It was an ALNAV, a message to the entire navy. The commander's selection list. "Page four, you might find interesting, Mr. Five-Percenter."

It showed, Lt. Comdr. Donald D. Sheppard, USN, deep selected for the rank of commander a year early. I'd made the five percent list, that percent promotion boards could use to recognize officers of high efficiency and drive who deserved selection from the next junior year group. Only five percent of the total officers in that year group could be considered. I'd made it. He offered his hand.

I hadn't expected early promotion, hadn't even considered it, and inside my cool exterior my heart sang, my feet danced. He smiled and handed me another message, a one-pager addressed to the ship, which, in effect, said, "When detached proceed to the U.S. Naval Post Graduate School, Monterey, California, for a course of instruction leading to a masters of science degree. Upon completion, report to U.S. Navy Transportation School, Oakland, California, for further studies in transportation management. Relief available Singapore."

Four hours later, the duty radioman handed me another message, a personal from the chief of the Bureau of Personnel, CHBUPERS. "Don, Bravo Zulu, lookin' good. Signed Vice Admiral David Baker." Ol' iron-balls Dave, my mentor, my first CO on my first destroyer, *Henshaw,* Commander David Baker, the captain who knew everything.

I soared on the thermal currents of delight as we got under way for operations and for Singapore. PG school, a master's degree, a commander. *Wow! Bloody wow!*

Ten days later, after being detached from the carrier group just off Vietnam, we headed south for Singapore and my relief. I really wanted off; it wasn't so much fun being an XO anymore. That evening, a priority message from COMSEVENTHFLT cut our stay in Singapore from five days to half a day for refueling and reprovisioning. We were then to proceed to the Persian Gulf for joint operational exercises with the British. What about my relief, surely one day with the new guy wouldn't be enough.

A fuel barge and supplies awaited our arrival. Some staffie, somewhere, had done his job beautifully.

Twelve hours in Singapore, ship loaded, I sailed with her. No choice. It was okay. We had a fuel stop scheduled in Cochin, India, where I would detach. Visions of adventure filled my mind. I'd fly from Cochin, located on the extreme lower tip of Western India, to Bombay. From there to Tel Aviv. From there to Paris, then New York, then Los Angeles. I'd spend a day or so at each place, soaking up the local culture. A dream trip.

I met him on the quarterdeck, he'd come aboard from a water taxi five minutes after we anchored. Lieutenant Commander Joseph K. Janis, USN, USNA, offered his hand as his quick-inspecting eyes measured the ship. The in-port OOD, cringing under his scrutiny, looked to me for relief.

I put my hand on his shoulder. "Petty Officer Whitney, this is the new XO, Mr. Janis," I said, waving my arm toward the ramrod-straight six-foot-one, naval academy officer standing almost at attention next to me.

Whitney saluted. I added, "Petty Officer Whitney just made first class, Mr. Janis; he's a damn good man." Whitney smiled.

The statuesque Mr. Janis frowned and with a cavalier disregard for protocol ran his finger across the small portable desk and brought it back with a smear of dust on it. He stared at his finger as he said in what might have been a snarl, "Well, we'll see about that," he said, his tone dismissive and grating, his affected superiority sticking out like a broken bone.

I put my hand firmly around his upper right arm, over his immaculately pressed high-collared full dress whites with its one ribbon depicting that he'd been in the navy while a war was going on in Vietnam. "Ease up, Mr. Janis. You've been aboard only thirty-nine seconds."

It would take about half that time for the word to spread that the *new* XO was an asshole and the *old* XO had cut him off at the knees.

At 2000 we painstakingly threaded our way out of the harbor without a pilot, none was available. We steamed west, clearing the many small islands off the tip of Malaysia and at 2317 came northwest into the narrow Strait of Malacca, the haven of pirates for a thousand years.

The clear outline of the coastline made radar navigation easy but the unending number of merchies and junks—none of which seemed to give a damn about the international rules of the road— kept us constantly maneuvering to avoid collision.

With twenty knots cranked on, the captain and I stayed on the bridge along with the ubiquitous Willie. Mr. Janis, having changed to a new set of khakis, stood in the background until about 0100, then disappeared. I had suggested to the captain he let him use his in-port cabin. At first he agreed, but after a ten-minute official welcome aboard meeting, he told me to put him aft with the junior officers. Boys town. I didn't question it.

Ship traffic dwindled by noon the next day as we entered the wider portion of the strait. At 0415 we came to port, our hull now cutting through the calm water of the Indian Ocean, six degrees north of the equator.

Joe Janis inspected the ship with the minute detail of an ORI team; nothing escaped his peering eyes. By gesture and the clicking sounds of his tongue, he criticized everything. The navy's new preventive maintenance system (PMS), with its voluminous paperwork requirements, came under even deeper scrutiny. It pissed him off that he could find no major fault. He soon found out I was a great advocate of the system, and being in charge of the entire program, I had ensured it was well supported by the men.

He also seemed disappointed that the charts were up to date, a tedious job for the quartermasters. And he showed further displeasure when he found the ship's office in 4.0 condition. God knows, he rooted through the paperwork enough, but never once wanted to go down to the engineering spaces or to inspect the guns or the ASROC stations even though he scrupulously scanned their paper records.

"I'm a by-the-book man, Captain, and that's how the navy should be, by the book," he proudly announced, standing on the bridge, frowning at the men.

The captain answered with a curt "Good for you, Mr. Janis," and turned toward me, raising his eyebrows. *By the book, spare me the type.*

The military services, unfortunately, tended to attract men who preferred to be ordered around rather than act on their own. The *book* was their crutch. They didn't have to think, just refer to the *book* and everything would be fine. If the *book* said okay, it was always okay. If the *book* didn't mention it, it wasn't allowed.

The Indian Ocean lay dead calm, with its heat-hazed surface dancing squiggles into shimmering distortion over its glasslike smoothness. Boredom, each day a blur of consistency. We thought about exercising at general quarters, at damage control drills, at engineering drills. We thought we would overhaul equipment and paint inside the ship.

But we didn't. It was too damn hot under the ferocious blanket of humidity. You could see it; you could almost move your hand through it like cutting soft butter. Talking was difficult, words coming out in gurgles.

Sudden squall lines formed, pushing their blackness to the sky. Then, like a dam bursting, deluged us with their pent-up collection of moisture from the hot sea. "Over all hatches and gun covers," the boatswain's mate of the watch would announce, advertising their coming, but always too late. And no one cared. The gun covers protecting the ends of the barrels were already in place, and the wetness coming through the hatches cooled the crew, who mostly ran out to accept its momentary relief.

Undaunted, Mr. Janis was on his second inspection of the ship's paperwork and fumed more nervously at his inability to find any but the smallest discrepancies.

I was on a stroll through the ship. I stopped just out of sight of the door to ship's office. I was doing some last-minute reading on a directive we'd received in Singapore. I was dropping it off, but wanted to read a particular paragraph one more time before I did. The yeomen's voices drifted out. "Yeah, you're right, Smitty . . . it ain't going to be pleasant. Sonofabitch is uptight, huh?"

"Sheppard's a ballbuster, but this guy . . ."

I heard the soft rhythm of an electric typewriter as one of them started typing. In three seconds it stopped. "Ya know what, Smitty, bet if you jammed a piece of coal up his ass, it'd be a diamond in a week." Laughter. I moved back three paces, coughed twice, and said good morning to an imaginary sailor before walking into the office.

Just after 1200, Willie and I were finishing the noon sight. "What does the crew think of the new XO, Willie?" I asked conversationally. Willie looked at me, the left side of his mouth curling up, his eyes twinkling.

"Great guy, XO, they can hardly wait till he takes over," he answered, his face now in a full grin.

"Glad to hear that, Quartermaster, seems like he's a swell guy. If he had been my first XO, I'd sure be a better officer," I answered through my false smile.

"Well, sir, you might be able to cut a fix smaller than the size of the Hawaiian Islands." I laughed, brandishing the points of a divider at him as if I were going to stab him.

"He cuts a good fix, XO, a natural, like the old guys. You'd be impressed," Willie taunted me in good humor, pulling my chain. I was still faking out that I knew what I was doing as a navigator, and the captain let the fiction pass. He had Willie, the best in the fleet. I signed the noon position report using, as always, Willie's numbers, and got up to leave.

Willie stood up with me, offering me a small, gaily wrapped box. "XO . . . ah, well, me and my boys . . . we, ah, just thought you might, well, just might have some use for this."

Quartermaster Reeves came into the chart house as I tore open the Chinese wrapping. An Omega Seamaster watch. I turned it over, looking at the finely embossed sea serpent on the back and read the tiny engraving: XO, YOU MAY NOT KNOW WHERE THE SHIP IS, BUT YOU KNOW WHERE YOUR HEART IS.

I put it on, then took it off. The lump in my throat prevented words from coming out. It had probably cost more than two hundred dollars in Hong Kong. I had casually mentioned my admiration for the Seamaster when I'd seen Willie on the beach in Hong Kong and had taken him to lunch, had a few drinks, and spent the afternoon together.

"I, ah . . ."

"Actually, XO, well . . . we found it at the fleet landing and thought maybe we should turn it over to you for, you know, for proper disposition. Would appreciate it, sir."

"Yes, yes, of course," I slobbered out, putting the Seamaster back into the box, not looking at them for fear that my emotions would run away. "Yes, I'll, ah, take care of it. Thank you."

Reeves wept unabashed as I shook his hand. Willie confined his emotion to moist, glassy eyes. I wiped away four of my tears as I squeezed Willie's shoulder, turned, and left.

"XO," the captain said to me on the fourth day out. "We're only six degrees north of the equator . . . let's dip down and have a bit of a pollywog shell back ceremony."

"Yes, sir." I was afraid he'd do that. A pain in the ass for me and a filthy ship later to contend with. I was tired of it. I tried to get Mr. Janis to relieve me. I would become a passenger, and he would get out of boys town, but he refused, and the captain wasn't greatly impressed with the idea either.

Captain Neptune and his court of shellbacks were easy on me, barely acknowledging that I was a pollywog. My degradation was little more than confessing my shameful status as a pollywog. Mr. Janis, however, got the full bag of *almost* mock beatings and eating slop. It was getting out of hand, and I called the CMAA to quietly lighten it up. They did, but Mr. Janis slept painfully that night and didn't inspect very much the next day. And the ship was dirty, and I was tired of it.

I felt us heel over in a turn. I called the bridge. "Orders changed," the captain said. "Brits canceled the exercise. We're heading back for Singapore. Sorry, XO." *Christ! Five more days of this abominable heat and Lieutenant Commander Janis.*

At my going-away party in Singapore, the officers toasted one another and got drunk. And I got drunk too while the captain got maudlin. He praised me to embarrassment while the other officers joined in creating a picture that I was a leader among leaders, an officer among officers, a man without peer, that I was John Paul Jones reincarnated, that I was the quintessential, unfailing, unerring, humanistic naval officer—things would never be the same on ol' *Kramer* ever again. Not without ol' Shep the mighty, the benevolent. Only Jim DeLeon meant what he was saying. The other praises were unequivocally for the new go-by-the-book XO to hear and to heed.

Chapter 7

Command

Dark clouds violated this September's morning in late 1973 as the sleek destroyer, *Cambridge,* the lead ship of two, turned smartly around the San Diego sea buoy, heading in for weekend liberty. The skies hung morosely over us as I ran my hand lovingly across my ship's smooth gray metal like a young man might do with his first automobile. I caressed her gently, floating on the euphoric sense of ownership. I am sitting in the captain's chair; therefore, I am the captain. This is my ship. Captain. I rolled the word around my mouth, savoring its richness. It tasted good, sweet, sweet like chocolate candy.

We were a mile and a half inside the narrow channel when the fog dropped over us. Point Loma disappeared into it. I could barely make out the bow as the fog's eerie domain of blinding dampness embraced us into its dangerous bosom.

I picked up the microphone cradled in its metal holder next to my chair. "Charlie Romeo, this is Quebec Foxtrot, fog's pretty thick in here, are you in the clear?"

"Roger, Quebec Foxtrot, we're just on the edge of it. We can still see around us, but the harbor is completely shrouded. Over."

The sweep on the bridge radar repeater swirled into a kaleidoscopic dance of orange, blinked once, bleeped, and went blank. "Bridge, Combat, surface-search radar is down," the kid wearing sound-powered phones to CIC blurted out, his face in a panic. I glanced over to the XO standing at the nav table. He shook his head, his bland expression showing he had no solution to the problem.

"Charlie Romeo," I radioed to our sister ship who had sailed down with us from San Francisco. "My surface gadget just went belly up, do you hold us on yours? Over." My hands sweated, but I refused to wipe them. I didn't want the bridge crew to detect my nervousness.

"Affirmative, Charlie Romeo, we paint you well. Over."

What to do? I should turn and exit the harbor; that would be the safest thing to do. Prudence demands I take that course of action. This is my first time under way with my new crew. I need something to get their attention. Something dramatic. The last CO was a fine captain, and I needed a spectacular act to get their attention and their loyalty over to me.

I leaned over and keyed the 21MC to the fire control director, asking if anybody was up there. In just a few seconds a hesitant voice answered they were manned and running a few PMS checks. I asked them how soon could they give me some range and bearings, hoping they'd say right away. They said in a few minutes; they'd have to put things back together first.

"Please do it as fast as you can; we're a little blind down here. Your machine any good?"

When they said best in the fleet, my heart beat a little slower. I wanted to turn to the captain and ask him what to do. But I was the captain. What'll I do?

"The XO's coming up with a chart. Pick out something prominent and give us ranges and bearings. . . . Can you do that?"

"Never tried it, but we'll sure give it a go, sir."

Turning, I said, "XO, get up to the director and start sending me fixes . . . ever done that before?"

"I've never done that before, Captain. I don't think it can be done." And he was right, if you don't think something can be done, it can't.

"Mr. Lawrence," I snapped, "do you think it can be done?"

"Yes, sir," the tall, thin, black-haired weapons officer said, glancing at the XO, then back to me.

"Move it, then." But he already had a chart in his hand, his feet climbing up to the fire control director on the deck above us.

I asked Sonar if their machine was any good. They answered yes.

"XO, take a chart down to Sonar and see if you can keep us off the rocks. You think that'll work?" I said, instantly regretting my sarcasm. His glance showed he didn't think so, as he scurried out of the pilothouse.

I told Combat to fire up their air search radar, and give me what they could. That wasn't much of a choice, but I was desperate. The air search antenna angled upward and usually only mountaintops showed. *Shit!*

What else? "Charlie Romeo, this is Quebec Foxtrot, can you give me my posits, the tide's going on maximum ebb, and I don't want to attempt a turn in midchannel. If you would, keep giving me my ranges and bearings from whatever good point you can get, and we'll take it from there. Maybe the fog'll blow away soon; winds are picking up in here, and I think this thing'll blow itself out soon. Over."

My bowels tightened into ice-aged pressure, and just as cold.

"Roger, Quebec Foxtrot." And he gave me my range and bearing to the south side of the Ballast Point lighthouse. I passed it up to the director. They needed a starting point. In seconds the director gave me my range and bearing to the tower on the naval air station, North Island. A good two-point fix. The ice in me started to melt.

All the land east of us as we steamed north into the channel was flat, and if we could hold the tower on fire control radar, we could steam all the way in on it. The USS *Jamison* kept the posits flowing, and each time the director crew verified them with their range and bearing. I trusted our hyperaccurate director more than I did *Jamison*'s surface search radar. After all, the director was designed to track small objects with great accuracy. It was meant to lay our guns against a moving target.

The quartermaster and Combat plotted the information and gave us courses to steer. Sonar reported bottom depths and solid contacts against the upward sweeps of the channel sides. The fathometer faithfully recorded the depth to bottom. The channel depth was well marked on the charts, and with all the aids going for me, my blood pressure eased, but just a little.

The fog lessened as we steamed farther in. I could now see at least fifty yards ahead of the bow.

Every time it roared out, the blast of our foghorn startled me. "JOOD, time the echo return, tell me how far off the cliffs of Point Loma we are." It wasn't necessary, but I wanted to impress my crew with my seamanship. The order baffled the JOOD, an ensign whose name I couldn't remember, and he confessed shamefully that he didn't know how to do it.

I called him over and hurriedly explained that sound travels at a given speed, and all he had to do was click the stopwatch when our foghorn sounded and mark the time when the echo returned, then divide by two and that was approximately our range, just like the sonars and radars do. His face lit with a broad grin in understanding, and he ran out to the port bridge wing as excited as if he'd just invented echo-sounding.

The weak sensation started in my toes and phlegmatically wiggled its way up my spine to the nape of my neck, remaining there, demanding attention. My skin flushed. It came from the ship, but it wasn't a friendly feeling as I had previously experienced on my other ships; rather, an incessant calling to an obligatory chore. "Come to all stop, Mr. Charles." Twenty seconds passed as we stood there waiting. Mr. Charles glanced at me as if wanting a reason for stopping. None came from my lips as the ebbing tide carried us astern ever so slowly. A feeling. Do I tell him a feeling?

"Your ship's heading is falling off, Mr. Charles, twist her to port."

Ten seconds later: "Bridge, Sonar, high speed screw noise dead ahead. We can't detect the range but they're getting louder." Good boys, they'd been listening on passive between pings. I should've thought of that. I hoped it was the XO's decision.

The thick fog absorbed the sound as darkness consumes the light. I couldn't hear the gentle ringing of the bells atop the channel buoys until they were almost abreast the bridge wing. And then they emerged eerily, like specters dancing on the water. *High speed screw noises? A power boat, a yacht?*

"Sound five short blasts, Boatswain's Mate." It was the international signal saying, 'You're standing into danger' or 'I do not understand your movements.'" In this case, both applied.

Five seconds later: "Bridge, fo'c's'le," came a shrill voice from the fog lookout stationed as far forward as possible in the *eyes* of the ship.

"Large power yacht coming in view fine off our starboard bow. She's on the wrong side of the channel, heading right for us."

"Five short blasts, Boatswain's Mate." The ominous, explosive sound shook the powerboat into action, and she veered off to her port, out of the channel, passing down our starboard side by no more than fifty feet. Four men, beer cans in their hands, shook their fists at us. "Assholes!" someone exclaimed, sparing me from expressing the sentiment.

At five knots, with absolute silence on the bridge, we tracked the muted ringing bells on the channel marker buoys. This was dangerously exciting, like mountain climbing or sport parachute jumping. You didn't have to do it but you did it for the thrilling highs it gave you. "Captain, there's no echo return," the JOOD yelled out. I got up and called him over to the nav table.

"Why?" I asked, excusing myself to the quartermaster as I pointed to the chart. He gave me his baffled look again as he stared in silence at the accusing chart. "What causes the echo?"

"The cliffs, sir . . . oh! The cliffs end and there's no echo, which means we were"—he banged his finger on the chart where the cliffs ended just off Shelter Island—"here when the echoes stopped," he announced as if he had just reinvented echo-sounding.

"You got it, but remember that's where we were, not where we are now."

"Quebec Foxtrot, this is Charlie Romeo," the radio cracked out in the silence. "You're fading since you turned easterly, can no longer paint you accurately. Request advise. Over."

"Roger, Quebec Foxtrot, we're okay, thanks for the assist. Out." I filled and lit my pipe, kept my face passive, and sat down in my chair, home free in a dangerous grandstand play.

We came east, leaving Harbor Island to our port side. Visibility increased to one hundred yards as we approached our berthing assignment at the Broadway Pier, which was now, according to the chart, only one thousand yards ahead of us. I asked Mr. Lawrence if he was comfortable with the fire-control radar up there. He said yes. "Okay, change your target to the end of Broadway Pier. Do you have it on your chart? If you have any doubt about acquiring it, stay on the tower."

"We got it, Captain, will switch when ordered," came the confident reply.

"Stand by . . . switch now!" I said matter-of-factly, knowing you could easily lose a target when you're shifting.

"West end of Broadway Pier bearing 098, range seven hundred yards," the director reported in a clipped tone ten seconds later.

"You sure you got the right one, there's four piers there."

"Yes, sir, *Broadway Pier* now bearing 098, range six hundred fifty yards," came the somewhat smart-ass answer. I'd offended their professionalism. Of course they had the right pier.

The fo'c's'le lookout reported the pier dead ahead, and my heartbeat dropped ten percent as my own eyes focused on its beauty. Mr. Charles paced nervously.

"How many landings have you made, Mr. Charles?"

"One, Captain, just one," he replied as if divulging a shameful secret.

"You wanna take 'er in?"

"Sir, it's tricky in this fog . . . maybe next . . ."

"Take her in, Mr. Charles," I said before he could say he didn't want to and degrade himself in my eyes. He squeezed his hands together, each one trying to crush the other. "The wind's dead now, and the current won't affect us as soon as you ease the bow in between the piers," I said, calmly trying to lessen his nervousness. "Hell, Charlie, piece of cake."

He came in dead slow. There were no line handlers. I guess someone figured no sane naval officer would come in through this fog. Lieutenant Ambrose E. Charles, USN, ROTC, put the bow softly against the pier. Boatswain's Mate Chief T. E. Eselun, USN, Chief Master at Arms and First Division Chief Petty Officer, sent two seaman over the side, dropping adroitly to the pier as Mr. Charles held our raked bow steadily against it. Number one line went over. "Moored." He twisted the stern in. Number six line went over, then two and three, four and five.

He looked at me for further orders. I shrugged; he nodded and doubled up all lines, secured the main engines, and secured the sea detail. He turned to me with a warm smile of accomplishment. "Damned fine job, Charlie," I said, walking off the bridge. The XO came up from Sonar. I told him to pass liberty call, then have all the officers assemble in the wardroom as soon as possible. There were some lessons to be learned from our little trip into the harbor.

The fourteen officers came to attention, stopping their laughter, taking on a serious view even though they thought they had done something great, which they had. I took my seat at the head of the table, my mind still having trouble realizing I was the captain of this ship. I told them this wouldn't take long, just a critique of the little drill we just went through.

"First of all," I started, "it wasn't the brightest thing to do. We could have turned when we first entered the fog and under *Jamison's* radar guidance exited the harbor. That is what I should have done. Waiting a couple of hours out there wouldn't have hurt anything, and we'd have been a helluva lot safer."

I made eye contact with each man, hoping each thought my words were meant directly for him. "We did it and everything worked out okay. But the individual actors in this drama didn't do as well as they might have."

Faces dropped as bewildered glances went from one to another. "When we entered the fog and the surface radar went down, the bridge team went catatonic. No one took any actions until I stepped in. It shouldn't have been that way. . . . I don't know if it was because I was new, and you didn't know me, or if you simply haven't had the opportunity in the past to act on your own. It doesn't make any difference.

"It is my fault that I hadn't discussed what I expected of you. My first captain on a destroyer once said if the captain has to do any work, someone's fucking off. A bit of an exaggeration, but essentially true." Every eye was on me. No one smoked. The hum of the friendly ventilation fans grew louder as the officers sat in silence.

"In the future I expect you to act on your own once you've thought out a situation. I expect every one of you to think ten minutes down the road and practice in your mind the action you'd take if something untoward happens. Be creative in what you think can go wrong. And ask me questions." A few gasps joined the hum of the fans.

"Let me explain. Some people think a ship's captain is above all that, that he's so busy he can't be bothered with questions. Bullshit, gentlemen. My first priority on this ship is to keep her in fighting trim. My second is to train you all to become admirals." A few smiles now.

"Keeping the ship battle-ready is easy. The admiral part is tough." I leaned back to let that soak in as I filled and lit my pipe. "When I was an ensign on my second day aboard, my captain told me to take the conn during tactical maneuvers. I was nearly petrified, and when we were coming into formation, I asked the captain how fast we'd slow when I took off our five-knot advantage to slide into station.

"I thought the XO and OPS officer were going to have a fit at the effrontery of an ensign with just two days onboard asking the holy of all holies a question like that.

"My captain smiled at the discomfort of the XO and OPS officer as he told me how many yards we'd coast. I listened and greased that mother right into our slot. That's what I mean; ask. If you don't know, ask.

"I've been around the navy for a long time and, gentlemen, I've done a lot of things and seen a lot of things. I know a lot. Help me with the job of making you admirals by asking questions." Still no one said anything, but at least a few cigarettes lit up.

"When you've got the watch, you've got the duty. Whatever evolution comes up when you've got the watch, you'll handle it. Getting under way, taking us alongside, taking us to station, mooring, coming into berth, whatever.

"And one more thing, a couple of good things happened today. The work of the Mark-56 Director was superb. I'd never heard of it being used for navigation before, and they did an outstanding job. Once those guys locked on the North Island tower the only reason I kept getting posits from *Jamison* was to not hurt her feelings. Well done, Mr. Lawrence, have the leading firecontrolman come to see me, please.

"And, Mr. Draco, you're the ASW officer?"

He answered yes, spilling his coffee in astonishment that I'd addressed him.

"Of Draconian fame?"

The laughter of the wardroom showed this to be an old joke. "A distant relation, sir," he answered with a grin. It wasn't true.

I asked him whose idea was it to go passive between pings. He said his, his face blanching.

"It was a brilliant move and saved our ass from creaming a large yacht. Thank you . . . ah, Dave, isn't it?"

He nodded yes, and I shifted my eyes to a hulking young ensign who weighed about two hundred thirty pounds. "Mr. Rogers, you're the first lieutenant. Great job on number one line. . . . You made it easy for Mr. Charles." Ripples of laughter filled the room. With a pathetic reply, he said it wasn't him; it was Chief Eselun. I asked him if he was in charge, and with a horrible blush he said he was.

"And one more last thing for all of you, when you're exercising your initiative, keep me informed. That's a no-shitter, gentlemen. And when you're on the bridge, tell me early enough when you think something is going to happen so I can be there to take action and not show up just to witness a catastrophe." I leaned my chair back on its rear legs and put my clasped hands behind my head. "Any questions, gentlemen?"

"Just one, Captain." Mr. Draco spoke up hesitantly.

"Yes, Dave?"

"How did you win the Silver Star?"

Laughter. "By going passive on the sonar and keeping my ship from hitting a large power boat," I chuckled. "Now you guys are dismissed. Have a good time in San Diego. We went through a difficult time getting in here, so you might try to enjoy it. The Admiral Kidd club is a great O-club and if I'm not mistaken, the naval station here delivers a car for the CO's use. Take it." Then, turning to the XO, I said, "XO, you and the department heads remain for a few moments, if you would, please." The junior officers left the wardroom laughing and joking.

It was good that they could laugh; life at sea is a bitch, and life at sea in the navy is harder. A good captain will try to replace the stress of dealing with superiors with simply the stress of doing their job. Men can handle that; it's something they can understand, but no one can understand the vagaries of a poor superior officer or petty officer. And especially if it's the captain.

A captain should be like a protecting father, someone to lean on when things get tough, someone to talk to when you need help. It doesn't always work out that way. The captain's power can go to his head. The responsibility can crush him.

Captains can become pompous, truly thinking they are masters under God. This may well have been true in the days of the early, oceangoing vessels, but hardly applicable now with our instant, unfailing communications. I hoped I could handle it.

We waited for a moment while the department heads got coffee. The XO handed me a cup. "Thank you. A few minutes if you would, gentlemen, some minor points." They sat down. Silence. They looked at me, not knowing what to expect. I waved my hand into the air as if it meant something. It meant nothing.

"Mr. Draco in Sonar should have informed the bridge before he went passive. The bridge should always know the status of the sonar search. Take care of that, Mr. Lawrence. And, Mr. Lawrence, we should never put a man over the side, like we did today, for number one line without the bridge giving permission."

He nodded, saying he planned to talk to Chief Eselun about that right after this meeting. I asked why not Mr. Rogers, the first lieutenant.

He flustered in embarrassment and said that Chief Eselun was a most formidable man and tends to intimidate Mr. Rogers, even though Rogers is built like a tank.

"Umm, well, anyway, encourage him to do it, a chief's bark is worst than his bite."

I turned my gaze to the sandy-haired chief engineer. He was a few years older than the rest of the department heads and about three inches taller. It impressed me that he smoked a pipe. "What can I say, Mr. Flanagan? Your boys answered the bells quite smartly. I'm impressed. Maybe we can figure out something a little more exciting for you on the way out." He smiled, twitched, sighed, and glanced at the XO.

Heads up, Mr. Flanagan.

"That's about it; thank you for your time." I rose, tamping the ashes out of my pipe, and turned to the XO. "You and Mr. Charles in my in-port cabin, please." They looked at each other, then at me. I walked out.

The steward brought up coffee. "Thank you, ah . . . Ramirez?"

"Yes, sir, anything else, sir?" I told him no, but that I would be having lunch and dinner aboard today.

"Gentlemen," I addressed the two next senior officers aboard as they sat down. "Let's talk about the surface search radar failure. It is perhaps the most reliable radar in the world when properly maintained. What happened?"

They glanced at each other for support, then back to me. A long ten seconds captured the room before Mr. Charles whimpered that it was a blower motor that had burned out because of a clogged filter in the power supply, which caused a transformer to overheat and melt down. He spoke as if confessing heresy in front of a fearful inquisition, his words barely audible, his head hanging low.

I asked him who was in charge of the PMS, the Planned Maintenance System, for the radar. It was he, and though I was angry at the failure, my tone level remained low.

The shamefaced ops officer answered that he was responsible, his eyes searching the rug for some tiny spirit to save him.

Then, turning to my second-in-command, I asked him who is in charge of the PMS program for the radars. He answered that he was. The correct answer. I gave him a begrudging credit and asked when was the last time he reviewed the equipment booklets for the electronics equipment.

He whined that he'd been really busy, what with just getting back from WESTPAC and the change of command ceremony and everything. The answer wasn't good enough, and I asked him when was the last time he reviewed the equipment booklets. His answer should have been last week. He said six months ago.

I turned to Mr. Charles, said thank-you, and dismissed him with a scowl as he scurried out the door.

"Planned Maintenance System"

"You disappoint me, XO, don't you realize the importance of the PMS program?"

Yes, came his sheepish reply, and he whined that he had no excuse, and it was his fault.

"Don't hand me that mea culpa shit, XO," I snapped. I felt my eyes narrow and, heard my voice going lower. "Let's get the radar fixed, that's the important thing, isn't it?"

Silence.

"Have you supervised any PMS documentation at all?" My question came out like an accusation. His face blanched as he confessed that he rarely did it, that he was very busy. At least he was being honest. "The department heads normally take care of those details," he said.

I wanted to tell him this was the exact reason the navy put the XOs in charge of the program, but I didn't, my goal being to establish a good relationship with him . . . needed to, he was my right hand, the taker-carer of a thousand things.

I asked him if he thought the surface radar would have failed today if proper PMS had been performed. He answered that it probably would not have. I told him softly that he put my ass on the line today. He whimpered, "Sorry."

I asked in a soft conversational tone if many breakdowns occur, was this just an isolated incident, or was it simply something that slipped through the crack. He answered he'd investigate, his manner showing more bravado than he probably felt. I felt like punching him. *The guy's weak.* I didn't like weakness in my officers and detested it even more in myself.

He sat there silently as I thought of the PMS program. The fleet didn't have a common policy, and the ships were going to hell. Each ship had a program of sorts, varying from none to outstanding, depending on the importance the various officers and petty officers put on it. Mostly, there was none.

The planned maintenance system is a simple program that works. The petty officers check the equipment for filters, greasing, cleaning, and tolerance specifications as the equipment book outlines for them. Then they initial it, the dailies, the weeklies, the monthlies, et cetera. The division officers verify the work is done properly, then the department heads view it and the XO oversees it, often checking the basic work itself.

The XO is the PMS Officer, because the navy thinks it takes an XO's horsepower to ensure compliance. Every filter, every grease fitting, every watertight door gasket, everything, absolutely everything, is under the XO's supervision.

As we sat there, woeful looks of pleading alternating with abject fear clawed their way across his pathetic face. I waited, too angry to let up, although ashamed for my use of brute mental force against him.

"Do you understand the program, XO?"

He didn't answer, which angered me more as he sat there, rubbing his hands together, darting his eyes to every rivet in the cabin's bulkheads.

"XO, I want to see all the PMS books for the electronics division right away before some sharpie gundecks the entries." A cheap shot, I shouldn't have said that.

"Yes, sir, right away. No gundecking, sir," he answered tentatively, standing to leave. I nodded. He bolted out the door.

Gundecking, falsifying official records—it was an old British naval term stemming from the sailing ship days when midshipmen, who lived aft on the gundeck, filled out their educational journals on the gundeck by talking to each other instead of touring the ship and learning it themselves as they should have done.

Just seven days aboard and I'd taken the conn away from him and already had a piece of his ass. Was I being too chickenshit? No! Damn him, damn him! His sloppy ship handling could easily be forgiven, but the PMS program was essential; ships that did it well succeeded and ships that didn't failed. *Cambridge* will not fail. I will not fail!

Waiting for him to return, I reflected on my ascension from executive officer to commanding officer. I had no problems with PG school, it had the same requirements as before: maintain a B average, and life was easy. The same social whirl of naval officers relaxing on their educational sabbaticals prevailed as we drank and caroused and socialized and maintained B averages.

At the transportation school in Oakland, California, I was surrounded by staff officers. They proved, on the main, a stodgy lot. They thought differently from line officers. Whereas we thought problem-solution-action, staff officers usually thought only problem, solution. The action part separated the staffies from the operators. Swift, decisive action hallmarked the line officer—it had to, that's how we survived.

I had to complete the school to get my master's in transportation management. Unfortunately, I hadn't known the Military Sealift Command, the MSC, sponsored the school, and for payback demanded a two- to three-year tour in the MSC, their pound of flesh.

The MSC is considered death row for a line officer; it was a staff officer's staff billet. In panic I called my detailer in BUPERS. He told me not to worry; they had better plans for me.

"What?" I whispered like a child questioning Santa Claus. He laughed, asking me what I had been putting on my duty preference card, my dream sheet, every year for the last ten.

"Command!"

"Maybe it'll happen," he hinted, his voice low.

I nearly dropped the phone. "You mean I've been selected for command of a destroyer?" I looked around for a chair. My knees needed help supporting the rest of my body.

"Whoa, Commander. Didn't say that, but keep your nose clean. Feel better now?"

"Yes, sir," I answered, fighting to keep hope from replacing reality.

Transportation school had been easy, and the workload was ridiculously simple compared to PG school. Four weeks before graduation, my orders came: Commanding officer of the USS *Cambridge,* a destroyer home-ported at Treasure Island, San Francisco, my favorite city, and to top it off, she had just returned from a WESTPAC tour. I would not have to go back there for a while. *Captain of my own ship, San Francisco. No deploying for a while. Could it be any better?*

I read my worn copy of *How to Handle a Destroyer* every night, read every book in the library on destroyer operations, and read meteorology books, oceanography books, engineering books. I read sea adventures and biographies of famous sailors. Everything, anything. I would be ready, and prayed only that *Cambridge* had a competent navigator.

It would be four weeks before I went to Prospective Commanding Officer School in Newport, Rhode Island—four weeks there, and then come back and take command. In the evenings, driving back to my BOQ room on Treasure Island from Oakland, I'd drive by her and just stare. God, she was beautiful.

My interest waned in transportation, and my thesis was a piece of junk: *The Commercial Aspects of the Amazon River,* a truly nonrigorous study, highly influenced by old copies of *National Geographic* and a large-scale map of the Amazon River. They took pity on an old sea dog, and with reservation accepted it. They'd never had a destroyer skipper as a student before.

As senior officer in the class, I was required to make a speech about how wonderful the school was. They gave me previous speeches to pattern mine after. It didn't come out as they had hoped. I spoke on responsibility for the overall task, and that the operator's mission is supreme. I pleaded for their understanding and begged them to fight their urge to have the staff tail wag the operational dog. It hadn't gone over well.

As I waited now in my in-port cabin on *Cambridge,* four minutes passed before a weak knock sounded on my door. I opened it to the harried lieutenant commander I called XO. He placed fifty to sixty letter-envelope-sized PMS performance booklets on my desk. I thanked him, and he replied with a weak smile as he backed out of my cabin like a beaten slave. I spent the next couple of hours minutely studying them, appalled at their incompleteness. I picked up the phone to the quarterdeck and asked if Mr. Charles was aboard.

A crisply efficient voice immediately answered yes, sir. I asked the voice to locate him and give him my regards, and ask him to join me in my in-port cabin. Then I asked his name. First Class Firecontrolman Kaplan, came the reply. I told him to come up and see me.

In forty-two seconds Kaplan appeared. I shook his hand, saying he did a fine job getting us fixes this morning. "You saved my ass, and I just wanted to tell you so. Thank you."

"Yes, sir, Mr. Lawrence said he would bring me up to see you. I appreciate it, Captain," he beamed, turning to leave.

I stopped him halfway out the door. "Petty Officer Kaplan, do your men do all the required PMS on the firecontrol gear?"

He looked at me as if I asked him if he liked young boys. "Why, of course we perform PMS, Captain. Of course, sir," he answered, insulted. "That's what we were doing this morning, Captain, don't you remember, sir?"

"Of course. Just asking, Petty Officer Kaplan, just asking. The performance of your director was superb." He said thank you, smiled, and left.

Mr. Charles knocked on the open door. I stood and shoved the booklets toward him. "Next Friday at ten o'clock, Mr. Charles, we'll look again." He mumbled thank you, blinked through the sweat on his face, and slunk away.

I paced in my small cabin, all my instincts telling me I'd handled that poorly. Using sheer power proved only that you had it. It worked only in the short run, and in the main it was wholly ineffective. Leadership was not a slash of the whip; it was a gentle touch of a feather convincing a man what had to be done and showing him how to do it. I'd blown it. I was shamed, degraded in my own mind. And I thought being a captain was going to be easy.

I went out to the 0-1 level a few feet down the passageway from my cabin door. Maybe a turn about the ship and fresh air would calm me.

Chief Boatswain's Mate Eselun stood on the fo'c's'le, peering over the edge at his men standing on a staging rigged from the main deck. Their paint rollers moved rhythmically, putting a cosmetic coat of haze gray over the huge gouges we took when getting under way from San Francisco.

"*Cambridge* Arriving"

Watching, my mind went back to seven days ago. I'd called the quarterdeck to let them know I would be reporting aboard at 0900. I figured this a small courtesy, I didn't want them flustering about by a new captain's surprise arrival. That would be rude.

Captain O'Brian waited on the quarterdeck of his immaculate ship and shook my hand. Over the next three days we chatted and inspected and told sea stories. I didn't deem it necessary to get under way to observe the ship at sea; it would be a bother to the crew, and it didn't matter anyway. We waltzed through the change of command ceremony, and he left, a lump in his throat.

Cambridge was different from the other destroyers I'd served on. She'd been reconfigured as a test class to fire homing torpedoes out the sides of her superstructure. It hadn't worked, and they were taken off.

Unfortunately, in the conversion she'd lost her after gun mount, Mount 52, and that had not been replaced. The upside: She was lighter by one five-inch gun mount and its ammunition; consequently, faster and more fuel efficient. The engineering plant was exactly the same as all other destroyers, and we were a knot and a half faster than any of them in the Pacific Fleet, and we could steam longer without refueling.

My cursory inspections showed Captain O'Brian ran a good ship, borne out by high crew morale and the ship's smart appearance. We didn't really have time, nor was it necessary, to go over all the records. It wouldn't have made any difference anyway, because a relieving captain who pointed out derogatory issues violated the brotherhood of command and that was just not done.

Captain O'Brian left with all items marked satisfactory. Squadron or division commanders, the commodores, usually knew the condition of their ships. A relieving skipper did not have to point them out, thereby embarrassing the commodore for not taking previous action. If something was bad, you fixed it; you didn't bring official attention to it. All in good time, anything bad or questionable would surface.

It was noted, however, that the ship had ample amounts left in her operating funds, the money used to pay for consumables other than food and fuel. It was called the operational target, the OPTAR, her target to stay within her budget. I found that odd but didn't comment. Ships were usually strapped for money.

Well, that part was all behind me now as I stood there in San Diego on the 0-1 level, on a beautiful Saturday afternoon, watching the chief boatswain's mate supervising painting the bow.

I recalled my trepidation when the ops officer had told me after I assumed command that we were due to get under way Thursday morning, only five days away. Panic had marched through me like Sherman to the sea as I realized there would be no captain aboard but me. And what did I know about being a captain anyway? I was one in name only. Real captains have been to sea with their ships.

Thursday came up mighty fast, and I remembered the morning as the first stabs of light punched the graying sky over the Oakland hills. A graceful sea gull glided low over the bridge. Heavy cartons of last-minute frozen stores made their way up the angled gangway on the shoulders of grunting sailors. Engineers snaked in huge hoses that had fed us steam from the beach. Thick electric cables, the size of an upper arm, were being pulled aboard by sweating electricians as the wire's weight fought them, begrudging them every inch.

Activity permeated the ship like a carnival breaking location. Each of the men did their job to the goal of shedding off the land for the cool purpose of the sea.

At the foot of the gangway, a young mother, shoulders slumped in sadness, held her daughter's hand as her petty officer husband stood at the top of the gangway, waving. His hand moved slowly in front of him at chest level, back and forth. The little girl cried. The woman dried her eyes with a small handkerchief as she took another look and slowly walked away.

On the pier aft, by the fantail, three other women, older, stood laughing, giggling, as they periodically waved to some loved one aboard.

Deck sailors in paint-spattered dungarees unfrapped mooring lines, triple strands of nylon the size of their wrists, while they cursed the engineers for sooting their decks from boilers too long idle. Last-minute mail sacks in their tattered gray canvas bags were handed off to the line-handling party assigned from the naval station.

"Now hear this, now hear this, set the special sea and anchor detail. The officer of the deck is shifting his watch to the bridge," boomed the 1MC into the placid morning air. Light gray, broken clouds formed to the south, the rising sun glazing their edges in golden hues and occasionally breaking through to kiss the water with a shaft of brilliant light.

The bridge team gathered, breaking out sound-powered phones, testing radio circuits, handing out binoculars, lining up the steering system. The quartermasters laid out their charts with the care of a mother laying out clothing for her child's first day at school. They sharpened pencils. They tested the pelorus and the gyro compass repeaters on the wings of the bridge and in the pilothouse. They tested the alarm circuits, the phone circuits, the lighting.

On the fo'c's'le, boatswain's mates clanged sledgehammers against the anchor chain stops, preparing the anchor for an emergency drop at a moment's notice.

The purposed hum of activity, the murmurs on the bridge, the throaty rumble of the engineering plant, the soothing hiss of vent blowers, all combined to awaken my stiletto-hulled destroyer to shed the surly bounds of land. We were ready.

It had been easy to be a captain sitting at the head of the ward-room table with your every word doted upon. Quite another thing getting under way and taking the ship to sea. This was my critical test, with all hands grading.

The tide and wind conditions combined to make this a simple un-mooring, a simple under way. As a courtesy, I asked the XO if he wanted to take her out. He hesitated, but said yes. What else could he say.

"All department heads except engineering report manned and ready for getting under way, sir," came the familiar report from the sound-powered phone talker to the OOD, who turned and reported it to me. Intuitively, my eyes swept the pilothouse for the captain. He should be up there. He wasn't. I was. *I am the captain.*

"Very well," I replied in what I hoped was the stoic tone custom demanded in answering formatted reports.

"Request permission to test main engines, Captain?" came as more of a statement than a question. I nodded yes, trying not to speak as my heart beat faster and sweat dampened my underarms as this nearly last link in the preparations for getting under way pushed against my eroding self-confidence.

"Engines test satisfactorily, Mr. Charles, ready to answer all bells," the sound-powered phone talker said, adding: "Engineering de-partment reports ready for getting under way, ready to answer all bells."

Mr. Charles, the OPS officer, acknowledged, passing the infor-mation to me as if I hadn't been listening. This redundancy was nec-essary to ensure the captain understood what was going on. Being present didn't always mean the captain was paying attention. Cap-tains, supposedly, had many things on their minds. All I had was ap-prehension and the hope that I wouldn't screw up.

"Very well, what's the tide doing, Mr. Charles?"

"Coming on max flood, Cap'n."

I, of course, knew this already, but it didn't hurt to ensure the

OOD did too. The XO appeared on the bridge freshly shaven, wearing clean, pressed khakis.

"Good morning, Captain," he reported. "Ship is ready in all respects for getting under way." The XO knew this from personal inspections and by talking to the department heads.

"Very well, thank you, XO, take her out," I said with a glance down the starboard length of the ship, the moored side.

"Take in all lines but number two," the XO ordered, and turning to the lee helm, said, "Main Control, stand by to answer all bells."

The bridge silenced itself as the action transferred to the scurrying deck force. *Why is he taking in all lines but number two? Number one is the logical one to leave over. I won't question it.*

The radar repeaters on the bridge etched their orange-yellow map of the bay. The cone-shaped light shields hadn't been put in position yet.

Even though I'd been through this hundreds of times, there had always been a captain I could turn to to save the day. He'd always been there, ready to pull my ass out of trouble. Waves of uncertainty splashed against the shore of my courage, eating it away, carrying it off to some never-never land, leaving me naked, exposed to the world.

We were moored on the east side, the back side, of Treasure Island in the middle of San Francisco Bay, almost under the Bay Bridge that connected San Francisco to Oakland. Since we were moored on the southern side of the pier and the tide was coming on max flood, all the XO had to do was let the tide push the stern out while holding number one line fast.

Then, with the stern pointing fair, take in number one and back down hard and let the flowing current push the stern down-tide as we cleared the dock area between our pier and the one a hundred feet to the south. This would leave us in a perfect position to go ahead standard and steam around Treasure Island and head for the Golden Gate Bridge and out to the sea.

The XO didn't wait for the tide to do its work, and as he tried to twist, he didn't do it boldly enough to be effective. Number two line hindered more than helped him, and thank God he let it go in time. To compound all this, he didn't back hard enough, and the ship scraped her bow along the pier face threatening to dig our anchor into the pilings.

I desperately contained myself, hoping he would correct. I worried about ripping out the pilings as well as the steam and electrical shore power fittings that ran down the pier face. "Back 'er down harder, XO," I whispered to him as he mutely watched the disaster taking shape.

Ten horrible seconds passed as I waited for him to take action. "Do something, XO, back 'er down harder," I said, now in a louder voice. He did nothing but stare at the bow raking itself painfully against the pilings. Another five seconds passed. *Shit!* I shouted, "This is the XO, no, no, belay that, this is the captain, I'VE GOT THE CONN! Tell Main Control to stand by for hard maneuvering bells . . . left full rudder. Starboard engine ahead full. Port engine back full."

I was home again and in command. I twisted the bow hard to port, away from the pier, without getting any headway on. I hoped the tide would push us out faster. I couldn't leave the ahead full bell on for very long or the bow would jam headlong into the pier. The screeching stopped and ever so slowly the bow twisted away from the insidious pier face that waited to be destroyed, waited to destroy us.

"Starboard engine back full, all engines back full," I ordered just before we gained headway. "Rudder midships." And we eased handsomely clear of the pier and into the bay.

"All engines ahead standard. Right standard rudder. Steer course three five zero." We were clear of the pier and heading fair.

I waited for several minutes, then called over the XO and told him to take the conn. He had to save face.

Ten seconds passed, then, finally, a less than enthusiastic voice came from my embarrassed second in command. "This, this is the XO, I, I have the ah, conn."

I didn't want this to happen; why didn't he react to my whispered suggestion? What an ignoble way to begin my relationship with my executive officer.

That too was behind me now, and the San Diego sun eased away my anger as I strolled forward to fo'c's'le on this now cloudless Saturday afternoon. "Good afternoon, Bosun." I said, walking up next to him. He acted surprised to see me, though I knew he saw me walking forward toward him. *Crafty bastard.*

He snapped to attention and saluted, saying good afternoon, and his smile filled his handsome young face. His immaculate khakis fit his muscular frame so well they seemed tailored. His unauthorized dark-brown leather aviation-issue flight jacket with the fur collar bore a gold-embossed, sewn-on leather name tag reading: BMC T. E. ESELUN, USN.

I looked over the side at the three seamen painting over the gouges and told them I was sorry for having caused the scrapes and sorry they had to paint them on a Saturday. They looked up at me from their paint rollers and smiled, but not too convincingly. I hadn't given the order to paint during holiday routine and wondered who did. The scrapes weren't that bad and could have waited until we got back to San Francisco.

I glanced at the side plating; it was only an inch thick, and I was concerned it might have been holed. The report had been no damage when the incident occurred, but I liked to make sure.

The chief bosun's mate gave me a half-smile and said, "Way I understand it, Cap'n, you saved us from a lot more damage."

And with an equal half-smile I told him it was just a rumor. "And, ah, Captain," he said, "I apologize for putting men over the side this morning without the bridge's permission. It was a foolish thing to do. It won't happen again. Yes, sir, Mr. Rogers had a piece of my ass about that," he replied as if he were serious.

"I'm sure he did, Bosun's Mate, I'm sure he did."

A third class came up carrying two cans of paint. He didn't seem to know what he should do about saluting with both his hands full. To help, Chief Eselun took the cans from him. The man snapped to attention, saluting, saying his name was Stone. "My name's Sheppard," I said, returning his salute and offering my hand.

I asked the chief to take a stroll with me. As we walked slowly aft, I unobtrusively inspected the watertight door gaskets, the fire hoses, the deck fittings, and the lifelines. "Our PMS is up-to-date, Cap'n," he said conversationally as if he weren't noticing my actions. "We got the message, Skipper."

I stopped and touched his shoulder, telling him that the appearance of the ship was the finest I'd ever seen, and that it was obvious that one fine chief petty officer runs first division. He flustered over the compliment.

We stopped at the quarterdeck for a second while the bosun's mate introduced me to Chief Petty Officer Samuel P. Whittlers, the OOD and leading sonarman. His dark-skinned face beamed as he answered my question on how good his ears were. "Finest in the fleet, sir." Every sonarman's ears were the finest in the fleet.

We paused on the fantail as I inspected the perfectly made up and new white-nylon mooring lines. "Very nice, Bosun's Mate, and I noticed in the bosun's locker all the lines were new. No old ones around." He flustered again, telling me he liked to keep up on things.

We continued up the port side, stopping at the open paint locker. I shook my head; the paint lockers were full of paint. A rare sight on cash-poor destroyers. I looked at him. He grinned and turned away.

I asked him who ordered the gouges painted out. He looked surprised and told me smoothly that he did, as if he had the authority to work the men during holiday routine. That call should have to come from the XO. He knew that. He shook his head. I understood and dropped the subject.

We passed the open door to the mess decks. Whatever was cooking in there smelled great. The bosun pointed to a closed wood-grained door. "We understand you're a mustang, Captain, would you like a cup of coffee in the chief's mess?"

In the chief's mess, soft, upholstered arm-chairs filled the spaces around their green-felt-covered mess table. Fake mahogany paneling hid the myriad cables and pipes that passed everywhere throughout the ship. The soft light of floor lamps cast a glow on the tasteful landscape paintings. The plush carpet looked a little worn at the door, but its dark blue color hid it well.

No one was there except the chief's mess cook, who immediately brought coffee. Every seaman had to be a mess cook at some time or other, and being the chief's mess cook was the best deal going because the chiefs pitched in and gave him money for good service every month. It beat being a regular mess cook, listening to the bitching of his ship mates three times a day.

Several unauthorized dark-brown leather aviation-issue flight jackets with fur collars and gold-embossed leather name tags on each hung from pegs on the bulkhead. I rubbed my hand over the supple leather, saying I'd wager there were several more of these hanging in officers' country. He didn't take the bet, his sparkling eyes hinting conspiracy. I took a sip of coffee and accepted a cigar from an ornate box the chief offered.

As I held it, I mentioned I was once an aircrewman, and had a jacket like those, but no captain I'd ever had on destroyers would let me wear it. "Unauthorized for nonflying personnel, you know," I said with a grin.

"Gee, Captain, didn't know that. Reckon I just don't understand all that officer stuff," he answered in mock surprise, throwing his hands into the air.

I rolled the five-inch black cigar through my fingers and sniffed its aroma. A good cigar. Chief Eselun handed me a silver end-cutter. Neither of us spoke. I snipped the end off the cigar and reached for my lighter. The chief offered his, a stainless steel Zippo. I took it, holding it in my hand, admiring it. I was two years old in 1932 when it was invented by a machinist named George Blaisdell, perhaps the finest piece of machinery ever invented. I thumbed it to life.

The chief's eyes never left mine as I lit the cigar and took a deep puff, letting the heady smoke meander out of my nostrils into a slight airstream and disappear into a wood-disguised vent. His eyes didn't blink, not even once, since we'd come into chief's quarters. After my next puff, I said, glancing around the room as if studying it, "I'll bet if a ship had a real sharp chief, he'd have a buddy over at the naval air station, Alameda Supply Center, who'd issue flight jackets to him if he had a proper requisition."

He looked at me with the innocence of a child. "I guess that could happen, but probably no ship's captain would ever let us wear them," he answered, affecting a pout.

I tipped the gray ash into a cut-off brass five-inch shell-casing ashtray. "Well, I tell you what I'd probably do, Bosun, if everybody had one, of course—" I paused, looking directly at him to let him know I knew that he was conning me. "What I'd do is have a man who the captain respected wear one and see if the captain said anything about it." The bosun sat there with a grin, knowing he'd succeeded.

I acknowledged his victory with a smile, but inside I fumed. The XO should have approached me on this, not the chief boatswain's mate.

"Gosh, Captain, that sounds like it just might work."

"It's a shame I don't have mine with me," I said.

"I'd say you wore a forty-six long."

"That's pretty close, Bosun. And you know what? I'll bet, if there were any extras, this real sharp chief could trade some of these unauthorized dark-brown leather aviation-issue flight jackets with the fur collars to the civilians in the supply center here for what, oh, say . . . new nylon mooring lines and paint and whatever else the ship needed. That'd sure make the ship's OPTAR and the chief look mighty good."

"No? What a good idea, Captain."

Chapter 8

San Diego Sea Detail

Monday morning, 0825: Under way, twenty-five minutes late. Lieutenant Pat Lawrence, the WEPS officer, twisted our stern out smartly, and when clear of the freighter behind, backed down two-thirds until he cleared the dock area. He kicked his engines ahead two-thirds to take off his stern way, twisted to port to line up with the channel, and came to all stop. We waited for a break in the channel traffic, waited for an opportunity to bolt ahead like a motorist waiting to race onto the freeway.

It was one thing to be under way with way on, that is, moving so you had control, but quite another to have to maintain position more or less stationary. It was difficult, and I thanked God for the mild winds and slack tide. I paced the bridge, hoping my nervousness didn't show. The unsure mood of a captain could contaminate the ship. I once more wished I hadn't had to take the conn away from the XO leaving San Francisco, and I regretted the unfortunate matter of the PMS failure. *I must rebuild my confidence in him. But how, he's already made too many errors.*

Ship after ship steamed by us, and since *Cambridge* was so junior, that is, her captain was so junior, we continually had to render honors to the passing ships. The book all ships carried listing who was in command of which ship still showed Commander O'Brian as captain, but that didn't help much, he was also very junior to most other destroyer COs.

The wind freshened a bit. I reproved myself for not waiting to get under way. I knew these Monday morning rushes occurred, and I should have waited.

I hated San Diego for this very reason, too many ships, too small a channel. All an enemy would have to do was sink a merchie off Ballast Point, which was the narrowest part of the channel, and all the carriers and cruisers, the destroyers, and submarines and the replenishment ships would be bottled up, easy to destroy. Even a simple thing like blowing the Coronado Bridge, which could be done by any simple-minded saboteur, would put the destroyers out of action.

Why not homeport more ships at Long Beach with its many piers and easy access to the sea, or even San Francisco; though at San Francisco, the Golden Gate Bridge is vulnerable to destruction, blocking the carriers homeported at Alameda. Several replenishment ships worked out of San Francisco, but there were only two destroyers, *Jamison* and us. North, about forty miles from the Golden Gate Bridge, several submarines called the Mare Island Naval Station home. They would fall easy prey to a blown San Rafael–Richmond Bridge.

These thoughts crowded my mind as I waited for some good-hearted skipper to let me enter the string. The wind picked up, and Lieutenant Lawrence maneuvered more and more to maintain our position. A steady stream of engine orders, bells, were fed down to Main Control, and the helm was in almost constant movement. Ships were meant to go forward, not sideways. Lieutenant Lawrence's sweat-beaded face gave no evidence of the pressure he must be feeling. The XO fed us continuous position reports. We knew where we were, and I didn't need his squeaky voice to tell me. "Don't call out the fixes, XO, we know where we are." *Damn, I just put him down again.*

I mulled over whether I should drop the anchor or not. The chart showed no underwater cables, but one couldn't be sure. If we snagged one of them, the navy would be awfully unhappy with me.

Questions would be asked on why I got under way twenty-five minutes late thereby guaranteeing a busy channel ahead of me. Since I was late anyway, why didn't I wait until the channel cleared? Why didn't I go back and moor? Didn't I, as an experienced naval officer, know the Monday morning conditions of San Diego Bay?

Couldn't I have handled my ship a little more skillfully? What had I instructed the skipper of *Jamison* to do since I was three days senior and thus also responsible for him? Why didn't I show more initiative on making my way into the departing vessels? Did I get on the radio and ask an approaching ship to let me in? *No.* I gave no instructions to Mr. Lawrence, he knew what he was doing. I couldn't have done it any better.

A lull. Lieutenant Lawrence looked at me, it was 0931. I nodded toward the channel. He smiled, ordering, "All engines ahead two-thirds, left standard rudder." And we swiftly eased into the line. Nine minutes later *Jamison* joined in two ships behind us.

The XO started singing out courses and times to turn. Lieutenant Lawrence dutifully obeyed as if he were a talking robot. I walked over to him, standing at the midships pelorus, the gyrocompass repeaters mounted inside the pilothouse and on the bridge wings. "Pat, do you really need all those recommendations?"

He looked at me, screwing up his eyes. "No, sir, but we always get them, and we have to follow them," he answered, not really understanding the question.

"You've just done a magnificent job holding us stationary for over an hour. I don't think you need any more recommendations," I said, placing a clipboard over the pelorus so he couldn't see what course he was steering.

"Just like a powerboat, Pat, steer her out. XO, knock off the recommendations."

"But, sir, I'm supposed to give recommendations," he answered. "Trust me, XO."

I recalled the first and only time I'd done this just after coming back from Engineering Officers School, and I made that ignobly poor landing at the fueling piers. What a difference, now as I sit here just like I know what I'm doing in my brand-new unauthorized, dark-brown leather aviation-issue flight jacket with the fur collar, size forty-six long.

That little show of steaming in here in the fog was a pure grand-stand play, and I berated myself for doing it just to impress my crew. I didn't have to impress them. I was the captain, master under God. They should be trying to impress me. I wondered why I wasn't doing this by the book. What if something happens, and they find out I wasn't using the navigation team but doing it by the seat of my pants—well, Lieutenant Lawrence's pants.

The soft stream of helm orders sounded great to my ear as I watched Lieutenant Lawrence steam out of the harbor on his own like a real sailor. Quartermaster Third Class Eric Von Lehman, USN, the helmsman, a young man in starched dungarees with a marine corps crew cut and a hard-chiseled face, accepted the orders easily and moved smartly to obey them. If Hollywood were casting him, he'd be playing the part of a Nazi storm trooper. He seemed to anticipate the rudder commands and was ready before they were given.

My confidence slipped back into my body like the sun lighting the earth after a storm. I glanced around to see the XO standing by the chart table, seemingly dumbfounded as he stared ahead with his arms folded across his chest instead of paying attention to his navigational responsibilities. "XO, keep taking fixes. I just said don't give recommendations." *Why is he idle when he should be hyper-alert, covering my ass?* He jumped as if I'd punched him in the ribs, his face confused as he twisted his body to the nav table, his eyes still on me.

The day and a half spent in San Diego allowed me to catch up on my sleep. On the night steam down from San Francisco, with an affected air of nonchalance and to impress the crew with my confidence in them, I went to bed early, but didn't sleep much, worrying if the OOD would call me before he smashed into something. It was stupid, but new captains, like new mothers, worry about their babies and things that can hurt them. I was just trying to show *my* boys how cool I was.

Most new captains, in the buoyant flush of their first command, often stayed awake much too long, thus robbing themselves of sleep; and when they were needed, their thinking was impaired.

We'd been told in Prospective Commanding Officers School that most new skippers got only about four hours sleep a night and only fitful catnaps during the day. I mused on the month-long school I had just graduated from. It was the most comprehensive and intense naval school I had ever attended, and it covered subjects from ship handling to consular duties we must perform in a foreign port if no U.S. legation were on hand and Americans were in trouble.

In a rush of bravado I called Lieutenant Lawrence over and said in a raised voice, "Let Petty Officer Von Lehman steer her out by himself. Von Lehman, can you handle that?"

"Of course, sir," his high Germanic tone answered as if I had insulted him. I expected his right arm to shoot up and for him to shout, "Sieg heil."

"This is Lieutenant Lawrence, the helmsman's . . . ah? . . . the helmsman's . . . ah?" Lieutenant Lawrence stumbled with the words; there was no standard announcement for this situation.

"Steering the ship," I said.

"Steering the ship," Lieutenant Lawrence added and stood to one side so Von Lehman could see out the pilothouse window midships. "Add three turns," Lieutenant Lawrence ordered to the lee helm as if trying to maintain some communications with the conn. This was new to them and something I'd always wanted to do myself, and Eric Von Lehman did it beautifully. Willie the Navigator, the first class quartermaster on *Kramer* when I was the XO, would be proud of me.

With no shouting of commands and recommendations, the bridge grew pleasantly silent, and in celebration of it, all words were whispered. A goodness started at my fingertips. Then a tingle, a warm tingle like an old friend extending his hand. We passed the southern end of Shelter Island. I could see Ballast Point ahead of us about a mile and a half. It stuck out from the Point Loma peninsula like the land giving us the finger.

Jet fighters started roaring off the runway from the naval air station, the flame and noise of their afterburners obliterating the bridge's tranquillity. Transport planes and helos joined the din. Ahead I saw submarines backing out of their berths at the sub tender moored at the concrete piers. *Would they give us services?*

"Mr. Charles." I turned and spoke to the OOD. Mr. Lawrence just had the conn, not the deck. "General Quarters, if you please. Pass to the fo'c's'le to have the bosun's mate stay there with three of his men in case I have to let the anchor go."

"But, Captain, we're at sea detail!" both Lieutenant Charles and the XO blurted out as if I'd turned insane.

"Boatswain's Mate, sound general quarters," I snapped, circumventing their objections.

He instantly depressed the 1MC switch and announced, "This is a drill. This is a drill. General quarters, general quarters. All hands man your battle stations. Up and forward on the starboard side and down and aft on the port side. Now general quarters."

A confused rush of men ran to their GQ stations, perplexed by general quarters at sea detail. I put my binoculars on Chief Eselun on the fo'c's'le, seeing his nod and sly smile of understanding. As trousers were tucked into socks and bulky cork life preservers were donned and gray helmets passed out, I kept a sharp eye on Von Lehman and the narrow outbound channel around us.

Mr. Charles yelled out he was the OOD and had the conn and for Von Lehman to belay steering on his own. A seaman I didn't know relieved him at the helm. Mount 51, our only gun mount, swung menacingly back and forth. The dull pitch of the director overhead showed it manned and testing.

Mr. Lawrence, now in his role as weapons control officer, stood next to me wearing his sound-powered phones to the gunnery spaces and asked timidly, "Instructions, Captain?"

"Track those aircraft taking off from North Island for a start, and when we get out a little farther, we'll track some ships—there's enough of 'em around."

"Sir," the helmet-bedecked general ship's talker said. "The fo'c's'le wants to talk to you, sir."

The bosun's mate's voice reported to me that the after lookout station was manned and ready. We didn't have an after lookout at general quarters, but we certainly needed one at sea detail in a narrow channel. I'd forgotten but the chief remembered. God bless him. "Very well, Bosun's Mate, but in the future please have him report on a more timely basis," I lightheartedly chided.

"Yes, sir. Sorry, sir," he answered, throwing me a salute from the fo'c's'le. I brought my hand to my helmet. He smiled. *Damn, this is fun.*

"Combat, Captain here, set a solution to shore-bombard the San Diego International Airport. On the double. Lemme know when you're ready to fire. Move it. Fire control, you copy?" Mr. Lawrence, standing next to me, acknowledged my statements and shifted his director to track commercial aircraft departing the airport.

"Mr. Charles," I ordered. "Report to Damage Control Central, we have two wounded men up here, and they're to be evacuated immediately. Tell them the starboard shaft alley is holed and flooding rapidly. Provide!"

In three minutes three men and the corpsman were on the bridge, bending over two giggling seamen lying on the deck. "Get 'em out of here," I demanded. "In the stretchers."

"Sir," the corpsman complained. "We didn't bring any."

I glared at him. "I said provide." Two of the damage control party sailors rushed out of the pilothouse.

"Bridge, Combat, we have a solution on the airport, but the guns are masked on this heading." *Shit, I should have realized that.*

"Shift target to the Coronado City Hall. Hurry or we'll mask the guns again. Hurry!"

The mount slewed around to the south. Ballast Point passed down our starboard side. I picked up the phone to the fo'c's'le. "Bosun's Mate?"

"Yes, sir?" came the reply as I saw the talker lean toward him so he could use the mouthpiece.

"Bosun's Mate, be extra alert. Right now I'm going to dump a boiler. I may need that little hook of yours." I knew that the other talkers could hear this, and they'd instantly pass it to Main Control. *That's okay . . . a little warning, a little teamwork would help them.*

"Aye, aye, sir" was his overly respectful reply. We were still in the channel, but the sides had opened up and it was much wider now that we'd passed Ballast Point.

"Solution. Request permission to simulate fire, Captain," Mr. Lawrence reported.

"Guns free!" I replied.

"Commence fire," he said in simulation over his phones.

I keyed the 21MC to Combat. "XO, come up here, please."

"Yes, sir," he said, out of breath, standing by my side in ten seconds.

"XO, go down to Number One Fire Room and have them declare a water out of sight casualty as soon as you can—right now. Tell 'em to wrap up the boiler." He stared at me for a second, then scanned his eyes at our position in the harbor. He quickly covered his frown with a drab, forced smile. I scowled.

"Aye, aye, sir." He spun around, heading aft. *I wonder if he knows where Number One Fire Room is.*

Mr. Lawrence reported ten rounds expended, no casualties before the guns were masked.

"Target destroyed," he cherubically reported as two stretchers appeared in the pilothouse, and the actors stopped giggling as the burly damage control men strapped them in and carried them precariously down the narrow ladders to the wardroom, now doubling as a battle dressing station.

Mr. Lawrence, in his role as the weapons officer, commenced tracking the jet fighters again as the director tried vainly to stay on them as they blasted out of sight on their magnificent afterburners.

The lee helm yelled out, "Water out of sight number one boiler. Boiler secured. Cross-connecting now."

"Very well," I answered in the standard acknowledgment of an omnipotent captain. We slowed almost imperceptibly as number one engine started to suck up the steam from number three boiler, whose blowers screamed in obedience to its increased demand for more steam. I could have slowed and let them have an easier job of it, but I wanted a good test under the pressure of them knowing we were in the main channel.

"Number one boiler secured, no damage" came the report from the engineering talker who was also the lee helmsman. In a few minutes I nodded agreement to the OOD when Main Control requested permission to light off number one boiler.

The XO returned in a sweaty shirt, walking over to me, saying, "Wow! That was really something. I'd never seen them do that before." Then he said it again as he wiped his face with a handkerchief, "That was really something." I looked away to avoid showing my disdain for an XO who had never witnessed casualty control drills before.

"XO, secure from general quarters and sea detail and set the 1-AS team."

In five minutes the ASW team reported manned and ready, and I briefed them over the loudspeaker. "There's a nuc attack boat two ships ahead of us, I figure he'll turn north and submerge after he passes the sea buoy. I intend to follow him out, and when he dives and kicks up speed we'll track him the best we can, and when we lose him we'll simulate firing an ASROC torpedo. Got it? And by the way, five minutes is much too long to get to 1-AS after just being at GQ."

We were a thousand yards behind the sub as he turned north passing the sea buoy. In fifteen minutes he came up on fleet common and said good luck, then dove. He'd figured out what we were doing. *Bastard.*

He gave us a patronizing wave as he went below seconds before the conning tower disappeared under the water. We should have had an ASROC solution by this time, but not hearing anything from the ASW evaluator, the XO, I ordered a simulated launch of an MK-44 homing torpedo. "He's fading" came the sonar report. I waited.

"Combat, you got an MK-44 solution?" I shouted over the 21MC after another fifteen seconds. I should have been more patient, but time went fast when waiting to fire.

"Sir, Sonar has a solution, I can fire from here," Mr. Draco shouted over the phone from Sonar.

"Fire from Sonar, Mr. Draco. Break break, XO! Solution?" No answer.

"Fire!" Draco shouted, and in ten more seconds reported all parameters good, evaluated a hit. "Great, Mr. Draco. Break. XO! You gotta an ASROC solution yet?"

"Wait" came his harried reply. I waited.

"Bridge this is Sonar. We're losing contact; he's hauling ass out of here at twenty-three knots. Captain . . . wait. . . . He's fading. . . . He's gone, Captain. Shit! . . . Oh! Sorry, sir."

I sat in my chair, pleased that the ship had done so well but angry with myself for expecting too much from the ASW team, too much on too short a notice. Draco saved the day. The XO failed again. *Christ!*

Ten minutes later Mr. Draco reported having the watch and requested permission to light off superheaters.

I told him no, but for him to set a course for our op area, thirty miles to seaward. Then, walking over to the ship's announcing system, I told the boatswain's mate of the watch, the man in charge of the enlisted bridge team, that I wanted to make an announcement.

His pipe shrilled attention over the loudspeaker, then he stepped aside. "This is the captain speaking. You men did okay on this morning's evolutions and I congratulate you. Well done.

188   Don Sheppard

"I know getting a new captain is disrupting because you don't know what to expect. My policy is to work our asses off at sea and have max, six-section liberty in port. Whenever we return from sea, I will attempt to have the next two days as holiday routine.

"I expect the duty section to be able to get the ship under way, and we'll practice that as much as we can. I am a fanatic about PMS and expect all, I repeat all, PMS to be carried out, and if it can't, I want to know about it.

"Also, going to GQ is not a drill; nor do you have to be reminded which way to move on the ship—up and down and fore and aft anymore. Once we're at GQ, or while we're going, the bridge will let you know what's happening.

"My door is always open, and I'd like you to know you can see me at any time. I'd rather you go through the chain of command, but if you don't want to, just come and see me. I am always available to you.

"I enjoy walking around the ship to see what's going on. But please, don't jump to attention when I come up to you. It's a waste of time and effort. A simple 'Hi, Captain' is good enough.

"I will keep you informed the best I can. Today we have an op area about thirty miles west of here, and we'll play with *Jamison* for a while, then head for home later this afternoon. We expect to get into San Francisco at about 0800 tomorrow or earlier. Wednesday and Thursday will be holiday routine. Thank you."

A murmur of understanding wafted through the ship; I could feel it, savor it.

Exercise at General Drills

The three line department heads, the XO, and I sat in the wardroom drinking coffee. We'd just cleared the abortive submarine attack area and were heading fair for our op area. *Jamison* was fifteen minutes ahead of us.

"I made a big mistake today, gentlemen. Once I saw we couldn't get under way on time at 0800 this morning, I should have waited until the traffic cleared. It was foolish, and we won't do that again." The three lieutenants sat relaxed under a comforting feeling of accomplishment. I'd made it tough on them, and they came through okay.

XO, you failed.

"Mr. Lawrence, you did a beautiful job holding us in position off the Broadway Pier, congratulations." He beamed until I asked, "You were the CDO, what prevented us from getting under way on time?" He looked at the XO, who blinked rapidly and averted his eyes. I waited for ten seconds before Mr. Lawrence answered, saying he was sorry, and it would never happen again when he had the watch. He looked back at the XO, who made himself busily unavailable stirring sugar into his coffee cup.

"XO?"

"I guess, sir, I guess just a lot of things came up and—"

"Never mind, I know all the reasons; sometimes shit happens. But in the future when we're scheduled for a certain time under way, I'd appreciate it if we got under way at that time.

"We've got about six hours on station before we head north, what plans do we have to utilize it?"

Silence answered the question, thickening the room with a pale of uncertainty. "Whaddaya need, whaddaya want to do?" I asked, trying to get them to talk. The department heads glanced around in confusion, looking at each other as if I were speaking Russian. The XO offered nothing but an addled smile.

Finally the chief engineer spoke up. "I'd like some engineering casualty control drills." Lieutenant Shawn H. Flanagan, USN, USNA, was the perfect picture of a chief engineer. He was big and had a bushy red beard. He'd been aboard for only three months. His trim body stood at six foot one with a slight paunch showing a degradation of his athletic stature—the seaman's peril on a small ship. I'd read his record. He'd fenced at the academy and had been a creditable quarterback on the second string football team.

"You did well on that boiler casualties drill, did you run it or did the chief?" I asked. Lieutenant Flanagan's quizzical face gave the answer.

"We didn't know it was a drill, Captain, and the chief had it under control before I could react."

"An honest answer, sir. You should schedule some drills and you run them. It'll give you a lot of confidence and raise your stature in the eyes of your troops."

He answered apologetically that Captain O'Brian rarely let them hold drills, afraid we'd screw up the plant.

"A common problem in the navy, but we'll change that. The plants are a lot tougher than nonengineers realize."

"Were you a chief engineer, Captain?"

"Yes, sorry," I answered with a grin. His face fell into an "Oh, shit" look and his department head mates suppressed their grins. "But I'm sorry, Mr. Flanagan, I'd rather not hold engineering drills while we have another destroyer to play with and a service-rich area down here off San Diego. What else?"

"There are a lot of things I'd like to do, Captain," Mr. Lawrence, the weapons officer, said after a short silence. "Hell, we need to fire our guns; we haven't done that in months, and under way replenishments . . . I can't even remember when we did that last. In WEST-PAC we spent most of our time in port or steaming around in circles five miles from a carrier. We didn't do anything. Really," he finished with a sigh as if he'd made a confession and waited for absolution.

"Did we request any gun-shooting services down here for today?" I asked him, knowing the answer was no. He looked at the XO for him to field the question. Nothing. Mr. Charles, the ops officer, and the one to request services, turned his head away. I let it go as I asked, "How was the ship-handling training in WESTPAC?"

Mr. Charles spoke first, he could answer this one. "Not much, Captain, we steamed alone a lot, and when we didn't we sailed in loose formation. We'd get in a few UNREPS once in a while, or go alongside a carrier or another can periodically, but not often. I guess we need a lot of training," he admitted.

I got up to fill my coffee cup and refilled the XO's and Mr. Flanagan's. My wayward stomach hinted a rebellion to the rising seas but the command insignia I wore over my left shirt pocket cowed it down.

As I returned the pot to the hot plate, I asked my nervous assembly, "How about damage control drills. Are they a joke here like on most destroyers?"

The taciturn XO glanced at the chief engineer, nodding for him to answer. "Ah, yes, sir, I'm afraid they are" came the reluctant reply.

"DCA any good?" The phone growled beside my chair at the head of the table before he could answer. "Yes, okay, ask *Jamison* if she still wants to play. He said he's ready . . . okay, pass the word; we'll be right up. Thank you, Mr. Draco."

"Now hear this," the boatswain's pipe called to attention. "Now hear this," bellowed the loudspeaker. "Stand by to tow ship, stand by to tow ship. First Division provide." The naval officers at the table looked at me in astonishment, then to one another.

I left them baffled for a few moments, then said, "My apologies, gentlemen, but I didn't think any thoughts or plans were being considered for today's exercises, so I took the liberty of talking to *Jamison*'s skipper, and we both agreed that ship towing was seldom practiced anymore, so we decided to try it. Have any of you towed ships before?" I asked, trying not to sound judgmental.

"When I was an ensign, my destroyer tried it once, but we gave up when the weather turned nasty on us," the XO replied, proud of his knowledge.

Jamison lay rolling, dead in the water, two thousand yards off our bow. The light wind and moderate seas drifted her south with her bow canted slightly to the north. I asked Mr. Draco his plan as I stepped onto the bridge with the XO and the ops officer following. I had briefed him before we went down to the wardroom so he'd have some time to think about it, and time to talk to Chief Eselun.

Mr. Lawrence went to supervise the towing setup. Chief Eselun smiled at me as his men, grunting and sweating, hauled out the huge ten-inch manila towing hawser. It wasn't new like the rest of his lines.

"Well, Captain, the book says to pass up her windward side and get a heaving line across as we pass her bow, then stop as they haul in the towing hawser and shackle it to their anchor chain. I've never seen it done before."

"That's a good textbook answer. I've never towed before either, nor have I ever seen it done. But I read a book about it. Did you talk to the bosun?"

"Well, ah, yes, sir, was that okay?"

"Of course, that's exactly what you should have done. Try this method," and I explained what I wanted to try.

"It sounds okay, Captain."

"Do it, then, Mr. Draco." And he kicked his engines ahead full— the kid had dash—heading for a point astern and to windward of *Jamison*. When there, he dropped his engines to ahead one-third and came around to her heading and slowly passed up her port side at five hundred yards. When ahead of her at four hundred yards, he backed two-thirds to take his way off and came to all stop five hundred yards off her port bow.

"Fantail reports ready to pass towing hawser," the talker announced. *Good work, Bosun.* Since we had about the same sail area as *Jamison,* our drift rate was the same, and we didn't get any closer ahead of her bow.

I started to say twist and get us over ahead of her, but the voice gave the orders before my words came out. In seven minutes he had us in position in front of her but too far ahead. He touched his engines back one-third for ten seconds. I felt my underarms grow moist and my heartbeat increase as I watched us close her dagger-looking bow.

Chief Eselun sent up continuous ranges. I didn't doubt they were accurate, but it looked a lot closer from up here on the bridge. Two hundred yards . . . one hundred yards, and we stopped closing. He kicked her astern again and took it off in seven seconds. We started drifting sideways faster than *Jamison,* and, as Draco and I had discussed, he twisted the ship to offer a smaller sail area for the wind to push against.

We backed again. Fifty yards. I heard the shot of the line-throwing gun. Eselun reported a miss. "All stop." "One hundred feet," came the cool report of the talker to the fantail. Two helos buzzed over us, came back, and hovered. I pointed to the JOOD and then to the fleet common net speaker. He told them we were exercising. They waved and veered off.

Another shot from the line-throwing gun. "They have it," passed the talker. The XO wasn't on the bridge. I hoped he was on the fantail, where he should be. From our canted angle I saw a small line go over attached to the thin string of the shot-throwing gun. Then heavier line. Then the towing hawser started its burdensome journey. Mr. Draco had the right angle and we drifted south together. Ten minutes and the hawser lay on *Jamison*'s deck, being shackled to their anchor chain by their sweating sailors.

The talker said Chief Eselun wanted to speak to me. I picked up my phone and heard, "Captain, it looks good back here, estimate thirty seconds. I heard the rattle as *Jamison* played out her anchor chain, dragging the towing hawser down with it. "Ready now, Captain," Eselun said.

"Signalman make to *Jamison*, we are commencing tow." Then, turning to the talker, said, "Clear the fantail." Then to Mr. Draco, I motioned ahead. He ordered ahead one-third on the port engine making turns for three knots.

"Leave the bell on, Mr. Draco," I cautioned as the entire rig snapped frighteningly out of the water with the sound of a hundred shotgun blasts screaming in protest, shuddering our ship and yanking *Jamison* ahead very slowly. Sweat beaded Draco's forehead. He'd told the JOOD to keep an eye out forward and chided him once when he noticed him looking aft.

The yanking almost killed our headway and the rig went limp, but we moved ahead again, snapping the hawser and chain out of the water one more time, then settled in as *Jamison* moved obediently behind us with the hawser and anchor chain underwater. I glanced at my watch; twenty minutes had passed from the initial start. "Well done, Mr. Draco. Well done."

In ten minutes we released the tow and began the backbreaking chore of heaving in the hawser. Then we went dead in the water for *Jamison*'s turn.

She went for the book approach of coming in parallel, close on our windward side, close enough to get a shot line over at the last minute as her fantail passed our bow. It was a tough way to do it, and she took three tries before she made it. In all, it took her almost forty-five minutes to have us moving.

A sandwich on the bridge was my lunch as we exercised at tactical maneuvers. We'd take the lead, then she would, each of us cautious as new conning officers got the feel of the ship. Mr. Charles and Mr. Lawrence took turns calling out the evolution when we were the guide. I'd had Mr. Charles bring up all the JOODs and let them have the conn in turn and have them stay on the bridge to watch their peers either screw up badly or grease a beautiful maneuver. I offered no advice letting the two lieutenants do it. As senior watch officer, it was Mr. Charles's responsibility to train the junior officers, the JOs.

I hadn't seen the XO for hours. I would have thought he'd want to be here.

At 1400 we turned north for San Francisco.

The ship's vibration sank deep into me. My mind assimilated every rivet, every weld, every molecule of her being. My thoughts caressed her as a lover. I was the ship; she was me, all in one blended entity, in a massive synergism of mutual trust and obedience. She is my ship; I am her captain, and it seemed I had always been.

On our way north we practiced going alongside each other for simulated high line transfers. We'd go alongside *Jamison* and hold our position long enough to get the distance line across and stay for five minutes. We'd break away and steam ahead and *Jamison* would make her approach on us and stay alongside for five minutes. In all we got ten of these leap frog practice runs each. I had briefed each JOOD, whose turn it was next, on the proper procedures while *Jamison* made her approaches. I stood behind them, offering advice when I had to, which wasn't very often.

The XO leaned over the nav table setting our initial course for San Francisco. We were ten miles south of San Diego and eleven miles to sea. *Jamison* steamed two thousand yards behind us in a loose formation. Tired from the day's exercises, we saw no further need for close-in station keeping. A time to relax. The phone buzzed, and the XO said something into it, then left the bridge.

It was 1700 as I walked over to the nav table to look at his courses. I should have had them thirty minutes ago, at least. The hair on my arms rose slightly and my face flushed as I saw he'd marked a course to have us skirt the northern end of San Clemente Island by only two miles when we had no reason to, and plenty of sea room to the east. My face grew cooler as I realized that probably one of the quartermaster strikers had laid out this course for practice and approval, and in a few minutes the XO would present me with a more realistic initial course to skirt the island.

I waited fifteen more minutes. Master Chief Petty Officer William J. King, USN, leading machinist mate, senior enlisted adviser and minority affairs officer, walked onto the bridge. He looked around in the waning daylight while strolling over to my chair. "Good evening, Master Chief," I said, looking at his ebony skin and six-foot, bullish frame.

The navy had recently created two more top enlisted ranks, E-8, senior chief petty officer, and E-9, master chief petty officer. King was the first "super chief" I ever had working for me.

"Nice evening, Captain," his resonant voice said. His neatly trimmed beard flecked with gray gave him the sophisticated appearance of a TV anchorman as his eyes danced around the bridge, taking in everything at a glance. Then he looked at me with an almost devilish smile, asking, "We chiefs would be pleased if you'd eat with us this evening, Captain."

"Why, Master Chief, I'd be proud to. What time?"

"At your pleasure, Captain."

"Eighteen hundred perhaps?"

"Done," he answered, standing tall in his tailored khakis. Most chiefs and officers wore wash khakis or the new—ugh—polyester ones while at sea or working. He looked magnificent in his beautifully pressed gabardine trousers and shirt covered rakishly by his brown leather flight jacket with name tag. I felt the compulsion to stand in his presence. I stood.

Still, the XO hadn't shown up. "I'll be in Combat," I told the OOD. "Captain left the bridge" came the swift reply from the boatswain's mate of the watch, and I saw the talker to CIC speak into his sound-powered phone, no doubt telling them I was on the way in. The crew deserved to know where I was, and where I was going.

The CIC watch officer, Operations Specialist Chief Horace M. Janski, USN, greeted me as I walked in. "Understand you're eating with us tonight, Captain," he said, standing up from the chart laid out on the DRT.

"Skunk Alpha Bravo bearing 010, five miles. CPA 7.2 miles bearing 075," the talker passed to the bridge. CPA meant closest point of approach. Skunks were unidentified surface contacts, designated by letters of the alphabet for a twenty-four-hour period. They started with alpha through zebra, then alpha alpha then alpha bravo, et cetera. Alpha Bravo was the twenty-eighth contact CIC had detected today.

"Skunk Zebra past CPA and opening," he finished, waiting for permission from the OOD to scrub Skunk Zebra off his status board. On the bridge CPAs were also computed, but with somewhat less accuracy than Combat.

The bridge used grease pencils, marking directly on the radar repeater screen. A little difficult during the day considering the large cone-shaped rubber hood placed over the screen to keep out the light, and to keep in the smell of a boys' high school locker room. I could imagine the bridge talker making his report and wiping his status board clean of the now nonthreatening ex–Skunk Zebra. "Bridge reports Skunk Zebra one of those new container vessels inbound to L.A. or Long Beach," the talker reported.

"Lemme see your course home, OOH ES SEE Janski," I jokingly asked. We both considered changing the name, radarman, to operations specialist, a little pretentious even though it better defined their work. The faceless intelligentsia on the staffs in the navy department were making their mark in naval history. The fine title of cook had been changed to mess management specialist. What a crock!

"Thanks, Chief, looks good." He'd lain a course to pass ten miles east, away from the northern tip of San Clemente Island. A prudent measure.

"XO," I said, returning to the bridge, seeing him bent over the nav table. "What's our course look like?"

"Here, sir," he answered, pointing to the chart with the close CPA to San Clemente. I studied it as if seeing it for the first time. There were no changes.

"Who laid this out?"

"I did, Captain."

"Why so close to San Clemente?"

He took a set of dividers and marked the distance. "Two miles, sir?" he asked more than stated.

"Why so close? There's plenty of sea room to the east. Why so close?"

"No reason, sir. It looked okay to me," he answered as if offended that I even asked the question.

"Too close, XO. Look at Combat's and plot the same course. I'll be in the Chief's Mess for dinner," I replied, curtly knowing the insult I'd just lashed him with.

"The Chief's Mess?" he answered, his mouth gaping open.

"To the captain," the eight chiefs toasted in unison, holding their wineglasses in salute as I entered their sacrosanct quarters. Seeing their glasses contained a dark red liquid, my heart stopped for a microsecond. My telltale expression caused a heady laugh as they handed me one containing the navy's ubiquitous "bug juice," that Kool-Aid–like beverage always available to sailors.

I'd been drinking it for twenty-five years. Strawberry was my favorite, mostly for the color. They usually all tasted about the same. This one tasted good, a little different, but good.

"We thank our illustrious Mess Management Specialist, Theodore H. Jones, USN, the world's foremost belly robber, for the blessings we receive tonight," the master chief toasted over a roaring laugh. He was not known for his piousness.

Mammoth steaks followed a delicate salad, and a rich baked Alaska topped the meal. The phone rang twice while we ate, both times dealing with a skunk whose CPA was less than five miles; standard doctrine. This Outer Santa Barbara Channel was the main route between San Francisco and Los Angeles and was always filled with merchies steaming north or south.

"To a captain who kicks ass and takes names," Chief Eselun toasted as two mess cooks cleared the table. I wondered what the "second" mess cook was getting for this evening's service. Chief Whalen, the leading gunner's mate, filled my wineglass again as eight o'clock reports sounded over the 1MC.

I answered, genuinely confused, that I hadn't taken any names or kicked any ass.

"No?" he said with that grin that could devastate a lesser man. "You've got Mr. Flanagan, the chief engineer, jumping through his ass because you told him he should know how to conduct casualty control drills, and he doesn't."

The master chief grinned as Eselun continued. "And Charlie, the ops officer, is having hourly chew-out sessions with the ETs for gundecking their PMS, and they're keeping out of your sight. And all the officers are in a panic, checking every PMS book on the ship." I didn't correct him for calling Lieutenant Charles, Charlie. "And what about the DCA, you've got him panicked by just asking if he was any good . . . which, by the way, he isn't. But I never said that.

"And we hear you chewed out the entire wardroom for not acting more positively on the way into San Diego when they should have, then you took the blame yourself. Some say the department heads, and the XO particularly, feel like shit for not having a plan for training today, and you had to come up with something yourself, and something spectacular to top it off. They feel like slitting their wrists. And the XO is hiding out in his stateroom. We only hear that, of course."

"Of course," I answered conspiratorially, accepting a cup of coffee from Chief Jones as the bosun continued.

"Mr. Lawrence late under way? It'll take months before the shame leaves him. It was the XO's fault.

"And poor Mr. 'Paul Bunyan' Rogers, my esteemed but timid division officer, actually got up the guts to tell me—in a nice way—that *he* didn't want *me* to put *our* men over the side without permission of the bridge. I was proud of him."

Eselun stood to pour another cup of coffee to all around. Chief Whalen passed out the beautiful big cigars from the ornate box, and we lit up in silence, filling the room with a pleasant fog of dense blue smoke. The mess cooks had been sent away after the meal. The master chief artfully twisted his cigar between his fingers to ensure an even burning as he blew a huge smoke ring into the ventilation fan, which sucked it in greedily. He made a temple of his fingers and rested its peak against his mouth. His majestic voice was the next to speak.

"Captain, the crew thinks you're great after that little fog thing going into 'Dago' and your speech about your open door and holiday routine, and so do we. Kaplan, the lead firecontrolman, and Quartermaster Von Lehman think you walk with God. And we understand Mr. Draco thinks you are God. Romeraz, the lead steward, is walking on air, having beaten you three out of five chess games Sunday afternoon—"

"Romeraz is a good chess player," I interrupted.

"Come on, Captain," the bosun laughed.

I flushed until the master chief spoke with solemn authority. "What we want to say, Captain, is simply this: We think you're damn good for *Cambridge* and we're behind you one hundred percent."

The other chiefs chanted, here, here, banging their cups down on the nearest hard surface.

On my way back to the bridge I suppressed the tear in my eye.

They didn't have to do that. They weren't trying to butter me up either. They didn't have to; they were chiefs, and, as a unit, tremendously influential on the ship. Nothing moved or happened *efficiently* without their consent.

I silently thanked them as I stood at the railing, taking in the clean, fresh sea breeze. I watched with magical fascination as the luminous chartreuse of the photoplankton, stirred up by our bow wave, danced gaily down our sides, first touching, then pirouetting away into the darkness like fireflies on a balmy night.

The loom of Los Angeles glowed majestically off our starboard side as my mind thanked the chiefs for reminding me what a powerful position I held. I had not considered that I had terrorized or chewed out anyone. But then I remembered what it was like to be a young officer wanting approval and success so badly and construing anything the least bit negative from the captain as a personal, career-destroying rebuke.

I realized there was more to being a captain than being a competent ship handler and being weird enough to think your ship talks to you.

I sat in my chair, absorbing the ship, the sea, the movement. There was a magnificent peace here, and I consumed it like a mother's love. The faint buzz of the radio speakers and the radar repeaters lulled me. Aft, the spinning force draft blowers hummed their soft tune only for my ears. The turbines, whirling, driving the screws through the massive reduction gears, tiptoed euphoria through my receptive body. The sea parting in respect to our passage sung its own melody of competence around this wonderful fighting machine. This is where I belong. This is where I live.

By midnight I was tired of watching merchantmen passing down the coast. I stretched and yawned, and got up from my chair. I looked at the quartermaster's chart. We were dead on our plot. I stepped into Combat. I came back on the bridge, squeezing Quartermaster Lehman's shoulder as I passed him. I could feel his smile.

"Mr. Flanagan, I'll be in the sea cabin, follow the night orders, gentlemen. Call me when in doubt."

"Yes, sir."

"Captain left the bridge." I loved that kind of talk.

Still awake at 0100 reading *Atlas Shrugged* by Ayn Rand for the third time, I heard the metallic click of the voice tube cover being lifted. The four-inch brass tube ran from just over the nav table on the bridge to the head of my bunk in the sea cabin. I listened, feigning sleep.

"The CPA is 4.9 miles," I heard the JOOD say. "Why bother the old man for a tenth of a mile? He just got to sleep."

"What do the night orders say?"

"Call him for CPAs of five miles or less, but 4.9, sir?"

"What do the night orders say?"

I heard something click against the tube, like a coffee cup, then the JOODs voice. "Captain?" There was a pause, letting me come awake to the call. I delayed four seconds before acknowledging.

"JOOD here, sir. We have a skunk at 6.7 miles and a CPA at 4.9 miles. She'll be at CPA in 12.6 minutes."

"Very well, thank you."

I heard the voice tube cover close and then fall open again.

"See!" I heard Mr. Flanagan's voice admonish.

Then the JOOD's voice, soft and garbled, as if the two men had risen up from bending over the nav table, asked, "The captain seems to know everything all the time, how does he do that?"

"Beats me," Mr. Flanagan answered, and another metallic click shut the cover.

I thought about the question. I knew so many things because I had a vast official—and less than official—reporting system backing me up. On *Kramer*, as XO I thought I had a fine network going, but as the captain I was awestruck by the volume and rapidity of the information coming to me. It was easy to appear sagacious, all-knowing. You just had to remember and correlate the data, and, of course, nurture your sources.

Chapter 9

UNODIR

Thursday morning the XO and the four department heads sat in the wardroom, drinking coffee. I had said we'd have these meetings, so this first one was no surprise. They looked at me in anticipation. "Gentlemen, welcome to our first Planning Board for Training. Though I don't intend to run *Cambridge* by committee, at these meetings we will discuss policy matters and what the ship should be doing for the next week, the next month, et cetera. I want you to be frank and open, and if you ever think I'm doing something wrong, I want you to have balls enough to tell me."

I'd found the Japanese *nima washi* concept of management very helpful in the past. *Nima washi,* a horticulture term, translated loosely, means "binding the roots." If the roots on a tree were well bound before transplanting, growth was reasonably assured. As a management style, it meant to get general consensus before proposing a plan, and by the time the plan was put forth, so much had been said about it, everyone felt a part of the decision-making process and easily accepted it.

The XO should have been chairing these meetings, but I couldn't get him to show the initiative. He had an indoor mentality, a mentality unmarked by beliefs or emotions and as smooth and pale as a bank clerk's. He was ready to receive orders and carry them out without delay or question. A conformist, always believing the last thing he heard. He wasn't too bad an officer as long as there was always someone to suggest, someone to guide.

But the XO's billet was the testing ground for command, the testing ground for initiative and drive. The massiveness and difficulty of the multifarious XO's job separated the good from the excellent, and it was the CO's job to record this.

After our return to San Francisco from San Diego, we'd had a little chat. I told him I was not pleased with his performance. "I know you're a good man, XO, but you just don't seem to be getting it all together. What's the problem?"

At first he stared at me with a hound dog look, hemming and hawing and looking around the cabin. "I don't know, Captain, I'm trying my best, but there just seems to be so much to do. Captain O'Brian helped me a lot, and I thought I did okay for him. I'm sorry you think I'm screwing off, Captain."

I answered that I didn't think he was screwing off, it just seemed he could take a firmer grasp of what's going on. You know, get into the trenches. Get on the deck plates.

"Captain O'Brian thought I was doing okay. My fitness report was real good. I'll try to do better, sir," he answered without fire or persuasion.

"Good, XO, I know you will," I answered with an equal lack of conviction, and the conversation was over, and so were his chances at ever getting a command. I would have to take care of the finer aspects of his job until I could get a replacement.

Later, I picked up the phone and dialed BUPERS. It wasn't hard to get a new XO, there were far more men qualified and waiting than there were billets. You couldn't waste them on an also-ran.

I'd been aboard for a month and just found out we were designated as a Naval Reserve Training ship, no longer a member of the active duty fleet. This meant we no longer came under the operational control of COMFIRSTFLT, unless for a special mission, and it meant we would not deploy to WESTPAC. At first it assaulted my ego like a bludgeoning of Thor's hammer. I felt abandoned, unworthy, not good enough to run with the big boys. Not a real captain. Not a combatant.

Our commodore came down from Seattle and explained the program. He said we had the best of all worlds, we keep our crews at the near maximum of a deployer and a full wardroom. We can pretty well write our own schedule and get under way mostly at our own discretion. Our OPTAR will be a bit higher than the regular cans, and we're here all by yourself in San Francisco to run your own little destroyer navy. We're the only gunship around.

The commodore had told me earlier that week on the phone that he was coming down and wanted to lunch in my in-port cabin instead of the wardroom. I was glad, because I need some private face time with the commodore. It was inconvenient for Romeraz and his boys, but they pulled it off as if I were an admiral always eating alone or with a guest.

"Your one and only mission is to take a reserve crew out once a month. And when they need their two-week annual training, you take 'em somewhere and train 'em."

The commodore fed me this line as if the blessings of the navy department gave us the enviable duty of ensuring the safety of the West Coast. While we ate, I noticed his right shirt cuff wasn't buttoned. It bothered me. Lack of attention to detail can cost lives.

He preceded me out of my in-port cabin. I saw the backs of his trousers at the knees were overly wrinkled. They needed pressing. He seemed to be a nice, textbookish-type guy, but showed little interest in the ship or the crew. He didn't want to meet the wardroom. He made sugary comments on how well we looked as he made a cursory walk around the ship, heading for the gangway.

"I know your record, Captain," he said, shaking my hand in parting after being aboard for only an hour. "You've got the picture . . . just keep me informed, that's all I ask, just keep me informed." He saluted and left. I didn't have the *picture* and didn't really understand what that little talk was all about.

What did he mean that we were the only destroyer here? What about *Jamison* tied up at the Naval Supply Center, Oakland. Didn't she have guns? She was in the same squadron as us. Did he visit her too, give her the same spiel?

"I guess it's not all bad, gentlemen," I told my officers, who from the beginning seemed to accept our plight more lightly than I did.

I guessed their egos were less delicate. "No one will be watching us," I continued. "No one will be planning our training sessions like they do down in San Diego and Long Beach. That's okay with me, we know what we need to keep current, and if you look around here, there's plenty of services from the carriers and replenishment ships at Alameda, and there's many a sub up in Vallejo just dying to give us ping time. My only concern is attack trainer time for our ASW readiness. But we can always go down to San Diego for a week."

They nodded in agreement, and the XO said he'd been to WEST-PAC enough and didn't care if he ever saw it again. Neither did I, nor did any of the rest of us. WESTPAC cities were now the same as any other big city. It was boring, and after the initial wonderment about being in the mystical Orient wore off, they became mundane. And very expensive.

"Also," I went on, "we might become ambassadors for the navy. I know a lot of people are interested in destroyers, and I think we can play that up big-time by becoming San Francisco's own. The Navy League is always looking for rides on naval ships, and we'll give 'em ours to play with."

"I don't understand, Captain." Lieutenant Junior Grade William H. Gunther, USNR, SC, spoke up, his jovial, unflappable manner giving way to furrowed eyebrows and a tilting head.

"Don't understand what, Bill," I answered, looking at his Teutonic face, amazed how young he looked for twenty-six. He'd just reported aboard a week before.

"All of it, the reserves, the nondeployment, the Navy League. Aren't we going to be a regular navy ship anymore?"

Mr. Lawrence spoke up enthusiastically. "As I see it, we got it knocked. No deployments, no flagship looking down our neck, no reduction of crew or wardroom and free to write our own schedules. Christ, that's great!"

"Oh?" was the supply officer's confused answer. "What about training?"

The XO answered, "Mr. Gunther, the most difficult thing we do on destroyers is getting under way and returning to port. Here in San Francisco we have one of the most difficult harbors in the world because of the narrow gap under the Golden Gate Bridge and the huge water basin that feeds through it." He stopped and filled his glass with strawberry bug juice. I waited for his conclusion, pleased with him for speaking up.

"The currents under the bridge are vicious and can get as heavy as seven to ten knots sometimes. Couple that with the all too frequent fog and you can see what we face. If the captain can get us under way as often as we want, we'll have plenty of training," he finished, sitting back in his chair with the smug look of a third-grade schoolteacher explaining the multiplication tables.

"Right, XO, let's test the theory," I said, proud of him for speaking up like a real XO. He hadn't improved much from our little chat, but he was trying. "Let's plan what we want to do. And, XO, you and Ops"—I pointed to Mr. Charles—"set up liaison with our reserve unit, and let's have a meeting."

Two days later, 0600. "Under way."

I'd sent a short teletype message to SOPA, a carrier CO, and to the Naval District Headquarters, and our commodore, stating, "UN-ODIR, under way for twenty-four hours on mission assigned." UNODIR, unless otherwise directed, stated you intended to do something if no one senior had any objections. Professionalism de-manded the message be sent early enough for someone to *otherwise direct* if they wanted to. I'd never seen anyone otherwise direct. It would be unheard of to send a message like this in San Diego or Long Beach. But here, no one knew our assigned mission and therefore no one could object. It worked.

Mr. Draco had the conn. He let go all lines but number one. The heavy running current from the tide on max flood pushed our stern away from the pier like a giant's invisible hand nudging us out. "Let go and bring in number one," he ordered and waited while First Di-vision let go the line and the current pushed the bow out. "All back full," he ordered, in a calm, even voice and waited for the twin sev-enteen-foot-diameter screws to bite into the water and pull us out of the slip.

The whine of the force-draft blowers jamming air into boilers filled the ship with a pleasant anthem of power. Then, "CHRIST!"

Huge bellows of black smoke spewed out of both stacks darken-ing the sky as the boilermen forced far too much fuel oil into the demanding boilers. The mark of a sloppy destroyer. An indictment of incompetency. They'd screwed up even though Mr. Draco had told them his first bell would be a back full bell. The wind, unfortunately from astern, blew the greasy black smoke across the bridge, driving the men into spasmodic coughing.

"MR. DRACO," I yelled even though I didn't have to. "Take us back in, we'll try again. Boatswain's Mate, pass the word." Then I grabbed the power megaphone and called out, "Line handlers on the pier, stand by, we're coming back in."

He went ahead full to break our stern way, then ordered right full rudder to get our bow in. This would be a tough landing with the strong current pushing us off the pier. What made getting under way so easy would make the landing extremely difficult. The ship twisted her bow slowly against the current as it pushed us bodily away from the pier.

This one was going to be a bitch. Draco couldn't line us up on the first try. He backed down two-thirds to get a better starting point, and when he judged it right, ordered both engines ahead standard. His face filled with question as he started his forward movement. He wanted help.

I walked over to him and in a low voice said, "Take her up boldly past the berth, twist sideways to the current, and when we drift down past the pier end, go ahead standard and get number one line over to anywhere as soon as you can, then twist your stern in. Next, depending where number one line ends up, walk it up to where we want to be. Piece of cake, Dave."

He did it as if he'd done it every day of his entire life. "Moored."

Dave Draco was a natural ship handler. He had the feel, *the seaman's eye,* that near-mystical communication with the ship and the sea that let him put her wherever he wanted. He was good.

Number one line went over too close to the end of the pier, but okay. He kept the stern twisting in with the engines while another line went over to a further inshore bollard. He let go the first line and steamed up so that the second line was perpendicular to the ship. He did this by adding a few turns to the going-ahead starboard engine to let us gain headway. With the windlass, the boatswain's mates warped the bow in, then stood ready to pass another line down the pier.

Three times they did this mule hauling, and in twenty-five minutes we had both number six and number one line over in our original berth. I picked up the 1MC microphone and keyed it. "On the fo'c's'le, on the pier, fine work men, thank you." Then, turning to Mr. Draco, I said, "Get all lines over."

I waited in silence, letting the crew wonder what was going on, letting the lesson sink in in Main Control. For as long as it took me to smoke my pipe, I waited with no instructions to anyone. The current's inexorable thrust against our hull, even though somewhat mitigated by the pier pilings, stretched and strained our breast lines, those that led perpendicular to the ship and pier. Their groan and wail would make the angels cry.

Through my binoculars I watched the sly, grinning face of Chief Eselun on the fo'c's'le. He knew this was for effect. In thirty seconds I motioned for Mr. Draco to take her out.

He told all stations to stand by to get under way and told Main Control that his first order would be a back full bell. All acknowledged. He let go all lines except number one. The current from the tide, still near max flood, pushed our stern smartly away from the pier. He had number one line slackened and brought in, and waited while the boatswain's mates heaved in the line and the bow pushed out.

"Under way."

Draco backed full, and one more time the heady whine of the forced draft blowers pulling max RPM filled the ship. Not even a hint of a haze came out of the stacks as we backed free of the pier and into the channel. This was almost our own channel, since few other ships ever came to the back side of the Treasure Island Naval Station. Draco threw on right full rudder and went ahead standard to line us up with our exit course.

I motioned for the boatswain's mate of the watch to pipe attention. After the shrill died down, I picked up the 1MC microphone. "This is the captain speaking. Today we're going to exercise at anchoring at a little spot we've picked out on the other side of the Bay Bridge. Then we're going out to sea to hold boat launching and casually control drills. At the same time, we'll do some damage control training.

"So as not to slight the supply department, we'll battle-feed at noon. I expect we'll get back in about 1900 with our asses dragging.

Tomorrow will be holiday routine unless we screw up today, and in that case we'll stay at sea tonight and practice again tomorrow."

I hung up the microphone and sat in my chair, confident now and ready to train my men in the fine nuances of destroyer life. I was ten feet tall. I didn't have to be a cowboy anymore.

"Two hundred feet to drop position," the XO stated without conviction as he crossed and plotted the bearings called in from his quartermasters on the wing peloruses. Anchoring was simple; the navy just made it hard by insisting that we anchor in a precisely designated spot.

"Fifty feet to position."

The weapons officer, Mr. Lawrence, was taking it in for the first drop. Theory was to steam over the spot very slowly, then back down slightly, then drop your anchor, then back down more to seat the flukes into the bottom—a seamanship evolution controlled ninety percent by the navigator.

"Position," the XO yelled.

Mr. Lawrence backed a touch, then ordered let go. The rumbling clatter of the anchor pulling the heavy chain out of the chain locker rattled and shook the ship in protest.

"Anchored," the 1MC advertised, and a round of bearings was plotted. It took ninety seconds for the report. Far too long, and to make it worse, we were fifty feet to the south of the drop point. Wholly unsatisfactory, and made worse by the XO's seeming lack of concern over his poor performance.

"Shit!" the weapons officer yelled, possibly the first cuss word he'd ever said in his life. He shot a disgusted sneer at the XO, who had just turned back to the nav table and looked at me in pained forbearance.

I tried to keep my voice under control as I told Lawrence to take in the anchor. It didn't bother me that the XO had missed, even though it had been a simple anchorage not complicated by winds, tides, or nearby ships. It was his indifference to failure that chilled me.

The ship inched forward as the brute strength of the massive anchor windlass hauled in the chain by pulling the ship over it.

Anchor chain up and down, came the report. There was a shudder. "Anchor aweigh." It had broken free of the bottom.

"Under way."

"Anchor in sight." With a fire hose, the anchor detail shot the mud off the chain and the huge anchor as it came in sight from the bridge.

Mr. Lawrence waited ten seconds, then ordered all ahead one-third. One could not get any movement, way on, when the anchor was hanging in the water, lest it draw back and smash the sonar dome or worse, hole the side of the ship. We came around slowly and lined up for a second run.

This time I surprised them by putting Mr. Lawrence on the nav table and giving the conn to the DCA, Lt. (jg) Ernest P. Strong, USNR, NROTC. He generally lined us up and headed in for the anchor point.

After a few moments of familiarizing himself with the nav set up, Mr. Lawrence gave an initial heading and distance to the drop point. Mr. Strong altered course slightly, but not enough, I judged. I held back from giving advice on these anchorings. I'd gone over it with the officers in a training session, explaining the basic procedures and figured it was best to leave them alone to try—to screw up or not.

The wind picked up a few knots and a slight chop visited the bay. Lawrence was good, and the nav team gave almost continuous recommendations, but Mr. Strong tended to ignore them. He was grandstanding, showing he was better than the nav team. I shuddered, thinking of my own brash junior officer days, but said nothing, letting him have his head, but my body started its warning tingle.

It wasn't too hard to make this particular anchoring by eye, there were several good landmarks he could use to visually sight on. But I didn't think Strong was good enough to do it.

"Drop position, one hundred feet, ten degrees off port bow," Mr. Lawrence reported, looking up first at the DCA and then at me, shaking his head. I hoped none of the bridge crew saw the look.

Mr. Strong ordered a port twist on the ship, his sharp voice betraying nervousness. I said nothing, and the silent bridge mocked him. The drop point lay fifty feet off the port bow. Strong increased his twist, allowing a slight forward movement. We slewed over the position with one or two knots forward speed.

"Let go the anchor," he shrilled, and I saw a seaman on the fo'c's'le swing his huge mallet against the quick release pelican hook and saw the anchor splash mightily into the water.

"THIS IS THE CAPTAIN! I HAVE GOT THE CONN!" I shouted, jumping out of my chair. "All engines emergency back full." The lee helm smashed the engine order telegraph handles forward against the stops, then yanked them back to full astern, the metal clanking in protest. This told Main Control we needed the bell right away, right away! The sudden high roar of the boilers' huge forced draft blowers told me the bell was being answered.

To back the engines full, the backing turbines demanded a tremendous amount of steam. To provide it, the boiler men had to jam huge quantities of fuel oil into the boiler fire boxes, and to support its combustion, an enormous amount of oxygen had to be forced in to make it burn. Too much air meant billows of white smoke out of the stacks, too little meant black smoke. Only a puff of white smoke eased out. Beautiful job. They'd learned.

In the same instant as I gave the emergency backing bell, I ordered the fo'c's'le to apply the chain brakes the best they could—which probably wouldn't do much good. The seamen cranked on the chain brake wheel as if the devil himself possessed them. We had dropped the anchor while turning into the chain and going ahead in shallow water—all the elements for a massive sonar dome crunch and volumes of correspondence with COMCRUDESPAC questioning my fitness for command.

Dry docks were in short supply.

Cambridge shuttered, groaning in obedience. I nervously waited, letting the massive forces take their course. Then, in seconds, I ordered all ahead two-thirds to squelch any backward movement. I waited a few moments, then calmly ordered all stop. We drifted slightly astern with the chain tending forward and the wind delicately kissing our superstructure. *Whew!*

Mr. Strong, his face downcast, his eyes begging for forgiveness, looked like a puppy dog caught peeing on the carpet. He knew he'd violated the cardinal rule of anchoring: going ahead when the chain dropped. I told him to take the conn, take in the chain, take us around, and try it again. A much-humbled lieutenant junior grade, his khaki shirt sweat stained under his arms, maneuvered us into position and made a creditable drop.

I motioned Mr. Charles over and turned to the talker, telling him to send my regards to Combat and ask Chief Janski to report to the bridge. I loved to affect the British naval style of sending respects and regards and compliments. It made me feel like I was Lord Horatio Nelson at the battle of Trafalgar, in 1805.

I asked the young, good-looking chief, puffing from his run to the bridge, how his surface search radar was operating today. He answered that it was fine and added that the ETs had it peaked to the best he'd ever seen.

I told him Combat was to guide us in to the drop point and we'd drop on their recommendation. He assured me he knew about anchoring: going astern when you let go the chain and all that good stuff. I asked him tongue-in-cheek if his boys were good enough.

Smiles danced around his cherubic face as he pointed his finger toward the door to Combat, saying his boys could do anything. Drop within twenty feet of the mark, I challenged.

He said piece of cake. I asked him if he wanted a practice run, because I wanted Combat to order the engines also. He bet a pitcher of beer at the Chief's Club that they'd put the hook within twenty feet of the drop point.

He turned to leave. I called his name. "Chief, is it you or your boys who are so good?"

He looked at me for a moment, then with a sly grin told me it was his boys, of course.

"That may well cost you a pitcher of beer, Chief." I stepped down from my chair and walked toward Mr. Charles, telling him to give the conn to Chief Janski.

This was a perfect setup for me to show Combat I had confidence in them. Too often on destroyers the radarmen, or operation specialist now, had low morale because they were poorly trained and ignored until things got hot. Then it was too late; they weren't able to help the bridge when they were sorely needed, such as in the case of a sudden fog or the bridge being shot up or when the machinery failed.

Mr. Charles snapped his head toward me as if he hadn't understood the alien words. He stroked his chin as if pondering a foreign language. His eyes narrowed to slits, pulling his lips into a cold grimace. The thought of an enlisted man conning a destroyer could not find validity in his academy-formed brain. He looked at the deck, then at the overhead, his eyes bulging. He looked at the chief, then at me. And he started pacing, as if existing in an unfamiliar world, walking back and forth like a caged tiger.

I told Mr. Charles again to pass the conn to Chief Janski. For five seconds he gazed at the chief as if the chief were an Australian aborigine, and then, almost at a whisper, gave the required report which a new conning officer needed: "Ah, all engines are ahead two-thirds, on course, ah, one seven five, exercising anchor drills."

He waited for five more seconds, then, as if fearful that the sky would fall, called out, "Chief Janski has the conn." The whole thing pissed me off, and chunks of my respect for Mr. Charles clattered to the deck.

The chief stood silently for a moment, looking at the door to Combat, seemingly wanting to jump through it. His eyes swept across the faces of the bewildered officers. His lungs couldn't seem to suck in enough air. He looked at me, then at the door to Combat again. I nodded, pointing my finger to the helmsman. The helmsman cleared his throat.

The chief pulled in his stomach and took in a deep swallow of air. "This is Chief Janski," he shouted, paused, then looked at me again as if this were some cruel game. Once more I nodded my head. "I have the conn," he yelled with the clarity of a centurion ordering his men to battle.

"Aye, aye, sir, steering course one seven five," Quartermaster Second Class Von Lehman sang out with pride in his voice.

The lee helm followed smartly with "All engines ahead two-thirds, turns for ten knots rung up."

"Very well!" Chief Janski answered, his voice composed. "Combat, give me a course to our anchorage and call out the distances," he ordered to the CIC talker. By now the entire ship would know he was driving. Mr. Charles, standing beside the chief like a mother hen, touched him on the shoulder and nodded toward me. Chief Janski remembered and called out, "I have the conn, Captain." Mr.

Charles's face lit in admiration of himself for helping this in-over-his-head chief petty officer. This enlisted man.

I acknowledged and ordered him to take us to anchor and told him he could have a practice run just to warm up. And then to comfort him—and myself—on this sudden turn of events I walked over to him, and when very close, whispered for him to remember to over-shoot the mark by maybe twenty yards, then back down gently through the point and let the anchor drop and the ship's momentum would dig the anchor in. I mentioned that when he backed, the stern would turn into the wind and it would throw him off a little.

"Piece of cake, Chief," I finished, patting him on the shoulder.

The chief took Combat's initial course recommendation. We were a thousand yards from the drop point. I called Mr. Lawrence over. "Go to Combat and make sure they don't embarrass the chief. Don't interfere unless you have to." I should have sent Charles, but he was still trying to recover from the shock of having an enlisted man conn the ship.

The practice run ended in a one-hundred-foot error. I told him to take it around again, explaining his errors and telling Combat to be a little faster with their fixes. Their slowness caused most of his problem.

On the second run, he ordered the engines back at the right time, the anchor detail dropped exactly on command, and the engine room answered the bells more smartly than I'd ever seen. The ship had come through magnificently for him.

"Anchored!" Eighteen feet to the drop point, the XO called out.

The CIC talker cleared his throat and reported too loudly, "Combat holds us seventeen point five feet, sir. Verified by the director, SIR."

I had earlier heard the director slewing around as if to acquire a target to mark us to the foot. *Great, they were a team.* "Well done, thank you, Chief Janski. I owe you."

Chief Janski practically floated off the bridge. In ten seconds he was back, heading for my chair. He saluted, even though the navy never saluted under cover, like in a ship or in a building. One could not salute without a hat on, and naval officers never wore a hat indoors. Never!

He extended his hand. I shook it. "Captain . . . thank you . . . thank you."

Battle Messing and Boating

By 0945 most of the officers had at least one anchoring, and their high spirits permeated the ship. We set course for the Golden Gate Bridge. "This is the captain speaking. As soon as we clear the sea buoy, we'll go to general quarters and battle mess. Afterward we'll hold engineering and damage control drills. We did well on the anchorings, and, if our skill holds, we'll moor around 1900 as announced." I took my finger off the 1MC microphone switch and settled back in my chair.

Rolling pockets of mist danced around San Francisco Bay. I informed Harbor Control of my intentions to exit the Bay and took Alcatraz Island a thousand yards to starboard. Mr. Charles had the deck and the conn, conning by eye while both Combat and the nav team stood silently, ready to back him up. Like a hummingbird flitting from flower to flower, he rushed from one bridge wing to the other. I got out of my chair and strolled over when he settled for a moment at the center line pelorus.

I covered it with a clipboard, telling him he didn't need it, and patted him on the back, then yanked my hand away, admonishing myself for being so damned paternal. "Just stand here, Mr. Charles, and point the bow the way you want it to go . . . piece of cake. Quit running back and forth. Your JOOD can do that."

His weak smile answered yes, but he wasn't convinced. He liked to do things by the book; it was more comfortable that way. I tried to let up on my department heads after my dinner with the chiefs, but dammit, I had to train these people to be flexible, to think ahead. The ship depended on it. *Or was it my ego?*

I asked him what the tide was doing, though I certainly knew. *Am I badgering him?*

"Quartermaster!" he shouted. "Tide condition?"

"Near slack water but still flooding, sir," Quartermaster Von Lehman shouted. Mr. Charles repeated it to me.

I walked over to him and whispered that he shouldn't have to ask the quartermaster. I pointed to a channel buoy. "See, it's tilted very slightly to the land and has a small swirl around it. The tide is still flooding. You should have remembered we got under way five hours ago at max flood. Keep it all in your mind, Mr. Charles. Trust your senses." A weak, aye, aye, sir, showed I hadn't gotten through to him. Naval officers tended to rely on their instruments far too much.

As we cleared the deserted island prison of Alcatraz, a nuclear attack submarine hove into view on the other side. Combat had been tracking it for the last ten minutes. The starboard lookout immediately reported it.

Our slightly ahead position warranted that we would go ahead of her under the bridge. I told the signalman to make to the sub that we would slow and let her go ahead of us if desired.

Our signal light clicked out the message, and the sub answered with a thank-you and yes; they would go ahead of us. Then in a minute another blinking light signal: "CO to CO. Didn't think there were any gentlemen left in the tin can navy."

Embarrassed, the signalman handed the message to me. I went back to the signal bridge and asked him to relinquish the light to me. I clicked out, "I'm the only one left. Interrogative your op area?"

"Get serious" was the instantaneous reply. Their skipper was on the signal lamp too. I knew it was a foolish question, subs never told anyone where they were going. I took a quick look around to ensure we were heading fair, then sent, "Can you give your tired old cousin some ping time once we're outside?"

"Sure. I didn't know you surface types could read and send blinking light. Are you brand new?"

"No, brand old. Could sure use an hour's worth of your time." He replied that regretfully he could allow only twenty minutes and that he would dive after we passed the sea buoy and head two six zero at ten knots. He added good luck and passed his portable signal lamp to another man. Good luck! That pompous ass, but he was right. He could run deep and scoot away from us in minutes if he wanted to.

Mr. Draco stood on the starboard bridge wing as I returned from the nearby signal bridge. He asked why I let the sub go ahead. His tone showing he really wanted to know instead of just making conversation.

I told him subs weren't as maneuverable as we are in confined waters, and even though there isn't much current here, one never knows what can happen under the bridge. They can use the extra maneuvering room. I was proud of him. It was working; the officers were asking questions.

Only a few eddies harassed us as we went through the narrow gap under the bridge. The first ground swells hit us as we passed out of the lee of Point Bonita. The ship rolled, and my wayward stomach churned. I ordered it calm; it fought me, not caring. I demanded, and in five minutes it reluctantly obeyed.

At the sea buoy the sub submerged and held her speed to ten knots, giving us thirty minutes of good ping time. The XO, as the ASW coordinator, didn't exactly do well in Combat. It was painfully obvious that Mr. Draco ran the show from the sonar shack deep down in the hull, as he had done in San Diego, my first time out. He had only limited assets down there, but he did a great job nonetheless. Over the gertrude, the underwater telephone, I thanked the sub and turned north to our op area.

By 1300 the wind came up, and the seas worsened as we went to general quarters. In a surprise movement I told Mr. Charles to launch the motor whale boat. I believed in using surprise during training evolutions. I was a firm believer in making training hard so the actual event would be easier.

Lowering a boat at sea is difficult, especially if you had a bad chop like we were getting. The bosun, Chief Eselun, was there directing as the davits swung out and the boat lowered to the rail. Mr. Flanagan, the chief engineer and now the OOD, maneuvered to put the wind on our port side to make a lee for lowering. Chief Eselun passed up word that he was ready.

I nodded yes to Mr. Flanagan, and he ordered the motor whale boat away. The coxswain jumped into the twenty-six-foot pointed-bow-and-stern boat, along with his two-man crew and Mr. Rogers. Chief Eselun had confessed that they had never launched at sea since he'd been aboard. We were doing it today at his request.

When it touched the water, it took on vicious twenty-degree rolls. I watched, remembering *Henshaw* when I was a lowly ensign so full of his own self-importance. And I recalled the boat launch to pick up the downed pilot. I remembered his face, his severed leg. I remembered the sharks, their feeding frenzy.

The motor whale boat's engine took charge, and with the sea painter taking a strain, the boat veered away from the ship. The bow hook, the forward man in the crew, yanked out the toggle on the sea painter, and the boat motored away smartly, free and clear. A textbook job. "Signalman, make to the motor whale boat, 'Bravo Zulu.'"

The hulking Ensign Rogers stood next to the coxswain, and I saw him pointing into the swells and the boat pitching energetically as its bow dug in and ripped through the waves. I saw him turn into the trough and roll violently. I saw him, a young lad with his first command, playing as if he were at the beach discovering surf for the first time. I felt proud of him. We steamed around them at a thousand yards. It was a great day for an outing on the water, except for the increasing winds and the rolling seas.

On the ship Mr. Flanagan went to his GQ station in Main Control as we continued our drills. Five minutes later, the lee helm yelled out, as if it were real, "Main Control reports water out of sight in number two boiler wrapping up the boiler now and cross-connecting."

"Very well," I answered, noticing a flicker of the control lights on our instruments. Good recovery. I waited for the next report while I kept an eye on the frolicking boat, its crew soaked and dripping. Perversely, I wished I were with them. "Lee helm," I called out, "ask Main Control what is maximum speed available." This was a required report after a causalty. I smirked, thinking the master chief screwed up.

In four seconds the lee helm yelled out, "Maximum speed available, eighteen knots. Number three boiler inspected with no damage, request permission to light off number three boiler."

I couldn't conceal my smile as I asked the lee helm if they really wanted to light off number three boiler, that I understand the low water was in number two.

"Yes, sir, 'sorry, sir,' they said. Request permission to light off number one boiler," the lee helm talker repeated.

"Lee helm, tell them I'd rather they light off number two if it's all the same to them."

"Yes, sir," he instantly replied, starting to key his microphone, then said with a confused look, "Fires lit in number two boiler, sir. I don't know what's going on, Captain."

"Tell them *permission granted* to light fires under number two boiler." And I chuckled as he did. *Things are just a little confused down there.*

The increased kiss of the wind on my cheeks counseled caution. I told Mr. Charles, now the GQ OOD, to recover the boat and secure the engineering drills until we had it aboard.

He made the signal and maneuvered to put the starboard side to leeward as the boat approached. He slowed to five knots as we came into position, and the boat nestled alongside, picking up the sea painter line as she did. In the trough of the waves now, we rolled fifteen degrees, and, as the falls hooked on and she lifted, her fiberglass side smashed into us once, then again, before she rested in her davits.

"Fifteen knots when you're ready, if you please, Mr. Charles," I said, slipping into my sea cabin.

"Captain left the bridge."

"Motor whale boat secured."

"Very well," I answered, coming out onto the bridge, carrying Oscar, the man-overboard dummy, stuffed with kapok and dressed in discarded sailor's clothing. I'd sent the messenger to sneak it up here from the bosun's locker while first division was busy with the boat and at GQ. I walked swiftly unto the bridge wing and threw it overboard, motioning with my finger to my lip for the lookout to keep quiet.

"MAN OVERBOARD, STARBOARD SIDE," screamed the signalman in a second, rushing forward to the pilothouse. "MAN OVERBOARD, STARBOARD SIDE," he yelled at me no more than three feet away as if the power of his voice could call back the man.

"Very well, thank you, Signalman."

The ship's whistle blared out her six blasts, indicating man overboard, and the 1MC roared out the call to every square inch of the ship and for two hundred feet into the surrounding air. Nothing happened. Mr. Charles stared at me, his mouth open.

"Man overboard, starboard side, Mr. Charles. This is a drill, Mr. Charles, do something," I said calmly. We should have already been turning. I couldn't wait. "Boatswain's Mate, pass the word that this is a drill, and we'll recover by boat."

As the XO ran onto the bridge, yelling, "MAN OVERBOARD, MAN OVERBOARD," Mr. Charles leaped into action as if a chain veil had been lifted. I could barely hear his command of right full rudder as the boatswain's mate screamed into the 1MC again.

The ship heeled around to starboard, throwing the stern and its huge screws to port, away from the hapless dummy. It might have been too late, and the screws could have chewed it up. We were around in minutes, and the port lookout spotted it ten degrees off the starboard bow. Mr. Charles backed the engines two-thirds as the boat station reported manned and ready. *Let's see how good you are in an emergency situation, Chief.*

We fetched up short by about fifty feet. I ordered a boat recovery, and the boat eased smoothly into the water, speeding for the dummy. I'd purposely stayed at GQ during all these drills to increase the difficulty and the confusion of pulling men from their general quarters stations and opening and closing watertight doors. The old saying, the more you sweat in peace, the less you bleed in war, constantly played in my mind.

"Oscar recovered," the signalman in the boat sent.

"Recover the boat Mr. Charles. XO, commence battle messing." Battle messing wasn't much more than a man from each unit going to the galley for a bag lunch of horsecock sandwiches and a piece of fruit and paper cups of bug juice . It didn't taste good. Horsecock was the time-immemorial name for bologna or any other circular loaf of processed meat.

I walked over to the port wing. "Son," I said in a low voice to the port lookout, a boyish-looking seaman with acne. "Your name's Moresly, isn't it?" He jumped to attention from his leaned-over position, where he rested the heavy 7x50 binoculars on the bulwark.

"Yes . . . yes, Captain, sir," he stammered.

"It was good work spotting Oscar in the water, but your lookout area is from the port bow to astern. Oscar was on the starboard side. You shouldn't be looking that way," I said softly in a fatherly tone. "You could have missed something on the port side while you were looking starboard. I know it's hard when there's action on the other side, and you haven't seen anything on your side, but it's really important for me to know what's happening on your side. Okay?"

His face dropped, then lightened as I squeezed his shoulder. "Yes, sir, I understand."

"Thanks."

I came back into the pilothouse. "XO, how come I'm not getting reports on all these planes flying around out here," I asked as he ate his dry sandwich.

"But, Captain, they're commercial flights from Frisco and Oakland," he answered, genuinely puzzled.

"Don't they give the same radar return as a Russian bomber?"

"Well, I guess so. I didn't think . . ."

"Mr. Charles! Mr. Lawrence!" I called out, ignoring the XO's attempted answer. "I want all those aircraft tracked and plotted, and I want the director on them, and I want the mount to simulate engagement. We fight like we train; remember that. Move it."

I went down to Combat to observe. There, I called for Mr. Gunther, the supply officer, to report to Combat. He stared in wonderment of this dark, mysterious, place. I took him to a quiet corner and in words barely above a whisper said, "Mr. Gunther, in all my years in the navy, I have never tasted a battle-messing ration as bad as what you just served: dry bread, a thin slice of horsecock, and no salt or napkins. And those cups of bug juice . . . didn't you realize they would spill as they were carried up and down ladders? The apple I had was nearly rotten. Jesus Christ, our men work their asses off, and goddammit, they deserve better."

He looked as if I'd kicked him in the balls as he stammered that the XO said it was what he should serve. "What's for supper?" I demanded, trying to hold my anger.

"Well, meat loaf. I figured everyone would eat aboard this evening, and I'd have a cheap meal."

"BULLSHIT! Your thinking is bloody backward." I slowly turned my head, dramatically looking at the huge clock over the plotting boards. "It's 1305, Mr. Gunther," I drew out his name, pronouncing it as if it were an insult. "I want prime rib for the crew tonight and ice cream and nuts for dessert. You got all that stuff?"

"Well, yes, yes, sir, but we're at GQ, you know, and I can't break it out to thaw. I . . ."

"Chief Janski," I called out, "my compliments to the XO, and tell him to have all cooks . . . no, all mess management specialists and mess cooks quit their GQ stations and report to the mess decks."

Then, turning again to the supply officer standing next to me, looking pale and a little seasick, I said, "Belly robbing is a sick joke in the navy, Mr. Gunther, and in my book a crime. I know you have a budget, and I know it gets hard sometimes, but I don't give a good goddamn about that. If we go over budget, I'll take the rap, but I want one thing quite clear: This ship is going to have a reputation as a real feeder, and you're going make sure it does. I don't know diddly-squat about running a mess, but you do—you can do it. Make the men proud of you. Questions?"

He whimpered understanding and backed away from me, his face even paler than before, his eyes lowered in shame.

Walking away, trying to hide my disgust, I headed aft to observe the damage control drills. I had received no reports from the damage control parties.

As I walked into the supply office, cum Damage Control Central, Lieutenant (jg) Strong sat there reading a paperback novel, his feet propped up on a desk. The leading damage control man sat next to him, reading a newspaper. The two plotters, wearing sound-powered phones, lay asleep on the deck.

I gripped the doorway tightly as hot blood surged through my body. "MR. STRONG!

He jumped up, slamming the paperback on the desk. If his plotters had been awake, he'd known I was on my way back here. The first class damage controlman whisked his newspaper into a shitcan. They all stood. I quivered, too angry to speak as they weaved in rhythm with the ship's roll. "Captain?" Mr. Strong offered, his face ashen, his body shaking. I turned and walked away, slamming the door behind me.

Dammit, I had talked to Mr. Strong on damage control just this morning. I told him how important I thought it was, how important his role in it was, how I depended on him. He concurred. He had told me what drills he was going to hold today. He failed me. He lied.

I fought my way through the barbed wire in my mind as I headed forward to the wardroom for a cup of coffee. My anger thrust ahead of me like a firestorm. I wanted my pipe to tranquilize me, for something to hold on to that I could trust. Something to occupy my hands. But the smoking lamp was out during general quarters.

"Doc" Pulaski, our first class petty officer corpsman, came to attention as I stepped in. He and his two seaman had the wardroom cleared for action, the way it was supposed to be, as the main battle-dressing station. The sterilized bandages and medical equipment were laid out perfectly, and the wardroom table was stripped to assume its battle role as an operating table. The only thing not done was the removal of the false plastic ceiling panels. These panels hid the fittings to accept the powerful operating room lights. We rarely removed them, and only then to test the lights. It was a helluva job to get the panels back in again.

"Sit down, men," I said, pouring tepid coffee into a cup. The hot plates were turned off during general quarters. "How's it going?" The battle-dressing stations were to be drilled with the damage control parties. Obviously nothing was happening here. The thought didn't help my mood. *It's not their fault; it's Mr. Strong's.*

"Boring, Captain, we've gone through our own drills twice, but we need some action from Damage Control Central."

I couldn't answer. I couldn't say anything to them as I silently finished the coffee, trying to quell my anger. I stood to leave, ashamed that they had been let down.

As I opened the door, the thought struck me; I had meant to tell the corpsman before. "Doc, whenever you prescribe a drug for the XO, you know, anything like aspirin, or cold medication, or anything like that, I want you to let me know, and the same thing, if you give anything to me, tell the XO. We both have to know." He nodded understanding.

As I dropped into Main Control, the confident voice of a sweat-soaked Lieutenant Flanagan was saying over the sound-powered phone, "Okay, Thornbear, put the second air ejector on the line and bring 'er up to full vacuum. I'll . . ." He turned and almost dropped the phone when he saw me standing there. "Captain, I didn't know you were down here. I was just wrapping up a low vacuum drill in number two engine room."

"You been running these drills, Mr. Flanagan?" I asked as he tried unsuccessfully to wipe the sweat off his forehead with his bare hand. The master chief standing behind him smiled broadly, nodding his head while extending his thumb up from his clenched hand in the well-done signal.

"Yes, sir, Captain, sorry about that boiler number confusion on the first drill. I guess I was just nervous on my first one."

"He did okay, Captain," the master chief said.

"You guys wanna run any more," I asked, "anything special? If not, I'd like to head for the barn and get these guys in at a decent time."

They both shook their heads no. Then, with a sly grin, the master chief added, "Unless, of course, the captain wants to run a few just for old time's sake."

I laughed. "Well, thank you, Master Chief, but I was taught to compete only on my own turf." I raised my arm, sweeping my hand grandiosely around the space, admiring his immaculate engine room. "And this isn't it anymore." The master chief smiled.

"Mr. Flanagan," I said, squeezing his shoulder in admiration as I started up the vertical ladder, "whenever you're ready, ask the bridge for permission to light off superheaters, and we'll kick 'er in the ass and mark this one a day." I was feeling better after seeing the progress of the chief engineer. *I'll talk to him about his DCA later.*

In thirty-five minutes we cut through the decreasing seas at 27.8 knots, our maximum speed on two boilers. The ever-expanding bow wave formed a spreading arrowhead followed by the white water shaft of the churning wake. We eased around the sea buoy as an old time racing aircraft sliding around the pylons and slowed to twenty knots once we got into the lee of the Marin Headlands.

Chapter 10

The New XO

During the next week we met with the Navy League, a civilian organization dedicated to supporting the navy. We offered the services of *Cambridge* to lend prestige and to enhance their task. We met with our reserve crew and laid out what we could do for them and established what they could do for us. They were decent chaps and welcomed our interest.

All UNODIR, we laid on a dependents cruise for our men and took the Navy League and the reserves and all their wives with us. The crew showed off—so did I. We fed everyone a fine meal, much to the chagrin of the penny-pinching Mr. Gunther. And they in turn invited us to parties and picnics, and my young men met even more young women. And a great relationship developed.

If the Navy League or our reserves wanted to impress someone with their navy connections, they were welcome to bring their guest to the wardroom for lunch or dinner. I always attended, and we dressed in our finest uniforms and paid deference to our guests.

I called on the captains of the carriers at Alameda and offered my services, which they gladly accepted. It was summed up by one of the carrier skippers by his saying, "We don't usually need a small boy, but when the shit hits the fan, it's nice to have someone who can move in fast to help."

I always requested a refueling and a token stores transfer just to keep our edges sharp. While in plane guard station one, I sat and counted the takeoffs and landings, just like Captains Baker and Macaby had done. Even though I contended in the past that it was useless, and the carriers could take care of themselves, I couldn't let it go. I counted and did not feel secure until the last aircraft trapped aboard.

To be different, to be cool, I started wearing tan Hush Puppy shoes with my wash khakis at sea. I allowed no one else to wear them, but the chiefs and officers were welcome to wear the black gabardine uniform that I wore whenever we had guests. It was completely authorized, but few men bothered, thinking khakis and dress blues were good enough. They were, but I liked the dash and paraded it in sartorial grandness.

In the beginning of my sixth month in command, Lt. Comdr. Charles S. Martin, USN, USNA, reported aboard to relieve the XO. The few phone calls I had previously made paid off. The sword of the old boy network swung both ways.

He stood six feet tall, his blond hair cut short, and his deep eyes penetrated to my soul when he looked at me. His immaculately tailored uniform accentuated his muscular body, and his grip radiated confidence. His Naval Academy ring glistened from the sun striking through my open porthole. He was the epitome of what a naval officer should look like. I sucked in my gut and tried to stand straighter as we shook hands.

We sat down in my in-port cabin. I lit up my pipe with a Zippo. "May I smoke, sir?" he asked. I nodded. With a gold Dunhill lighter he lit up a thin three-inch-long cigar. He held it with three fingers on top and his thumb on the bottom, and he let the gray smoke curl languidly up his handsome Nordic face as his eyes remained on mine. The whole scene smacked of intimidation. I liked it. Clint Eastwood would have been proud.

My life changed. I could now be a full-time captain without being a part-time XO. I quit attending the Thursday Planning Board for Training. He ran them well without me; it was his job anyway. I quit reviewing the PMS books a month after he came aboard; they were perfect. His fixes crossed in a one-hundred-yard square, and though I kiddingly intimated I could do better, I knew I couldn't. And I buried my shame of not being a good celestial navigator.

Chuck Martin handled *Cambridge* as if she were a speedboat, and he could lay her into a tough berth as if he were simply parking a car.

I had failed to make Mr. Strong a competent DCA and had transferred him off, without replacement, a month before the new XO arrived. He shouldn't have lied to me.

Mr. Flanagan was in fact the damage control officer—the A in DCA, was for assistant. Assistant to the chief engineer. Under the shame of having failed with Mr. Strong, Mr. Flanagan absorbed his duties. The old XO never did get it, never understood.

I gave my new XO only one instruction: Square away the damage control parties. Three weeks later, with Mr. Draco as the new DCA, they were. With Chuck Martin running the ASW show from Combat, Mr. Draco's strength was not needed in Sonar.

After the XO settled in, the ship ran better. Now when anything came to me for a decision, I'd answer yes or no in serial order on the theory that by the time it got to me, the answer didn't make any difference. With a good XO, all avenues would have been explored, and if it was yes, it would have already been taken care of. If the correct answer should be no, it wouldn't have been brought to me.

My answer simply gave official notice to something that made no difference. Commanders Baker and Macaby taught me that one.

I had a good XO. He used the time-tested method of General Grant in the Civil War. Whenever Grant wrote an instruction or a message that might be misunderstood, he'd give it to a junior officer to read and explain what it meant. If the junior officer understood it, Grant would issue it. If the JO didn't understand it, Grant would rewrite it. General Grant's man was a Major Smith, who was at best a little dull. When Grant *Major-Smithed* something, everyone thereafter understood it, as they did with the XO's messages.

The XO brought the eight o'clock reports. We were twenty miles south of Monterey and had just been detached from a carrier's plane guarding and a refueling. We hauled out to starboard and kicked on twenty-seven knots. It wasn't necessary, but we sure looked good dashing away like a speedboat.

In an hour we would cut our speed to arrive at the sea buoy at 0600, enough time that liberty could go down by 0900. The ship had to be cleaned first. The seas had been rough and we were salt-encrusted. We'd been with the carrier for three days, and after detaching us, she headed south for San Diego.

The XO brought up the eight o'clock reports. This was a quiet time for us to chat about events of the day and plans for tomorrow. I'd missed it with the previous XO. He never quite seemed to understand. I mentioned the last dependents cruise wasn't very much; it was thrown together in a hurry and consisted of only steaming around the bay and serving lunch.

I said I'd like to do something big, maybe go outside the sea buoy and shoot the guns or cruise up past the Richmond Bridge, make some high-speed runs, and impress everyone with how great *Cambridge* really is.

My phone buzzed. It was the officer of the deck telling me the coast guard called on fleet common, wanting to know our posit. I told him to comply, and we'd be right out. The XO rose, his muscular frame and close-cropped hair giving credence to the navy's recruiting posters. Quartermaster Von Lehman could have been his clone.

"This is Coast Guard, Monterey. Roger your posit, *Cambridge.* Have unsubstantiated report of sailboat in distress 10.3 miles, zero one five true your location. Request you investigate. No cutter available on scene for one hour. Over." I nodded to the XO. He nodded to the OOD.

Lieutenant Rogers answered: "Wilco, Coast Guard. *Cambridge* on the way. Out." He replaced the microphone and looked at me. I pointed to the bow. He smiled and ordered the engines ahead flank, making turns for twenty-seven knots.

The XO keyed the 1MC and announced to the crew what we were doing. Mr. Rogers glanced at him, a question on his face. "You've got the watch, Mr. Rogers," the XO answered his silent question.

The hair on my arms eased upward. A little lump played tag with my vocal cords and a shiver tickled my body. Mr. Rogers turned to the bridge team. "Lee helm, tell Main Control to commence lowering superheat—maintain best speed available. We're on a rescue mission." He glanced at the CIC talker. "Combat give me a time to station, at, oh, say, twenty-four knots." The speed available would be reducing as the superheat temperature was lowered. Superheat had to be lowered slowly, or we'd crack the insulating bricks in the furnace. His guess on the average speed available of twenty-four knots was a good one. Superheat had to be secured before we could come to all stop.

The XO pursed his lips to me and nodded his head once. I returned the gesture, both of us knowing we had a good OOD here. The bosun walked onto the bridge and said deck division would be ready in a few minutes. "How long before we get there, sir?" he asked of Mr. Rogers.

Mr. Rogers turned, telling him about half an hour and that sunset was at 2045. "We'll have just enough light to take care of that mother," he said, his voice deep and strong and confident, as if he were General Eisenhower ordering the D-day invasion of Europe.

The bosun gave me a quick look. I winked.

"*Cambridge,* this is Coast Guard, Monterey be advised, exercise extreme caution. I say again, exercise extreme caution. Over."

"Monterey, this is *Cambridge.* Interrogative extreme caution. Over," the XO radioed.

"This is Monterey, regret, cannot amplify. Exercise extreme caution. Detain as necessary. Helo on the way from Frisco. Out."

Here I was again, classified intelligence not available to the man on the scene. I thought of *white knight* in Vietnam. I thought with disgust of the compartmentalization of the intelligence community. It was happening again. Extreme caution to me meant staying out of the line of fire.

"Mr. Rogers, get Chief Whalen, the chief gunner's mate, up here," I said, and to the XO added: "What a bunch of bullshit, what are we supposed to do?"

The XO left the bridge. I went to my sea cabin's safe, removed my .45-caliber automatic, and strapped it on. When I returned to the bridge, the XO had done the same. I didn't know he had one. *Good man.*

The sailboat crept through the water, rolling five to ten degrees. Her mainmast lay fallen across her open bridge in the stern. Strange, the winds had been high, but certainly not enough to break a mast unless the crewmen had been woefully inept. Three men with axes hacked away, trying to clear the debris. We lay five hundred feet off her windward bow, not wanting her to drift into us. The three men looked at us, waving us away as we approached.

Over our bullhorn the XO shouted, asking if they needed assistance.

A loud hailer appeared on the dismasted thirty-foot yacht. "NO ASSISTANCE REQUIRED. WE ARE OKAY."

A small churning froth of water kicked up off her stern. She was running her engine. A stupid thing, she'll foul her screw. The XO shouted again, "DO YOU NEED ASSISTANCE? WE ARE THE UNITED STATES DESTROYER *CAMBRIDGE* STANDING BY TO TAKE YOU IN TOW."

A voice came back on the edge of hostility. "WE DO NOT REQUIRE ASSISTANCE . . . GO AWAY . . . EVERYTHING IS UNDER CONTROL." Chief Whalen and two gunner's mates waited out of sight in the pilothouse with M-14, 7.62mm rifles.

The wind freshened; it had a bite. The white-hulled sailing yacht rolled more heavily in the seas. Our bridge stayed silent. A cough from the helmsman drew frantic shushes. Through my binoculars it appeared a man lay askew in the rudder flat. The XO concurred. We were losing the sun. We called Monterey again. They answered for us to detain her, and that the cutter would be on station in thirty-five minutes.

The men quit hacking, ignoring us as they grunted the broken, sail-fouled mast into the sea. A young woman appeared from below. She wore red shorts and a yellow halter top. Even at this distance we could see her unsteady weave as she made her way forward.

On the bow, the wind whipping her long blond hair to a frenzy, she started to dance. As she did, she released her halter top. Her breasts swung free in cadence with her undulating hips. She wiggled her shorts down. She wore no panties.

One of the men in the boat rushed forward and backhanded her. She crumpled to the deck and lay there, not moving. A collective groan oozed off *Cambridge*.

The boat pulled away heading for sea. "ON THE WHITE BOAT: STOP. YOU ARE UNDER ARREST. HEAVE TO AND PREPARE TO

BE BOARDED. YOU ARE UNDER ARREST," the XO shouted, then turned to me, raising his arms in question as the low-hulled boat continued seaward in defiance to our order.

"This all seems sorta, well . . ."

"Mysterious, XO?"

"Yes, sir, a little mysterious and a bit tawdry, I'd say."

I called for Chief Whalen, and his two men, their M-14s at the ready. "Chief, put a burst across her bow—all three of you. Fire when ready." We were two hundred feet from her now, and she was moving mighty fast for just using an auxiliary engine. As she moved past us, her wake showed two engines. She had some power under that cabin.

The sound of helo engines droned in from the north.

The XO called the coast guard. "Monterey, this is *Cambridge,* yacht without mast is under way heading out to sea moving at about twenty-two knots. Fast for what she appears to be. We paint her poorly on our surface radar and might lose her if the seas get any higher. We're staying in close. Have put shots across her bow with no effect. We hear a helo coming in from the north. We hold a high speed contact coming in from the south. Is that your boys? Request further instructions. Over."

A man crawled forward and dragged the limp, naked girl back to the rudder flat. The other man lying there hadn't moved.

"Stop her, *Cambridge.* We're fifteen minutes from your location. Stop her . . . break, break. Helo Two Five, interrogative your time on scene. Over."

The return call from the helo, with the whoop-whoop-whoop of her rotor blades distorting her message, said she be overhead in zero five minutes.

If I were in Vietnam I'd have no trouble stopping that sonofabitch. But I'm not.

"Chief Whalen, across her bow again . . . fire at will."

The three M-14s with their high velocity .30-caliber-sized slugs let loose at once. Fifteen splashes sprayed her hull. They reloaded. "Again, Chief, again!" Nine more splashes. She slowed. Her stern wave dropped. "Again, Chief, again. Make sure she understands she's fucking with the United States Navy." Six rounds laid across her bow at about ten feet. From her aft steering flat, a frenzy of boxes were being thrown overboard.

I told Chief Whalen to put a few shots across her stern, close aboard.

Twelve rounds shot from our bridge. Nine splashes. Three holes in her hull. They got the message. They stopped and raised their hands. *What to do now? I'm not going to board the bitch. No way.*

A white helo with an orange stripe across her fuselage zoomed low over the yacht and turned to seaward. The radio crackled over the wind, "*Cambridge,* this is Cutter Three; we have you in sight. We are ready to take over."

We'd been tracking him from Combat for the last fourteen minutes. The sun had deserted us five minutes ago. We moved in to one hundred feet and put our searchlight on her. The helo came in again, hovered over the yacht, and lit it up with their huge spotlight. The crewmen still had their hands up. "PUT YOUR HANDS ON THE TOP OF YOUR HEADS," the helo's loudspeaker boomed like the voice of Moses from the mount.

The cutter pulled up along side the boat, machine guns aimed at the surrendered men and the now-stirring naked woman. "*Cambridge,* thanks for the assist. We got it now," came over the radio. "Thanks again. Out."

I pointed north toward San Francisco and walked toward my chair hearing Mr. Rogers ordering superheaters lit, and Combat recommending a course for the sea buoy.

I turned. "XO, don't forget the dependents cruise."

"I won't, sir."

My boys had done well. I had given them their head, and they came through for me—for *Cambridge.* It felt good, warm, and cuddly.

Outside of That Captain, How Was Your Day?

Three weeks later, Sunday morning, UNODIR, ninety-eight guests ambled about the decks, trying to stay out of the way as *Cambridge* slipped her berth. We started early: 0700, not a cloud in the sky. My coal-black uniform, absorbing the sun, warmed me against the cool breeze across the bay. The XO had done it again, a perfect day. We'd gone around Treasure Island and steamed slowly under the Bay

Bridge, the rumble of the cars crossing overhead sending an eerie low thunder to our guests. We headed for Alameda to show off the mammoth carriers stationed there.

The XO, also in black uniform, ran his nav team in coolly mono-toned voices. It wasn't necessary, but that's what the people expected. That's what we planned to give them. A visual representation of their men at work. Show-and-tell time.

The sound-powered phone talker to the main deck touched my shoulder and moved in close to me, his face pale. He whispered, "Ah, Captain, from the fantail, sir, after lookout reports, ah, reports a dead body floating in the water off the fantail. Starboard side." He probably thought he said it quietly, but every head turned toward him.

The XO's eyes rolled up almost out of sight and his arms moved up in a what-now gesture as he asked the talker to repeat the message. He did, this time louder, as if we were deaf. The XO left heading aft.

"Mind your helm," Mr. Draco said to the helmsman when he noticed him looking at me.

I keyed the harbor common net, "Harbor Control, this is the destroyer *Cambridge.* We are one thousand yards south of the Bay Bridge. There seems to be a dead body floating next to our fantail. Request instructions. Be advised, I'm on a dependents cruise. Over."

"Roger, *Cambridge,* understand dead body a thousand yards south of Bay Bridge. You're standing by. Wait. Out," Harbor Control answered smoothly, sounding bored, as if he received these reports all the time. Maybe he did.

Word passed swiftly; the civilians and off-watch sailors rushed aft to see the show. We took on a slight starboard list. "Main Control," I phoned, "we got a little spectacle on the fantail, lots of gawkers. Shift some water to take off the list, okay?"

In seconds Harbor Control came up on the net. "*Cambridge,* this is Harbor Control. Be advised Coast Guard is on the way. Request you maintain position until arrival."

In ten minutes, a yellow, thirty-foot civilian powerboat roared under the bridge full out, a siren screaming its arrival. It came in fast, reversing its engines fifty feet from our fantail and coasting to a stop fifteen feet off our screw guard. Its bow wave nudged the body. The body rolled once and disappeared under the water toward us. It was a coast guard auxiliary vessel manned by civilians who donated their time and their boats to augment the regular Coast Guard on the weekends.

From the bridge it seemed all ninety-eight guests crowded the lifelines aft, and half the crew stood there, gawking, with their loved ones. I chuckled, watching the hapless XO trying to get them back off the lifelines; all we needed was a man overboard. The list came off the ship as Main Control pumped ballast water into the port side wing tanks.

"Where's the body," a short, fat man wearing a captain's hat and dressed in a flowered bathing suit yelled from the forward deck of his yellow boat over a power megaphone. Fifty voices yelled they didn't know. He was trying to sound important as the ranking Coast Guard official on the scene. A middle-aged, suntanned, bikinied woman stood easily on the teakwood bow, brandishing a boat hook, poking it into the water as if to spear a fish.

In a few seconds the body popped up under our starboard screw guard and the same fifty voices yelled, "Here it is! Over here!" Fingers pointed from the thirty or so viewers lucky enough to have a front row, lifeline view. The XO briefed me on the phone as if I couldn't see anything from the rear of the bridge with my 7x50 binoculars.

"You want me to twist our stern out of the way, XO?"

"We'd suck it into the screws if we did that, Captain. . . . I'll try pushing it away. It's crazy back here, it's . . ." He went off the line as a seaman ran up with a boat hook. The bosun, along with the master chief, both in their immaculate gabardines, cleared a path.

A dirgeful wail of fifty laments saddened the ship as the seaman eased the carcass out into the open water for all to see. The young, sun-bronzed man on the controls of the thirty-five-foot cabin cruiser eased his boat in deftly to four feet of the screw guard. The front-side-up body, arched in its center, its eyeless face staring blankly to the sun. Bloated like a basketball; its facial features garbled in a macabre caricature of a man. Deep pinkish-white scars crisscrossed its bald head and what used to be its face.

With a good view of the body, a silent pall, like the presence of God, settled over the fantail. The onlookers touched themselves to verify their immortality. Only the soft rumble of the boiler force draft blowers interrupted the increasing wind. The bikinied girl reached out with her boat hook to draw the body in.

The pointed tip penetrated the microthin skin.

She drew back as if from a striking serpent as the exploding body spewed blackened, rotted guts onto her and the yellowed-hulled boat, and onto our fantail. She drew up into a knot and vomited as the wretched odor gripped her, and the wind blew it across us. Fourteen of our guests rushed to the port side to throw up. Eleven others didn't make it.

"Mr. Draco, all ahead one-third, if you please."

We pulled away, then increased to two-thirds, ten knots. At fifteen, the odor disappeared. I keyed the 1MC microphone. "Attention please, guests, this is the captain speaking. I'm sorry this incident happened. We will be passing out wet towels and show you to the rest rooms so you can clean up. Anyone who had their clothes messed up, please report to the mess decks and our supply officer, Mr. Gunther, will pass out different clothes and will get yours cleaned up. My men will show you where to go. Please accept my apology for this little unpleasantness. It's never happened to us before. Thank you." Click.

In about a half an hour, when the XO reported the guests somewhat settled down, I announced to them, "We're heading out toward the Golden Gate Bridge now. We'll steam under it, and soon we'll be on the high seas, where we'll fire the guns for you. The wind and waves are expected to be relatively calm today, and we expect to have a nice, pleasant voyage." I felt like an airline stewardess giving her pre-takeoff spiel to a bunch of shell-shocked soldiers.

The XO stepped unto the bridge; it reminded me of the schedule of events. "And, oh, yes, we'll be serving breakfast in about twenty minutes. I hope you'll enjoy it."

The XO grimaced. "Breakfast?" he sneered. I wanted to yank back the words as the moans from our guests assaulted the ship.

We steamed smoothly under the Golden Gate Bridge, gapes of wonder following us out, the horror of the dead man apparently forgotten. Deep swells lifted the bow rhythmically, but not uncomfortably, as we passed under the lee of the Marin Headlands. The more experienced seaman, the old hands, braced their legs and rolled easily with the ship's movement. I'd warned our guests, but they hadn't really understood what to do. The rolling passed quickly as we turned the sea buoy. We fired our superheaters to max and cranked on twenty-seven knots, heading for our shooting area twenty miles out to sea.

The smooth sea and our high speed cut an impressive example of the navy's finest. A coast guard helo buzzed up our port side at thirty feet; he was part of the show the XO arranged. He flew circles around us, hovered at our speed, and did helo acrobatics for our guests. The coast guard figured they owed us one for the assist with the sailboat; and besides, I had three Coasties with their families aboard as a courtesy anyway. Officially, the helo was there to ensure our firing area was clear.

Ten minutes later, two F-4 fighter jets flashed silently over us, yanking all heads up as they cleared our mainmast by twenty feet. In their wake, like rolling thunder from stage left, came their deafening roar.

They were part of the cast, the XO had arranged it with an aviator classmate of his at Alameda. The jets cleared to the south, turned, and headed back. One thousand feet off our port side, they yanked up, torching their afterburners to a flaming crescendo as they shot vertically for the sky. The children screamed, clapping their hands over their ears in agony. The older guests followed.

The XO looked at me and shook his head. I raised both hands, palms up. *Scratch that part.*

In another half hour we were on station; the main deck forward, cleared and roped off. Guards patrolled to keep our guests from wandering into the area of our gun turret. The bridge was so packed with guests, so packed, the OOD could hardly move.

This was unsafe, a mistake, but we were too committed to change now. I stayed in my chair, keeping a smile on my face while the XO ran the show. The barometer inched down a point or two. Low squall lines formed to the north, but still it was a marvelous day.

Our weapons officer, Lt. Pat Lawrence, dramatically, wore a set of sound-powered phones. The XO stood by his side, both of them with binoculars trained aggressively at an imaginary enemy force to the west. The safety of the free world stood in balance.

"Fire Control, this is Combat. Enemy force bearing two seven zero, range six miles" came the amplified voice from CIC. Every inter-communications system was crossed with every other to enhance the noise and realism. We'd never do that for real, too much confusion and chatter over the line. But now we played the game.

"Captain, enemy force bearing two seven zero . . . range six miles . . . break, break . . . Fire Control, acquire and track target bearing two seven zero . . . range six miles," Mr. Lawrence said, his face drawn, his jaw tightened in mock determination.

"Bridge, this is Fire Control . . . on target and tracking."

"Captain, this is the weapons officer; on target and tracking. Request permission to engage."

"Very well, Weapons Officer. Permission granted to engage; guns free," I said, looking very serious.

The XO, in all his efficaciousness, had choreographed this thing last week and had insisted we rehearse our parts. During the steam to our op area he had given a dramatic running commentary of the imagined enemy force approaching the coast to ravage San Francisco.

"*Cambridge,* this is Coast Guard One Eight, your area clear. We'll stand by until firing run completed," the helo reported, whipping over us again and spinning off eastward.

"All stations, this is the weapons officer. Enemy force in sight. We are engaging." All heads turned to the west as if an enemy force really existed. I would have believed it.

"All stations guns free. COMMENCE FIRE! COMMENCE FIRE!" Lieutenant Lawrence yelled, then, with a smirk, turned to his wife standing next to him. She shook her head with a boys-will-be-boys look and smiled in appreciation of her great big man and his great big toys.

The resounding blast of the guns, the heat, the smoke, and the bittersweet bite of cordite sucked in all the emotional coinage on the bridge. We fired again and again until thirty rounds cleared the barrels and boiled the water, throwing great geysers into the air, to the west, exactly six miles away.

The women, a few of them, twisted, undulated, swayed to the rhythmic blast of the naval cannon. I'd heard about it, but had never seen it. Contented, faraway looks covered their faces, their lips creased into smiles as they grasped something to anchor themselves to.

We turned east. The squall lines grew darker. The seas freshened. The XO appeared at my side. He touched my shoulder and bent his head to the north. I nodded. He left. A few drops of rain splattered the windshield. I whispered to the OOD to make turns for twenty-seven knots. *I've gotta outrun this mother and get these people back in port.* It looked bad, skies darkening by the minute.

As the pit log eased up past twenty-five knots, a forboding twisted itself around my neck. I opened my mouth to order speed reduced, to order a turn.

Suddenly, something like a giant hand grabbed the ship, shuddering it, yanking it to a near stop. It threw me forward out of my chair. There was no sound, no crash, a thud, that's all, a thud. Sailors and guests catapulted forward against the wheel, the compass housing, the engine order telegraph, and the cluttered bulkhead. Coffee cups, books, charts, and instruments, all flung against the windshield. Screams and what-the-hells blasted my ears. A collective disaster's wail flung itself at me.

I fought myself up, my head trying to ensure me it was still there as it ordered my muscles to obey. I grabbed my phone yelling for Main Control to slow to ten knots. If I went any slower, I'd burn out my superheat furnaces.

Von Lehman, the quartermaster, grabbed the helm.

Globs of blood splattered our windshields. Screams. Shouts. Moans. A boiler safety valve lifted, adding its banshee screams to the confusion and disorder. "WATER OUT OF SIGHT, NUMBER TWO BOILER—WRAPPING IT UP NOW," the lee helm yelled from the deck, as he pulled himself up.

"A WHALE, CAPTAIN, THERE'S A WHALE DUG INTO OUR BOW . . . A WHALE, CAPTAIN!" the starboard lookout bellowed. I limped over and rang up all stop on the starboard engine and ahead two-thirds on the port and picked up the dangling 1MC microphone.

"This is the captain speaking. It seems we, ah, hit a whale. Nothing to be alarmed about. Ah, we've got the situation under control.

We'll be free in a few minutes. All guests please report to the mess decks. We'll keep you informed." Keep them informed, hell, I didn't even know what was going on. I knew the XO would be taking care of things on deck as I keyed the microphone to Main Control.

The master chief answered, telling me the plant was okay, that they almost lost number two boiler but caught it in time. The checkman got tossed away from his check valve and lost sight of the water in his gauge. But it was okay.

I thanked him and said to light off whenever he was ready. Any casualties?

His answer was fast and concise. A few burns and cuts and bruises, nothing serious. A couple of guests got shook up, but they were okay. He'd be ready to answer all bells in about ten minutes, and superheat was coming down nicely on number four boiler.

A few more drops of rain fell, larger now, smearing the blood on the fo'c's'le even more, as if buckets of red paint had been dumped over it. Charnel houses were cleaner. The bosun was there with three seaman. About twenty feet of black, shiny whale clung tenaciously to each side of our bow. We'd hit her broadside, cut her open three quarters the way through. She must have weighed at least twenty thousand pounds. Her skin glistened to the splotchy sun breaking through the rolling black clouds.

I put my binoculars on her. Her tiny left eye looked at me balefully. Condemning. Her baleen clearly showed through her rounded face. Her useless flipper twitched twice, then fell limp. On the starboard side her flukes waved uselessly in the air, then fell like a limp rag into a pail. She aimed one more pleading cry at me and went silent.

Her weight dragged the bow down. I could see the bosun trying to keep the crowd back.

I called to Mr. Charles, the OOD, who held on to the midships pelorus watching the guests crushing onto the bridge. *He should be doing something.* I pointed at him and jerked my thumb aft. "Get 'em away from the bow, get 'em off the bridge," I ordered. He looked around for the boatswain's mate of the watch. There he was, busily helping two teenage girls back to their feet, giving them more attention than their predicament warranted.

Mr. Charles shrugged and keyed the 1MC, announcing for all guests to clear the fo'c's'le, to clear the bridge. He repeated the message and asked all guests to please return to the mess decks. The XO appeared in front of Mount 51, gesturing with his arms and talking to the guests, indicating with his courtly manner for them to move aft.

"Bosun wants to talk to you, Cap'n," the talker said. Mr. Rogers stood by his side now. The bosun passed the phone over to him as I picked up mine. I looked at my watch, only four minutes since the collision. *Christ, it'd seemed like all day.*

Mr. Rogers reported the whale embedded in the anchors on both sides. Dug in deep, and maybe, maybe, if we backed down, it would pull itself free.

I told him I couldn't back down yet because of the superheaters still lit on number four.

He said something to the bosun, who nodded. "Maybe, Captain, if we did some tight turns, she'll shake off."

"Maybe. Lemme talk to the XO." The XO walked to the bow and looked over as he accepted the phone. "How's it look, XO?"

He said no one was hurt bad, just bruises, cuts, some sprains. He put his hand, palm out, in front of his mouth as he looked at the whale, then mentioned one of the guests was a doctor, who was helping our corpsman. Nothing bad . . . people shook up a little.

"Ship?" I asked.

"Lots of broken cups and plates; it looks like a bomb exploded in the messing areas; it's getting cleaned up. People are wailing on the cruelty of us smashing that whale, like it was our fault. Gotta get rid of that thing and head into port. You been lookin' to the north?"

"Yes, we're in for a blow. Get the fo'c's'le cleared, XO, then bring Mr. Rogers and Mr. Lawrence up here."

In five minutes the three of them came into my sea cabin. I had a few options, but I really didn't know what to do. They'd been up there and seen the whale. I hadn't.

If you can't make up your mind, ask one of your subordinates what they would do; they may come up with a good idea while you're thinking about it. Mr. Rogers came up with the plan.

At fifteen knots the sea tore at the pinioned whale, driving it into us, forcing our bow deeper into the water. Our bow wave splashed and careened around the beast. Ugly mess, not a destroyer's smooth anthem of beauty. I hated that whale, and deplored myself for killing it. I should have seen it and should have done something to avoid it. She encumbers my ship. . . . I must cut her in two and let her drift away. Is it a her?

I turned into the sea, the lifting and dropping bow sawing into the whale's slimy hulk. The fo'c's'le was clear and roped off. The crimson water flung itself back onto Mount 51 and the forward breakwaters, splashing the bridge and painting our windshields a gruesome red. *This isn't working. Am I some latter-day Captain Ahab; Queequeg, where are you?*

I increased speed to twenty knots, whipping the ship into tight turns, fighting like an angry jackal twisting its quarry, trying to tear the meat off the bones. Only the increasing smell of vomit from the guests answered my effort. *What must they think of me?*

Superheaters were secured. I backed down, one-third, two-thirds, full, but the mammoth beast wouldn't let go as if it were a millstone around my neck damning me to the world for killing an innocent creature of God. Woe be unto a sinner who kills something that big, something that beautiful.

We moved forward again into the rising waves. The ship shuddered. The whale shuddered. We were at five knots and increasing when she parted. The port half drifted away. The starboard half clung to our side, sticking, as its yellowish-white, blubbered mass oozed astern, greasing its passage blood-red. Our guests crowded the lifelines, reveling in the morbid scene. Eyes gawked. Cries shrilled.

Oh, my God, it dawned on me. "ALL ENGINES STOP!" Too late. Ten thousand pounds of meat thumped through the knife-edged blades of our starboard screw. Ground blubber leaped into the air, over our fantail, over our guests . . . and littered our wake astern.

A hundred gulls dipped down to feast.

Three hours later, in the gloom of a darkening sky and the push of a gusting wind and the sting of the pelting rain, the master chief, the XO, and I stood at the head of the gangway, forcing our smiles and saying good-bye to our green-faced guests. Their averted eyes and obligatory thank-yous hollowed as they waddled ashore, heading for the stability of the pier.

As nearly half the guests had left, a girl of about eight, frowning under the wet bandage covering her head, offered her hand reluctantly to the master chief and the XO. When she got to me, her eyes screwed into a question. She pulled her hand back and turned away. In a second she twisted around, her face puzzled, and asked, "Are you the captain?"

I nodded.

"Why did you kill that whale. . . . Why did you kill that man?"

Suzy Ann

With the XO's fine hand administering the ship, the rare discipline problems we had all but disappeared. The XO screened and investigated all violations, and I gave him the power to attend to them *unofficially* as he saw fit. The authority given to me by the Uniform Code of Military Justice, the UCMJ, was used only for repeat offenders or serious cases. For the serious cases, a court-martial could be ordered, but we never had any offenses serious enough to warrant that. Or I could hold a captain's mast, the *mast* referring to the old days, when defaulters were read off forward of the main mast.

I often bragged to the department heads that no innocent man ever came to captain's mast on *Cambridge,* because the XO would have investigated it thoroughly and determined guilt before sending him to me. He and I had the same resources for investigation, and I could find out nothing more than he could.

In one case, a seaman had been continually late two or three times a week for the last month. The XO, having exhausted his prerogatives of extra duties and one or two nights restriction to the ship, scheduled a mast. The seaman asked if his girlfriend could be there.

I came to the lectern placed on the bridge waiting for the man to be brought before me so I could formally read the charges against him. As I waited, I glanced across the bridge, seeing the grinning faces of Master Chief King and Chief Eselun, the CMAA.

What's so goddamned funny?

In thirty seconds the duty MAA brought Seaman Billy Joe Landry into the pilothouse followed by the XO leading a crying young girl by the arm. On command, Landry stepped forward, saluted, and I read the charges. "Do you have any comment on the charges of failing to be at your appointed place of duty at the proper time," I asked with all the dignity of a powdered-wigged, English judge of the eighteenth century.

He looked at me with hound-dog eyes and admitted his guilt, but said it wasn't his fault. It was Susan Ann's fault. "Just look at her, Captain, sir," he said, glancing, red-faced at the girl. Her face glowed in radiant innocence as she listened to his long vowels draw out.

And I looked at her. She couldn't have been more than seventeen. Her long red hair fell recklessly over her small shoulders, framing a magnificent baby face. She wore cut-off jeans and a tied-up man's shirt, which barely concealed her ample breasts. I asked him how it was the young lady's fault.

"Mr. Captain, sir—" she interrupted, blurting out with a drawl that would make Scarlett O'Hara sound like a New York debutante. "It sure is ma fault."

How, I asked, trying not to stare.

She looked around the bridge, unintimidated by the legalistic setting and strange equipment. "Well, Mr. Captain . . ." She glanced around again at the tall men acting as if they weren't looking at her. "Can I talk to you private like . . . it's sorta . . ."

"I'm afraid not, Miss, ah . . ."

"Susan Ann Balfour, sir, from Louisiana and right proud of it."

I told her she could come to the lectern. She oozed over, the smell of jasmine and fresh soap wafting in the air. A breeze through the pilothouse blew a few strands of her flashing red hair across her face. She took one and ran it through her mouth, biting on it.

The XO and the others tried desperately not to grin at my discomfort or stare at the girl. Only the XO was able to pull it off.

"You see, Mr. Captain, sir, I've been up here with Billy Joe for only a month or so . . . shucks. We been sweethearts since second grade . . . and in the morning . . ." She paused, casting her eyes downward as if she were going to tell me a secret. "In the morning I get this here squishy feeling—you know all cuddly like and warm—and good ol' Billy Joe is there, and I just plum won't let him go until, well, you know, until . . ."

Uncomfortably, I told her Seaman Landry had to be back on the ship at the proper time. She moved back away from me, taking Seaman Landry's arm as tears formed in her eyes.

"I understand, Mr. Captain, sir. You reckon you'll put 'im on bread and water?" Billy Joe wouldn't like that; he needs red meat," she sobbed, openly wiping her tears away.

I turned to Mr. Rogers, his division officer, and asked him if he had anything to add in the boy's defense. He cleared his throat and told me Seaman Landry was a good man and that these problems never came up until about a month ago. "He's a good worker and has never been in trouble before."

A screeching sea gull perched on the open bridge bulwark as I pondered for a minute this great judicial problem of cause and effect. The awesome weight of military justice hung heavily on my shoulders. I accepted the load and stood straighter, pulling in my gut as I pronounced majestically that based on the circumstances involved in this case and the good recommendation given by his division officer, I would let him off with a warning: "Don't be late again, Seaman Landry. XO, dismiss the mast."

Susan Ann rushed forward, grabbing my arm, wrapping her body around me, hugging me. "Oh, Mr. Captain, sir, thank you, sir, I'm going to try real hard—you know, in the morning—I'm going to try really really hard, you'll see. You'll see."

I lifted her head from my chest and gently pushed her away, stammering, "Well, ah, thank you, Miss Balfour, we're, ah, counting on you."

"Ma friends call me Suzy, Mr. Captain, sir," she answered, winking as she wiggled off the bridge.

Eselun, sotto voce, spoke first. "Wow! Master Chief, ol' *Mister-Captain-sir* is one rough-assed sonofabitch, eh?" The XO glared at them and had enough control not to laugh. I didn't.

Doc Savage

Three weeks had passed since our abortive dependents cruise, and I was still licking my wounds. I reported the whale incident to the

Naval District Headquarters, but since the death-dealing newspapers hadn't gotten onto it, the affair passed into memory unpublished.

A ship stationed at Alameda had had an incident where they suspected two men of being homosexuals. Their skipper asked me to convene a field board to investigate and recommend. I was bored. The XO did all the work. I accepted.

"He's a roarin' fag, Captain, if I ever saw one," Bosun Eselun said as he came to get me for the field board.

Homosexuality warranted a general discharge from the navy. This meant you didn't get an honorable discharge, whereas millions of American men had gotten honorable discharges in the past and looked askance at those who hadn't. A general discharge could screw up a man's whole life. Because of this, they weren't given lightly. Anytime a general discharge was being considered, a field board was convened from a different command not affected by the act.

Lieutenant Lawrence sat at my right, Lieutenant Flanagan on my left, and Lieutenants Rogers and Draco flanked them. Field boards, per se, were not courts of law, but all the rules applied. Lieutenant Paterson from the man's ship was the prosecutor, and Lieutenant (jg) Gunther, our supply officer, was appointed for the defense.

I shouldn't by all rights have been sitting as the senior member. It could unduly influence the board. I wrote their fitness reports.

Lieutenant Paterson was an average-looking man in every dimension, except that his hair was too long. He lumbered to his feet in the finest Darrowinian tradition. He straightened his perceived loose tie and picked up a pencil from the table, tapping the eraser against his chin. He'd watched too much TV.

He cleared his voice. "Seaman Hank B. Savage is the accused," Lieutenant Paterson pronounced, his voice twangy, as if he had a nasal disorder. His eyes narrowed as he repeatedly stabbed the pencil toward the nineteen-year-old seaman as if it were a saber fending off the Mongol hordes.

"On the night of Wednesday, nineteen October, this year, Seaman Savage—he likes to be called Doc—was observed climbing into another man's rack with the intent to commit oral sex and/or sodomy. He brought neither act to fruition because the duty master-at-arms caught him before he could," Lieutenant Paterson pronounced, sitting down, smirking, as if he had just summed up the Stokes trial and proved, irrevocably, that man had indeed descended from the apes.

Doc Savage, in immaculate dress blues, looked at him, then at Mr. Gunther, then at me, his eyes questioning. "Oh . . ." Paterson grunted, standing again. "And his partner is sitting on your mess decks right now, waiting for us to find Savage guilty, or in case you might want to talk to him. He's next but hasn't been charged yet. He's at least a class two, but he'll beg off to a three." He sat down again, his face dripping with self-satisfaction. He lit a cigar.

The navy had four classifications for homosexuals: Class one was the rapist, the psychopath who molested children and murdered his victims. The military or civilian courts dealt with them. A class two was the cruiser, the guy who went to gay bars and picked up men on the streets. An active homosexual. Class three candidates were those who would accept sexual advances if it was convenient, but never were the aggressors. They experimented and usually gave it up before they were caught or escalated to a class two.

The class fours were those who performed homosexual acts before coming into the service and who lied on their enlistment forms. Or it was the man who had been forcibly, raped. If a man had been coerced, he was ipso facto a homosexual, and to be general discharged out of the navy to make room for untainted, real men. Penetration, however slight, was sufficient to culminate the offense.

"Is that it?" Mr. Gunther asked, his eyes scrunched, his head twisting to Paterson.

"What more do you need? It's all in the log, and Savage admits he was caught in the other guy's rack."

"What about intent, for one thing?"

"*Intent,* Mr. Gunther, is not an element in homosexual cases such as this," Mr. Paterson snapped back.

"Well, you say Seaman Savage *intended* to have a sexual relation with the other man. Why bring it up if it's not an element?"

"Well, I'm not a slick-tongued, supply officer like you, I guess." Lieutenant Paterson sneered, leaning his chair back on its two rear legs, seemingly proud of his quick retort as he blew a smoke ring toward Savage.

Lieutenant Gunther looked at Lieutenant Paterson as if the lieutenant were a not-too-bright child and said slowly, "If I may suggest, Mr. Paterson, *slick-tongued* is not quite a term we should be using at this hearing." I bit my lower lip to keep from laughing. My fellow board members did not.

I banged my gavel down hard. "Enough!"

Mr. Gunther flashed his right first finger at the man in dress blues and asked, "Seaman Savage, what do you have to say for yourself?" He ignored Paterson's harumphs. I liked the way Gunther was handling this. The XO told me he'd be good, but I was still biased over the battle-messing episode where he had served stale, dry bread.

"Well, sir, I got back late that night and was a little drunk. Well, a lot drunk, sir, and I didn't rightly remember where my rack was. I wandered around until I thought I was at my rack, then got in it. Honest, sir, I thought it was my own rack. I didn't mean anything by it. I didn't know anyone was in it. That's the God's truth, sir," Seaman Savage explained, then added in a low voice, "They don't like me on that ship. They say, ah, I, ah, drink too much." I watched his soft-featured face sag as he put his hands into his lap, holding them in comfort.

"SEE! See, he admits he got into the other guy's rack. He's guilty," Mr. Paterson yelped, slamming his chair back onto its four legs.

"Guilty of what, Mr. Paterson," Lieutenant Gunther asked with all the solemnity of the Queen's Bench. "Being drunk, mistaking his rack? Does that make him a homosexual? Doesn't there have to be some kind of contact?"

Lieutenant Paterson jumped to his feet, jamming his finger inches from Mr. Gunther's face. A drop of spittle ran down his chin. "LISTEN, GUNTHER, Savage is a queer, and you guys know it. He's admitted getting in the other guy's rack. Whaddaya want, a little show right here. SHIT! You guys are just a rubber stamp anyway. Now, let's get on with it."

My officers jumped when my hand smashed down on the table, popping cigarettes out of their ashtrays and rattling coffee cups. "NOW, MR. PATERSON! I remind you that you are a naval officer. Need I remind you that you are required to act like one? And in the future you will address all questions and comments to me." I let it soak in for a few seconds, then added more calmly, "Do you have a personal interest in this case, Mr. Paterson?"

"Well, no, not really. But I am, well, his department head, and he's trouble . . . drinks too much. Rotten worker."

"May I call your attention to the fact, Mr. Paterson, that we are here to determine if he is a homosexual, not to judge his work habits or your leadership," I said, composed again and regretting my sarcasm.

"Yes, sir, sorry, sir."

"Mr. Gunther?" I questioned. "Do you have anything to add, anything for the defense?"

"Well, Captain, I . . ."

"Mr. Gunther, I am here as the president of the board not as your captain. Please continue."

"Sorry, Cap—Mr. President, but I see nothing has been proven here except a man, well known for his excessive drinking habits, got drunk and by mistake tried to get into a rack that already had another man in it. That's all. Nothing sexual." He sat down, expelling a flush of air from deep down in his lungs.

"Mr. Paterson?"

"I think my case has been well proven—and besides, listen to this—he was wearing purple silk boxer shorts." He hammered his final words out as if putting the last nail into a coffin.

I winced, my mouth went dry. I glanced to my left and then to my right. Each officer of the board shook his head slightly, indicating they needed no more information. "Seaman Savage, Mr. Paterson, Mr. Gunther, you're momentarily excused. Please remain in the vicinity until we call for you."

We voted by secret ballot. I counted: two for being a homosexual and two for not. I hadn't voted. "Let's look at this situation," I said, just short of pontification. "I don't want to influence your vote, but think of the consequence on Seaman Savage's life. All we really know is that Savage, a known heavy drinker, got drunk and crawled into someone else's rack. In my book, that doesn't spell homosexuality, just sloppiness. Please think of this, and let's vote again."

I didn't want to be a tie breaker.

"Well!" Mr. Charles squeaked. "What about his purple silk undershorts? That should tell us something."

"Does the color of a man's undershorts determine his sexual inclination, Mr. Charles?"

"Well, it can. I mean, well, what kind of *real man* would wear purple silk boxer shorts anyway?"

Mr. Draco and Mr. Rogers snickered. Lieutenant Lawrence looked bored. "Let's vote." I collected the small pieces of paper again. Three against, one for. I didn't have to vote, one of them got the message. I was ashamed of the hammer of rank I had used.

The bosun led me back to my in-port cabin, as custom demanded after any legal proceedings. "You nail 'em, Cap'n?"

"No, Chief Eselun, we let him go—not enough evidence," I answered curtly, not in the mood then for his jocular familiarity.

"Shame, Cap'n. While you guys were deliberating in the wardroom, those two lovey boys were hugging and kissing on the mess decks. I looked at him, knowing my face showed utter despair at his statement.

I closed my door and locked it. I filled my lungs with air and blew it out. I undid my trousers, lowered them, sat down, and took them off. I pulled off my purple silk boxer shorts, put them in a manila envelope, and secreted them away in my briefcase—to be destroyed, never to be worn again.

Chapter 11

Eureka Port Visit

As our rapport built, the Navy League became more active and arranged goodwill visits to cities up and down the coast. About once a month we'd operate locally with a carrier, and I bugged COM-FIRSTFLT's staff to include us in their big exercises off San Diego, and we always took some of our reservists with us. We ended these sessions with two or three days on the Attack Teacher; at which, of course, the XO displayed his normal proficiency.

The months passed swiftly as I watched my officers mature and grow, and we were lookin' good.

I loved the trappings of command. I enjoyed the smiles of recognition, and the attentiveness of the crew when I passed. I beamed when the young sailors brought their visiting parents aboard and introduced me as *their* captain.

The announcement, "*Cambridge,* arriving," and the four rapid rings of the bell whenever I came aboard ran surges of pride through me. And to see my absentee pendant being hauled down from the yardarm to show the fleet I was on my ship never ceased to enthral me. Their wasn't much of a fleet in San Francisco, but that was okay, autonomy was my big suit.

Whenever I left the ship, the four bells and the words "*Cambridge* departing" saddened me; for each time I left, I felt I was deserting my crew. My three-foot long, white-and-black triangular pennant always fluttered smartly to the yardarm the instant my foot touched the pier.

But mostly, I loved my men.

I loved training them, seeing them learn their trade, seeing them grow as I shared their enthusiasm and burgeoning self-confidence.

We trained to the razor's edge. We had our sea legs. All systems up. We were ready for war. There was no war. There was no enemy to pit ourselves against. I was but a grape of wrath withering on the vine of peace.

The worldwide fuel crisis hit the navy hard in 1974 and 1975 and under way time was cut back drastically, and we had to account for and justify every gallon of fuel used. But *Cambridge* had friends in high places, and our local steaming continued. Public affairs and the support of the civilian hierarchy ensured extra money for the navy at budget times. The Navy League spoke directly to the Secretary of the Navy. I was their man in San Francisco. I did, however, stop cowboying around at twenty-seven knots.

The Navy League requested we visit their brethren in Eureka in northern California, and with an UNODIR, we got under way.

Humbolt Bay in northern California, with the city of Eureka sitting to the north of it, didn't look like a difficult steam; especially when you're sitting in San Francisco Bay, looking at a chart.

Saturday, 0800. Our pleasant cruise up and the promise of parties perfumed euphoria throughout the ship. Sunshine glistened off the Pacific Ocean, and the sky shone blue as we hove to off the Humbolt Bay sea buoy and the harbor pilotboat pulled along side our starboard quarter.

Harbor pilots were the experts for their area. They knew the water, the shifting bottoms, and the vagaries of tides and currents. But few destroyer captains liked harbor pilots handling their ships. Harbor pilots rarely handled ships as powerful or as quick-reacting as a destroyer. We feared they'd order too much rudder or too much engine and dent our babies up.

A slim man stepped out of the pilotboat's wheelhouse, swinging himself gingerly onto the fantail as the XO offered his hand to help.

I saluted him as he stepped onto the bridge. He smoked a cigarette in a long ivory holder, the ash the color of his hair under his Humphery Bogart 1940s felt hat.

"Good morning, Captain. Fine day," he answered, wiping his wire-rimmed glasses with a red silken handkerchief as he looked around the pilothouse, seemingly trying to orient himself.

I asked him if he'd ever conned a destroyer before as I admired his four-hundred-dollar gray suit and his black Gucci loafers.

The pilot took another puff on his long holder and looked around for an ashtray. Quartermaster Lehman handed him one. The pilot smiled, and as if in afterthought, answered, "Yes, ten, maybe fifteen years ago. All ships are the same to me, I can handle *anything.*" His voice came out a little higher, seemingly offended by my question. The XO glanced at me, then stepped back, shaking his head.

"She's not like a merchie, Pilot, she answers her rudder and engine orders very rapidly, like a speedboat," I said, reminding him we had sixty thousand shaft horsepower at our command and two huge rudders astern. From the chart, I was aware that the L-shaped channel demanded a ninety-degree turn to the north after we steamed in for a mile.

"Don't be nervous, Captain, everything will be all right," he answered condescendingly, dismissing my statement as if I were a midshipman on my first cruise.

Lieutenant Charles passed the conn to the thin-faced man, who immediately ordered ahead standard and took up a heading for the initial leg in.

Too fast, we're picking up speed too rapidly.

"A little fast, aren't we, Pilot?" I asked, trying to control my uneasiness. He ignored me.

He ordered left full rudder while we still had land forward of our bow in this narrow channel. *Too soon. He thinks he's handling a bigger, a less maneuverable ship with a greater turning radius.* The XO tapped my shoulder as if I hadn't noticed.

"Too much rudder, Pilot. She'll run aground. We turn fast," I warned him again, my voice rising.

"Nonsense, young man, I know what I'm doing . . . WHAT?"

He realized we were going aground, and before I could react, he screamed, "BOTH ENGINES BACK FULL!" The lee helm yanked his engine order telegraph handles back to the stops and the hyper-efficient engineers answered the bell immediately, dragging our stern down and toward the south bank.

"THIS IS THE CAPTAIN, I'VE GOT THE CONN. ALL ENGINES AHEAD FULL. RIGHT FULL RUDDER."

"YOU! You can't take the conn away from me . . . in thirty-two years as a pilot, no smart-assed skipper has ever taken the conn away from me. NEVER! YOU! YOU . . .!"

I felt the stern rise as the ahead turbines battled to cancel the effect of the backing turbines. The XO rushed to the starboard wing, peered aft, shouted, "One hundred feet to the rocks . . . closing . . . seventy-five . . . closing." The stern sunk again as the ahead bell took effect, sucking water from just ahead of the screws.

The water, how deep? "Depth?" I called out. Someone answered; I didn't know who. The precise depth didn't register on me. It was okay—the number was good enough.

"Fifty feet . . . opening," came the XO's relieving voice.

We were clearing. *Take off the ahead full bell.* "All engines ahead one-third. Rudder midships, steady as she goes," I ordered, holding on to the bridge bulwark so no one could see my hands shaking. *Safe!* A rectal urgency clawed my bowels. *Go away.*

"Mr. Charles, take the conn."

The frozen-faced pilot babbled repeatedly that I couldn't take the conn away from him as the XO pulled him away from the midships pelorus, where he bear-hugged the compass repeater in defense of his position.

"Yes, yes, sir, it's okay, Pilot. Okay," the XO soothed, leading him to the nav table, where Quartermaster Von Lehman offered a cup of coffee. The pilot took it, staring at the shaking cup as if he didn't know what to do with it. "The conn. I must have the conn. You don't know what you're doing." Spittle ran from the left side of his mouth. His hate-filled eyes darted around the pilothouse like an angry raptor seeking a kill.

"There, there, sir. It's okay, sir. You can have the conn a little later. Okay?" Von Lehman cooed with all the sincerity of a mortician as he patted the pilot's shoulder. The bereft man couldn't focus, and he puffed violently on his long ivory cigarette holder that held no cigarette.

Mr. Charles maintained his course passing the South Spit on the starboard hand and the tip of North Spit on the port. At the precise moment, he came hard left around the ninety-degree turn, staying to the right of the center of the channel. *Good job, Charlie.*

The safety of the ship ensured, and the beautiful day with its small, fluffy clouds and its beguiling light winds, chased my adrenaline back into its holster. The XO and I stood together on the port wing, staring ahead and out to sea, our proximity comforting.

After five minutes, the XO tapped my shoulder, pointing to the flat ocean horizon, the blur at the end of the world. Delicate, wispy high cirrus clouds with their featherlike plumes formed at about forty thousand feet. Below them, at perhaps twenty thousand, rippled cirrocumulus grew. They had the look of mackerel scales and the high cirrus could be likened to horses' tails.

The XO repeated the old sailors ditty: "Mackerel scales and mare's tails make tall ships carry low sails." We looked at each other and shrugged. The weather report insisted we'd have clean weather for at least three days.

Down our port side passed a huge lumber-processing plant, the major industry of Eureka, and in thirteen minutes we entered Eureka Channel.

The mayor and several dignitaries witnessed a textbook landing as Mr. Charles laid the ship satin-smooth against the city pier. The boatswain's mates had the lines over and doubled up in a waltz that only a master could have choreographed. We were lookin' good, like a seagoing drill team.

Women in summery dresses and men in slacks and polo shirts came aboard, laughing and joking, waiting for tours, friendship, and refreshments. The townspeople wandered about the ship, meeting my men and inspecting with them my marvelous war machine. One could see liaisons forming as the crewmen singled out ladies, or they singled out them, for their special attention. A picnic that afternoon, followed by a reception and dance that evening, sparked the enthusiam. The local car dealers furnished automobiles for those wanting to tour the city and the surrounding forests and beaches.

After the first rush of people came aboard, I went back to my sea cabin where the pilot paced the eight-by-twenty-foot cubicle, his lips muttering over and over that no one has ever taken the conn from him—no one. He'd refused to leave the bridge and be the first one ashore, as was the custom with pilots.

I told him again that I was sorry, apologized again for taking the conn. But we were in extremes and I had to act. I reached out for him. He jerked his body back as if my hand were a hungry tiger's mouth.

"I'm sorry, Pilot," he mimicked in a loud falsetto voice as his tongue darted back and forth between his lips. He pulled up his loosened tie. His hands flashed over his suit coat, brushing off imaginary lint. He took a deep breath of cigarette-smoked air, flung open the sea cabin door, and marched out.

It made me sad. *Had I been too quick to take the conn? Did I really give him enough time to recover on his own?* My instincts said yes. *Cambridge* was safe and happy. No one was hurt. My ship, my crew, and my career were still intact. Only his ego—seemingly delicate at best—carried any bruises.

I put it out of my mind and thought about tomorrow morning. Then it would be our turn to host the townspeople with a leisurely cruise out to sea, topped off with a five-inch-gun shoot. And I prayed for no errant whales.

By this time the whale incident had dimmed, and we'd put together another dog and pony show. It served the navy well: Each attendee came away with a strong, positive feeling for the navy, which could manifest itself as support for larger fleet budgets. One never knew with whom these people might associate. We were nice to everybody, as the custom of the navy and the tenets of a gentleman demanded. And I liked people—especially those who liked the navy.

A bevy of unattached ladies, young and old, attended the picnic along with half as many men. They welcomed my crew with beer and drinks and food. I couldn't believe a town this small could have mustered up so many women.

That evening the dancers whirled to the band, smiling laughing. The camaraderie of loud toasts echoed off the walls. Mardi Gras, New Year's Eve, the junior prom and graduation night all wrapped into one.

The duty radioman came in and scanned the dance floor, sadly realizing what he was missing. He spied the XO, walked up to him, and handed him a note. The XO grimaced, said something into the man's ear, and looked around for me.

Shit!

He handed me the message. Fleet Weather Central was predicting a slow-moving low pressure front to hit Sunday, about 1400, with heavy winds and high seas. And the winds expected would be about fifty to sixty knots in driving rain. Seas expected to be ten to fifteen feet.

I asked the XO for a recommendation, my voice trying to appear nonchalant.

He stoically said in his concerned-about-something, flat voice that prudence demanded we get under way this evening and run south to beat it. He was right. It was a localized condition and we'd be free once we got far enough to sea so we could turn south, clearing Cape Mendocino.

I looked around at my crew. They were damn good sailors and deserved the great time they were having. I pointed to the mayor, and with the XO sauntered over to him, showing him the weather forecast. Being the mayor of a northern California coastal town, he was well aware of the storms that could blow up seemingly out of nowhere with little warning. "Whaddya think, Mayor?"

He looked at me with the eyes of baby being pulled away from its mother's breast. "We're scheduled under way at ten," he said, more a question than a statement. Neither the XO nor I answered. The mayor looked at the revelers. He looked at us. Only the drums in the blare of the band penetrated our minds.

I looked at the XO. He pursed his lips. *Hell, my boys and I could weather any storm on good ol' Camby.* "Jim," I addressed the mayor, "suppose we change the under way time to seven, we could be back in by, say, ten and get under way right afterward. We should be able to miss the brunt of the storm. Whaddya think, Mayor?" The mayor said great. The XO grimaced, the plan sucked, I didn't have to ask.

And bravado nudged out common sense.

The mayor's shoulders drooped from the relief of not having to make a decision as he walked to the microphone on the bandstand.

He announced the storm and the change of plans. There were moans. There were cheers. Sailors moaned that we were leaving earlier. Townspeople cheered that we were still going.

A prickly tingle on the back of my neck announced that a wrong decision had just been made.

At 0700, in our starched dress whites and the civilians in what could pass as their yachting togs, we pulled smartly away from the pier. Several roasts of bear meat were brought aboard, a gift from the local hunters. It had been well praised and tasted great last night, and they rewarded our enthusiasm with fifty pounds of it.

Dark clouds formed ominously out to sea even though over us it was still a grand day. The wind had picked up, but not enough to bring concern. We cleared the harbor in our festive, though somewhat hung-over mood, heading for the open sea to fire the guns. That always impressed the civilians; me too actually. It was like a mini-orgasm every time they went off.

By 0800 the winds freshened appreciably, backing to the south. *Oh, Christ!* The skies darkened. The seas picked up. I keyed the 1MC. "Attention all guests and crewmen, this is the captain speaking. You can tell the seas are picking up. Regretfully, it is too dangerous for us to carry out the shoot in such bad weather. We must return to Eureka as soon as possible, then get under way again. I'm sorry, but we'll be back." Groans and cheers.

We turned for land cranking on twenty-two knots heading back for Humboldt Bay. We rolled badly, maybe twenty degrees to the side as we skirted the sea buoy heading in.

With the greatest attention, the conning officer threw the rudder hard over to port to make the turn conforming to the channel as we steamed into the bay. We turned early, knowing that the wind would set us on the eastern shore once we turned broadside to it. The tide, coming on full flood, sloopied our rudder commands. Dave Draco had the conn; next to Chuck Martin, my XO, he was my best ship handler.

Visibility decreased. One thousand yards.

Not much.

The XO called the pilot station requesting two tugs to help us make the landing. But the dapper man, so badly offended, refused to have them under way in this weather.

I could envision him wiping his glasses with the silken red handkerchief and smiling. The mayor angrily ordered his compliance; he too was refused. The mayor swore he'd have his job ten minutes after we landed. Rightly he should; this was a gross violation of the custom of the sea.

To fight the set of the wind, Dave hugged the left side of the channel as we crabbed up the four-mile bay into the narrow Eureka Channel. Dave made a twisting turn under full power and had the ship parallel twenty feet out from the city pier as the first line went over.

The howling wind, now full off our starboard bow, jammed us into the pier, and Dave twisted, muscling the stern in. Our side plates groaned from the grinding impact as a wild gust smashed us into the wooden pilings. Even though the wind kept us firmly against the pier, I demanded all lines over before we rigged the gangway.

I prayed another freak wind wouldn't set us off and dump the people of Eureka into the bay. With the gangway over and secured, the moaning, seasick townspeople charged off into the driving rain, stampeding for the shelter of their cars in the parking lot.

For an instant, I debated staying here, but quickly gave it up as the wind ground the stern hard against the pier, portending the destruction of the port-side steel plating or worse the port screw. We'd surely sink if the wind continued its pounding fury against us.

The mayor, the last civilian aboard, gave me a weak wave and a weaker smile and scurried off over the gangway. As he stepped off, it was instantly hauled aboard and secured.

With the wind pinning our bow firmly against the pier, Dave left number one line over and ordered left standard rudder and opposed his engines: port back full, starboard ahead full. Number one line tended aft with a tremendous strain from the forward turning full bell on the starboard engine. We pivoted against the bow set firmly against a piling. The stern twisted out agonizingly slow as it labored against the fury that now gusted to fifty knots, and held steady at forty—a five-minute job taking twenty.

The stern cleared. "Let go number one line. All engines back full." We surged astern, away, free of the destructive pier. The wind yanked farther to the south, blowing directly into us as we took it head-on, reaching for the turn out of the bay and into safety. At sea, a much more powerful storm would be required to daunt us.

The wind increased to a steady fifty knots full on our bow. The water churned forbiddingly, rubbed and abraded by the wind into a treacherous and insecure surface. We passed the wood-processing plant to our starboard. Just as it passed off the quarter, the wind jumped to eighty knots, stopping our forward motion like a giant hand grabbing us.

"Drop the port anchor, Mr. Draco."

The anchor clanked—though I couldn't hear it—out of its hawse pipes and dug deep into the mud and sand bottom; the worst holding ground there could be. The boatswain's mate of the watch, in his finest naval tradition, announced, "Anchored."

We steamed into the anchor chain, trying to hold our position. Losing. "Drop the starboard anchor, Mr. Draco."

The wind, aided by its sister element, the incoming tide, combined, rendering us impotent. Even though the engines were ahead standard, which would speed us to fifteen knots in the open sea, we were moved slowly, inexorably astern, dragging, plowing both anchors across the bottom.

The wind, gusting to eighty knots now, thrust relentlessly against the huge vertical expanse of the forward bulkhead of our bridge.

The XO brought a chart showing we were but one hundred yards from dragging the anchors across all the power cables from the mainland to the wood-processing plant. *Shit, Im about to shut down the city of Eureka's economy.* I hoped the crew got a lot of ass last night, because I sure had mine stuck out a mile.

"Button up the ship, XO." He set condition ZEBRA—battle conditions. I told Main Control, over the howling wind, to light off numbers one and three boilers and for the chief engineer to report to the bridge.

We'll fight our way out by brute force.

In fifteen seconds he stood beside me, puffing. Light off super heaters in two and four, I told him. He looked at me, astonished, breathing hard from his run to the bridge. He said he couldn't light off the superheaters at this rate of steaming, the forced draft would blow out the torches.

"Don't gimme that shit, Mr. Flanagan, I know what you can do. At the right moment, you tell me when you're ready. I'll cut power on starboard engine for ten seconds to allow you to torch the super-heaters in number two boiler. . . . Do you understand? I can't give you any more time."

He knew the chance we were taking; if someone screwed up and we lost number two boiler, we'd be hard up on the rocks in minutes. And the same with number four boiler and the port engine. It was delicate. "And throw the fire to 'em . . . get 'em up to temperature as fast as you can. . . ."

I'm sorry, boilers, about what I'm going to do to you . . . take it; you can take it.

I waited as the anchors dragged closer and closer to the undersea cables. The cables were already under the hull midships. I ordered more anchor chain out. I felt helpless, imagining the disaster if we lost an engine.

You poor bastards on the fo'c's'le—it must be murder up there lashed to any-thing you can get a lifeline on to. Take care of 'em, ship. God, will you help?

We were two hundred yards from yanking the undersea cables out when the phone talker reported ready on the starboard engine. "If you please, Mr. Draco, decrease starboard engine to ahead two-thirds."

The ship lurched back as the starboard engine slowed its steam-ing rate. After what seemed like hours, the lee helmsman screamed, "On! On!"

Within a heartbeat Mr. Draco ordered, "Starboard engine ahead full!" The forced draft blowers whined. The starboard screw thrashed into its water and dug in. We moved forward ever so slightly and waited for the extra power of the superheat to take hold.

From the corner of my vision I saw the bridge messenger shuffle reluctantly toward me, his eyes not leaving the looming rocks on our port side. "Ah, Captain. Are you scared, Captain?" I whirled around to chew his ass out for such an impertinent question at a time like this. I caught myself. The messenger, a young seaman who probably didn't even shave yet, was powerless to alter his destiny in this situa-tion. He was looking for comfort from his captain, who he believed could do anything and knew everything, his captain, who quite ob-viously held his young life in his hands. I knew the feeling.

"A little, son, but *Cambridge* is a good ship, and we got one helluva crew. Piece of cake, boy," I answered, reaching my right arm out, hugging his shoulder. He smiled, muttered thank-you, and turned away with confidence.

On the word from main control, the same slowing took place on the port engine. It had taken them only six minutes. With both engines, with growing superheated power, we moved ahead.

"Take in the anchors, Mr. Draco."

CIC reported our stern passing over the undersea cable. We were on the way out. The nav team concurred. We were making good, maybe a knot or two, as the chains groaned their way back into the chain locker.

"Anchors aweigh," the talker repeated from the bosun.

"Under way," came the 1MC. A cheer filled the ship. It was 1100 but as dark as late twilight. I could barely see the anchor detail in the streaming rain as they made the anchor ready to drop again. I told Mr. Rogers to secure as many men as he could and send the rest aft to the dry comfort of the ship. He and the bosun and three sailors stayed on the fo'c's'le, braving the hiss and claw of the wind, in case we needed the anchors again.

We were still in danger; I'd need at least fifteen knots to give me enough control to clear the rocks on the northern side of the exit channel. I asked the lee helm how were boilers one and three coming. He spoke into his sound-powered phones.

"Mr. Flanagan wants to talk to you, Captain."

"Captain, we're losing vacuum on both engines . . ." came his choppy voice, fighting down nervousness, trying to appear cool. "The main circulating pumps can't push enough water through the condensers without any forward motion. Sand and mud from the bottom is being sucked up into the pump, clogging the tubes. . . . They're heating up. Bad, Captain!"

Shit! I hadn't thought of that.

I ignored the statement, knowing there was nothing I could do about it. "How's the pressure coming up on numbers one and three boilers?" I calmly asked, squeezing my hands together until they hurt.

"Captain, I can't hear you over the noise. Say again." I yelled out the question again. I could hardly hear myself as the rain smashed against the pilothouse like shotgun pellets, and the wind screamed into every crack.

"Okay—he pumps?"

"Forget the fuckin' pumps. The boilers, throw the heat to 'em. You can do it."

"But, Captain, the plant?"

"You can do it, Mr. Flanagan. Don't worry about the plant; it'll take it. We'll be getting some speed soon . . . condensers'll clean themselves out. . . . It's okay."

I had to absorb his fears by keeping myself calm as the virus of doubt spread through my body. I wanted to run and hide in my sea cabin and pretend this wasn't happening. I wanted to blame the XO for something. Or the OOD. Or my mother.

I asked him again how the extra two boilers, one and three, were coming, hoping my voice didn't betray my fear.

"They're at three hundred pounds, about halfway to pressure. We—"

I interrupted with the instructions to cut in bleed steam from numbers two and four boilers to one and three when one and three's pressure reaches four hundred pounds. I cautioned him he'd hear a lot of groaning and snapping from the unequal pressures, to alert the men to it. Do it slowly, nice and easy, and start bringing down the superheat on two and four. "You got that, Chief Engineer?"

"Aye, Captain, it'll work; it'll work. I remember stories of Pearl Harbor, that's—"

"That's interesting, Mr. Flanagan, maybe we can chat about it later. Apologize to your troops for me. We're going to be popping gaskets like they've never seen before, and they'll be busting their balls repairing them. It'll be like a rain forest down there. Sorry!"

In thirty seconds my phone to Main Control buzzed. "Not to worry," the master chief said, "piece of cake."

"Thanks, Master Chief." *Yes, thank you, Master Chief. I need your strength.*

Well clear of the undersea cable, I ordered the anchors let go again to give us time to bring the other two boilers on the line. They made a good drop; the anchors dug in and held. The wind backed farther, forcing us at an angle to the narrow bay against the straining anchor chains. They held. Mr. Draco played his engines and rudder against the wind to minimize the angle on the ship and the uneven strain on the anchors. Though most of my officers would have done it by feel, Dave, a nuclear physicist by education, was, I'm sure, calculating all his moves mathematically. *Good enough!*

I walked over and squeezed his shoulder, showing my confidence in him. He looked at me, smiled, and had the audacity to wink. I winked back; it was too noisy for words.

Howling winds slicing through the rigging screamed for prominence over the sharp, loud-crying crashes of different pressure steam at different temperatures, pounding, punishing the innocent steel of boilers one and three. Their piping groaned in protest as the engineers bled high-pressure, superheated steam into them, forcing them, driving them to equalization. And it drove me crazy on the bridge.

It must be god-awful scary down there. I'm sure they think I was crazy for torturing their prima donna plant. I whispered to the plant my sorrow at what I was doing. But it had to be done. It would be a lot worse if we piled up on those hideous rocks over there. I looked at the rocks, willing them away. A haze moved in and covered them. *Rocks, you're still there, aren't you? You'll not touch me.*

"Bridge, Main Control, all four boilers on the line, superheat coming up. Ready to answer all bells," came the triumphal voice of Mr. Flanagan.

"Well done, Mr. Flanagan. Well done."

With four precious boilers on the line, we had the power. I ordered up anchors. The clogged main condensers were losing vacuum dangerously fast. We had to get moving, had to clear the junk out of them. Had to.

In an eon of time, the port anchor broke bottom. "PORT ANCHOR AWEIGH!" screamed over the phone. With only one anchor down, the slashing wind and the flooding tide shoved us astern. Dave Draco rang up ahead two-thirds; it took, our drifting astern eased and stopped. The port anchor housed. We could feel it. Rogers and his men shifted the starboard chain to the windlass. We could handle only one chain at a time.

It seemed like hours. I watched the fo'c's'le through my binoculars and fought heroically to keep from yelling at the men to hurry. I was ashamed, ashamed of what I was doing to them, what I was doing to the whole ship on the straw horse I rode to self-aggrandizement.

The acrid smell about me offended my nose. I felt the dampness of my sweat-soaked shirt, hoping it came from there, hoping it wasn't the smell of my fear.

"STARBOARD ANCHOR AWEIGH!" We were free of the bottom, I nodded to Dave. No words were needed; communications existed on a different level. The ship surged astern. Dave rang up ahead, standard-adjusting the rudders to keep us aligned with the channel. A tough job.

He smiled, maneuvering the ship, attempting but failing to stay stationary, and waiting for the anchor to clear the water.

If he had gone ahead right away, we could have driven the anchor back into us, seriously holing us. A lesser officer might have pushed ahead the moment the anchor pulled free. I had prepared to countermand his order if he had fallen into the trap. He hadn't.

His calmness soothed me. This was the first time he had ever been tested, seriously tested under pressure, and he rose magnificently to the task. With the starboard anchor now housed, he cranked on full four-boiler power. We steadied on fifteen knots. We couldn't hold this for long, as the southern shore of the channel raced toward us. The battering rain smeared visibility to two hundred yards, each drop of it mocking my stupidity for not getting under way yesterday, like any prudent captain would have done.

The constant voice of Combat called out our position from the groaning surface search antenna high above us atop our whistling mainmast. I couldn't hear it, but I knew it was taking punishment.

Chief Janski and his boys in Combat carried the day. The XO's nav team was useless in the low visibility, but they were trying. Mr. Flanagan's snipes gave us our maneuverability, and Draco's bridge team was steering us to safety. There was nothing else I could do.

Organize, deputize, and supervise.

The wind, abating ever so slightly, shifted more to the southeast. Dave, his face grim, came in fast on course one nine zero, dead toward the rocks on the South Spit. He had to; he needed the power and the speed for rudder control. And at the right moment, with split-second timing, he would have to come hard right into the exit channel, precious inches to spare.

No one spoke on the bridge, but heartbeats could be heard giving cadence to the sound of fear geysering out of frightened pores.

I fought the overwhelming urge to take the conn. I gripped the arms of my chair until the pain forced me to stop. Even in this poor light I could see sweat rolling down Dave's face. I wanted the conn, wanted to be in direct control, but I couldn't.

If I took the conn, it would destroy everything I'd worked for in building my officers' confidence and skills. I would be no different from the multitude of commanding officers who preached leadership but failed to put it into practice, especially when the chips were down. I would become the kind of man that drove good men out of the navy, but were promoted for their timidity, labeled prudence.

I could hear the XO's smooth breathing as he stood next to my chair in his best Clint Eastwood style, smoking his thin cigar, his feet spread, his hands at his sides as if ready to throw off his serape and draw a six-gun. There was nothing he could do, but he was ready if there was.

He probably felt the same as me. Dave was doing the best any man could hope for. What we could do was leave him alone. His fitness report and the accolades of the crew would well publicize and credit his skill.

My mind hammered the seconds through my body as we raced to the southern rocks. At the last moment, not a second to spare, Dave threw on right hard rudder and backed the starboard engine full.

A massive gust of wind nudged the swinging stern from the rocks on the southern shore as we jerked around sloppily to course three one five.

A thunk echoed throughout the ship.

We'd touched.

The XO glanced at me. I shrugged and nodded yes. He left the bridge, both of us apprehensive of what he might find.

We were on the way out, but the relentless wind drove the stern toward the shoals on the northern side of the channel. "Watch the stern—the stern, Dave," I whispered but knew he couldn't hear me.

The adage of taking care of your stern and everything else will follow pounced into my mind.

He gave her a hit of right rudder to kick the stern out, then backed the starboard engine full and the port two-thirds to pull us back into the channel. We waited the eternity it took to take effect.

It did, and we cleared into safety. Dave ordered both ahead full and we crabbed out of Humboldt Bay with an eighty-knot wind battering our port quarter. *Safe! Thank you, Ship. Thank you, God, for that last gust of wind.*

The tension drained from Dave's body, slumping his shoulders, drooping his head. I walked over, putting my arm around him, squeezing. His clammy shirt smelled. "Not too shabby, boy." He tried to smile. Blood returned to his face.

Several cars parked on the North Spit blinked their lights in farewell. I blew five short blasts on the whistle in salute. Thanks for a great time, I hoped it said. *Can a whistle be sarcastic?*

With the wind now on our port quarter and the four boilers kicking out their best, we rapidly picked up speed, crashing soundly into the fifteen-foot waves trying to destroy our bow. Dave looked at me. I nodded. He slowed to ten knots, the minimum, I figured, we dared go with four boilers on the line.

It was not critical now. I'd wait. I didn't want to face the insidious chance of failure by adjusting the engineering plant this close to land with the furious, confused winds hammering us from behind and the heavy seas forward fighting to fling us ashore.

I had had no choice within the harbor.

But even at this slow speed, with the seas dead ahead, the bow raved on the edge of self-destruction. Twenty minutes more of groaning torture. We were out far enough. "Dave, commence lowering superheat and take two boilers off the line." *No sweat now, a routine evolution easily done.*

I waited for the XO to report, like a kid outside the principal's office waiting for a beating. *Did I hole the ship? Did I hurt you, baby? No, you would have told me.* Nonetheless, I wanted to hear it from the XO.

We came far enough out so we could come left and run south with the seas to clear Point Mendocino. We had no choice, I wanted to clear the point by ten miles. This would take us at least six hours. The tension eased as we turned away from the head-on seas, substituting the rolls for hammering.

The ever-changing, never-changing sea rocked us twenty degrees to a side in the vicious south-running ocean. The bellowing waves, each rising, each falling in the dim light had a life of their own, rising to perfection, holding, then collapsing to feed life anew to an embryonic brother.

The party hangovers, the adrenaline plummet, and the angry seas combined to render two-thirds of the crew wretchedly sick. Men limped to their stations weak from fighting the brutish tossing, the impotence, the frightful ordeal of the harbor, and the gut-wrenching seasickness.

I fought it down.

The XO finally returned from his inspection tour, his head shaking no, his face beaming a smile. I sucked in a gulp of air, my lungs allowing me to breathe once more. Dave Draco did not miss the implication. The news drained the adrenaline from my bloodstream, robbing me of energy and willpower. My body slumped in my chair. *Home free.*

One more time I had scaled the high wall of Command, its top lined with the horrible spikes of responsibility waiting to entrap the unwary captain.

"Mr. Rogers has the watch, Captain." The words triggered me. I sat straighter. "Request permission to leave the bridge," Dave said, saluting, even though under cover. I returned his salute, even though under cover, and held it longer than custom required.

"Permission granted," I said softly, and he grinned, lookin' good, walkin' ten feet tall off the bridge.

"I've got the watch, Captain," Mr. Rogers reported.

"What's that smell, Mr. Rogers?"

"I ate some bear meat before coming up, Captain, a little fatty, but still great—love it. Want some?" He offered me a grease-covered plate with chunks of blackened meat on it.

I barely made it to my sea cabin's toilet.

"*Cambridge* Departing"

"Captain, we just got a call from the new CO saying he'll be aboard at 0900 tomorrow," the in-port OOD reported.

The next day I stood on the quarterdeck of my immaculate ship and shook his hand as he came aboard. Over the next three days we chatted and inspected and told sea stories.

He asked me if I minded him talking to my department heads. This implied alone—without me. "No, Don, you don't have to be there," he said, "just a friendly chat with the boys . . . know you're busy."

"Of course it's okay," I replied. "Yeah, sure . . . I gotta lot to do. Go ahead; the XO'll set it up."

In my in-port cabin I had nothing to do but seethe at the perfidious navy department for robbing me of my child, my love. *What are they talking about down there? I don't care? Yeah, I don't care.*

I paced, hating this pretender who thought I would give him my destroyer. *The guy probably doesn't know the first thing about ship handling—or leading men. He'll run her aground. I know it, just know it.*

My cabin grew warm. The bulkheads glowed a mellow white. I placed my open hands on its invitation. "Your time has come, Captain," it murmured. "Your time has come."

The new captain didn't deem it necessary to get under way to observe the ship at sea. "It'd be a bother to the crew," he said, "and wouldn't matter anyway."

We waltzed through the change of command ceremony, and I left, lookin' good, walkin' ten feet tall, my heart dragging heavily behind me.

Two days later, the wind flung its damp sea air across San Francisco Bay. I shivered from its biting cold as I stood shrouded in melancholy's gray cocoon. *Cambridge* backed smartly from her berth and in painful clarity glided past me a thousand yards away. I was no longer in command—no longer her captain.

I felt her power whisper a saddened farewell as she maneuvered slightly to starboard to avoid an incoming tanker. Her lights faded. She was gone, and I was alone.

Epilogue

I reported to the Commander in Chief, United States Naval Forces Europe, CINCUSNAVEUR, London, U.K. Admiral David P. Baker, my first captain on my first destroyer, *Henshaw,* motioned me in, wearing his four stars like beacons of success. Ol' Cap'n Dave, he'd made it.

He had followed my career and heard I had orders to some budget group in the Pentagon. A set of orders I hated. Staff duty always got me in trouble. He had had his chief of staff call me to see if I wanted to come to work for him. I did. I was now in London.

"Cap'n, goddamn, Cap'n, it's good to see you." I blurted out as I stepped toward him. He rose, walking quickly around his massive desk and took my hand, putting his arm around me as we shook in greeting. The old feeling of being wrapped in Superman's cape again warmed my body.

"Don good to see you. Charlie, have the steward bring in some coffee for us, okay?"

I kept addressing the admiral as captain, so powerfully ingrained was his image in me. Charlie, his chief of staff, winced each time I did it. "It's Admiral, Commander, not Captain. You address him as admiral," he corrected me every time the word slipped out.

He wasn't pleased with me, an upstart ex-destroyer CO being asked for by name by the admiral, and being called Don to top it off. It was his job to ensure good officers were sent to the staff, not the admiral's. I had already screwed up and hadn't been there an hour yet. I walked too straight; I walked too tall. I was a destroyer captain.

Admiral Baker laughed. "Captain's okay, Charlie, best job I ever had. Ol' Don here was one of my boys." His eyes went to a large picture of *Henshaw* framed on the wall. "Yeah . . . one of my boys." His saddened eyes came back to me.

"It was easier then, Don, easier," he whispered. We sat silently for several seconds, each of us living again the adventure of *Henshaw*: the screw-ups, the good times, the pirates, the Foxtrot submarine, Typhoon Mary, and a thousand other things.

CINCUSNAVEUR didn't have a real job. The Sixth Fleet in the Mediterranean reported to him, but when anything even remotely warlike happened, Sixth Fleet came under the command of NATO, and we had less to do. I was the fleet exercise officer and was supposed to watch over the Sixth Fleet to see that all their qualification requirements were met. They didn't need anyone to watch over them; they were big boys, fleet sailors.

We were staffies. We were an irritant.

I was bored and eventually appalled at what I was really supposed to be doing. I was a NATO briefer on the views of the U.S. Navy, its deployment, and current mission in Europe.

I didn't do it well. My edited briefings didn't always agree with the facts, and I was judged by how well the two meshed; that is, my fitness reports depended upon how well I lied. It may have been called misdirection, or putting a favorable spin on something, or shading the truth, but they were lies, lies nonetheless. The state department got into it, admonishing me to get with the party line.

I couldn't. Too many years in the fresh honesty of the sea weighed heavily upon me. Naval officers do not lie; it is not honorable to lie, even if it is couched in the euphemistic, bureaucratic rhetoric of the state department.

Every wardroom I'd ever seen carried the words of John Paul Jones on a placard. I knew them well:

> It is by no means enough
> that an officer in the navy
> should be a capable mariner.
> He must be that, of course,
> but also a great deal more.

He should be as well a gentleman
of liberal education,
refined manners,
punctilious courtesy,
and the nicest sense
of personal honor.

There was no placard in London.
I retired.
The admiral looked at me, his face sad as he shook my hand in departure's silence. He knew.